Language Policy in Africa
Perspectives for Cameroon

MAP
Kansas City, MO (USA)

Language Policy in Africa
Perspectives for Cameroon

Edited by

Pius W. Akumbu and Blasius A. Chiatoh

Centre for African Languages and Cultures (CALAC)
University of Buea, Cameroon

Foreword by
Beban Sammy Chumbow
Emeritus Professor

Language Policy in Africa: Perspectives for Cameroon
Ed. Pius W. Akumbu & Blasius A. Chiatoh

First published 2013

Miraclaire Academic Publications (MAP)
8400 East 92nd Terrace, Kansas City, MO 64138, USA

Copyright © 2013 by Miraclaire Academic Publications

All rights for this book reserved.
No part of this book may be reproduced, stored in a retrieval system, or transmitted, in any form or by any means, electronic, mechanical, photocopying, recording or otherwise, without the prior permission of the copyright owner.

ISBN-13: 978-0615795591 / ISBN-10: 0615795595

Printed in the United States of America

MAP is an imprint of Miraclaire Publishing LLC
www.miraclairepublishing.com

Miraclaire Publishing makes every effort to ensure the accuracy of all the information ("Content") in its publications. However, Miraclaire and its agents and licensors make no representations or warranties whatsoever as to the accuracy, completeness, or suitability for any purpose of the Content and disclaim all such representations and warranties, whether expressed or implied to the maximum extent permitted by law. Any views expressed in this publication are the views of the author and are not necessarily the views of Miraclaire.

Foreword

At a time when many African countries are dreaming and strategising for *economic emergence* in the arena of global development, this book is a welcome reminder of the need to take on board the language factor as a central element in the social, economic and political transformations that characterise development in the twenty first century: ***the age of knowledge economy.***

The book is about language policy and language planning in the interest of Africa's development. Why is this an issue and why must development strategists and African policy makers at all levels and the entire African population consider it as a matter of extreme urgency and a ***sine qua non condition for emergence?***

Policy, in a sense, is the articulation of a **vision and strategies** for the implementation and materialisation of that vision. *'Without vision, the people perish'*; this truism of the *'good book'* summarises the tragic situation of Africa without an effective commitment to a language policy as a vision that makes use of African languages for the effective development of the masses of the rural population who live and use essentially or uniquely an African language.

On a continent where the official language of government action is, for the majority of countries, still an exoglossic and foreign language of the colonial legacy (such as English, French, Portuguese and Spanish) spoken at a reasonably functional level by a minority 10 to 40 percent of the population, it follows that government action in the official language leads to the **marginalisation** and indeed the **exclusion** of the majority 60 to 90 percent of the population that uses African languages from the benefits of development initiatives. We have consistently and persistently emphasized this fundamental predicament of the African continent. In the present millennium, the development and underdevelopment divide is a function of the quantity and quality of cultural, economic, scientific and technological ***knowledge production, knowledge dissemination and knowledge appropriation by the population.*** Not only is Africa tragically behind in knowledge production it is paradoxically unable to

disseminate and **appropriate** locally produced knowledge and the avalanche of available free access knowledge from the global community because of a retrogressive language policy that favours the hoarding of knowledge in an **official language** that is mastered only by the elite, beneficiaries of this policy of exclusion. The consequence is that the knowledge which is crucially relevant for development in terms of poverty alleviation, food security, reduction of the incidence of HIV/AIDS, infant and maternal mortality and roll back malaria, etc is **available** (to some elite) but not **accessible** to the majority who do not share the (official) language. Any doubt therefore that the implementation of the millennium development goals in sub-Saharan Africa has, generally, a low level of implementation success rate despite meaningful and spirited government action? The Language and communication factor has been shown to contribute to this sorry state of affairs (Chumbow, 2012).

The lessons are clear. Only commitment to a language policy action that is geared towards the **democratisation of access to knowledge** by making knowledge *available and accessible* in African languages has the chance of mobilising the majority of African people from the zone of **ignorance (where they have been sentenced)** to become agents of change in the initiatives for national development.

The book, ***Language Policy in Africa: Perspectives for Cameroon*** edited by Pius Akumbu and Blasius Chiatoh is a volume of ten chapters preceded by an illuminating and insightful editorial introduction to the case for the use of African languages in education and national development that deplores, *inter alia,* observed generalised lethargy in the implementation of language policy (where policy exists). A succinct summary of each of the ten chapters is provided and constitutes a well articulated abstract of the book.

The chapters are well researched presentations and analytical assessments of language policy and language planning initiatives in seven countries of Africa (Cameroon, Ethiopia, Malawi, Nigeria, South Africa, Sudan, and Tanzania). The chapters conceived and articulated by a crop of dynamic and committed linguists of the rising generation bring out the specificities of the experience of individual countries in language policy and policy implementation from pre-colonial times through the colonial period to the present with a focus on current initiatives and an evaluation of these against the back drop of what may be called the ideal orthodox paradigm policy for Africa inspired by UNESCO and African Union consensus positions. The countries in this study each have a rich and unique tradition of language policy that will provide students and scholars with insights into the diverse options and possibilities of facing the challenge of multilingualism in the enterprise of nation building in Africa. Thus, for instance, while Tanzania under Nyerere took a bold option of choosing and promoting one of its languages, Kiswahili, as national/official language along with English as official languages, Nigeria proposed regional lingua franca, (Hausa, Yoruba, and Igbo) with English as the official language. Cameroon adopted the two languages of it colonial legacy (English and French) as official languages to the exclusion of indigenous languages. Sudan opted for Arabic, and Ethiopia adopted Amharic initially. However, under the influence of the challenge of UNESCO's position, each of these countries is currently constrained to review the original policies of linguistic imperialism and to reduce the impact of the hegemonic dominance of African mega languages. Among the consensus observations that emerge from the evaluation of the various policies are the following: the enthusiasm of some to develop and use African languages is paralleled by negative attitudes of others towards their own language, unbridled language loyalty that breeds intolerance and negative attitudes towards other languages and a gap between the provisions of language policy and the facts of policy implementation; a gap attributable to inertia, lip service to policy, desire to protect the **de facto dominance and advantages** of the elite class and lack of political will.

UNESCO 2003 in its seminal position paper, *Education in a multilingual world* and the African Union in the 2006 revision of its language policy document, *Language Plan of Action for Africa* clearly requires that member nations should have language policies that envisage the use of African languages in education and national development with the official languages as partner languages.

The last chapter of the book provides perspectives for a new policy in Cameroon that is congruent with the more realistic multilingual reality of the country and the exigencies of the UNESCO-AFRICAN UNION prescription. The authors provide insightful descriptive and analytical elements of language policy relevant to the enterprise of a new language policy, not only for Cameroon but for all countries of the continent.

Indeed, on the whole, the book is a compelling and compulsory *reader* for language planning and language policy implementation in Africa.

Professor Beban Sammy Chumbow
Distinguished Professor, ICT University, Cameroon
Emeritus Professor, University of Yaounde 1

Table of Contents

Foreword.. i

Introduction:
Language Policy Implementation in Africa – What is Holding Us Back?
Pius W. Akumbu & Blasius A. Chiatoh 1

The Cameroonian Situation

Chapter 1
An Overview of Language Policy and Planning in Cameroon
Gabriel Mba...12

Chapter 2
Cameroonian Languages in Education: Enabling or Disenabling Policies and Practices?   Blasius A. Chiatoh............................32

Chapter 3
Literacy in Cameroon: The Case of Mungaka
Beatrice Lima Lebsia Titanji 52

Experiences from Across Africa

Chapter 4
The Tanzanian Experience in Language Policy and Planning
Josephat Rugemalira..62

Chapter 5
An Overview of Language Policy and Planning in Nigeria
Linda Chinelo Nkamigbo 98

Chapter 6
The South African Experience in Language Policy and Planning
Kathleen Heugh 108

Chapter 7
The Malawian Experience in Language Planning
Atikonda Akuzike Mtenje 129

Chapter 8
An Overview of the Ethiopian Language Policy and Planning
Bekale Seyum 145

Chapter 9
An Overview of Sudan Language Policy and Planning
Abdelrahim Hamid Mugaddam 179

Perspectives for Cameroon

Chapter 10
Towards a National Language Policy for Cameroon
Blasius A. Chiatoh and Pius W. Akumbu 194

About the Authors 215

Introduction:
Language Policy Implementation in Africa – What is Holding Us Back?
Pius W. Akumbu & Blasius A. Chiatoh

African multilingualism is well recognised across the world (Wolff, 1999: 333; Obanya, 1999: 82; Trudell, 208: 1) and multilingual and multicultural practices on the continent are real and current. Yet the policies which regulate language treatment and use as well as the linguistic attitudes are essentially exoglossic in nature because they accord primacy to and promote external languages (Ruiz, 1995:75) in a vast majority of countries. As offshoots of colonial perceptions and treatment given to African indigenous languages vis-à-vis foreign languages, these policies have tended to undervalue and so disregard the former. Over the postcolonial decades, therefore, colonial languages have continued to be perceived as the most acceptable instruments for nation construction. Coupled with this orientation has been the determination to uphold the "one-nation-one language" approach to language policy and planning. Consequently, except for a few countries that have defied generalised practices by adopting multilingual policies based on the realities of linguistic diversity, most of the countries have maintained the colonial legacy of the supremacy of foreign languages. In fact, even when the need for multilingual policies has been recognised, the putting in place of appropriate policies to cater for this need has not proven to be an easy task. While governments openly acknowledge the necessity for a shift in linguistic behavior, their actions on the ground reveal a completely different reality. Their actions demonstrate that they are either unconvinced of the need to undertake fundamental language policy reforms based on linguistic diversity or that they are simply unprepared to embrace a change in policy. Whatever the underlying motivations for this behavior, the impact of the maintenance of foreign language-based policies for Africa is not only increasingly being felt but also it has become the focus of debates in recent times.

Whenever the need for alternative language policy and planning has been expressed in society, education has been at the centre of the debate. The debates have been even fiercer in settings where a majority of the languages have minority statuses. In these contexts, demands and advocacy for more contextually-relevant approaches to language policy and planning been observed to be greater. Long years of dependence on hegemonic languages, usually but not limited to foreign languages, have bred serious misconceptions about the value and functions of indigenous modes of communication. Faced with the challenge of innovation, both governments and the general population, probably due to limited understanding of the potential multi-dimensional gains of educational reforms based on indigenous African languages continue to resist change. A look at ongoing practices suggests that either Africa is uncertain of the benefits of any such innovations or that it simply wants to maintain the status quo by choosing the path of convenience rather than that of necessity. While the path of convenience has to do with the maintenance of foreign languages and the resources available in them for learning and other purposes, that of necessity entails radical overhauling of present policies and practices through obligatory integration of indigenous languages into all language policy and planning processes especially with respect to education. Obviously, the latter is more challenging because it involves changing long established linguistic attitudes. It entails the development and promotion in learning and other functions of languages hitherto considered as not good enough for these functions.

By opting to persist in the pursuance of foreign language-based policies for a multilingual Africa, governments have failed to realise that effective development of nations depends greatly on the choices and options made with regard to educational planning and delivery. Clearly, on this continent, where multilingualism is the norm rather than an anomaly, these concerns are even greater. Regrettably, the linguistic choices that have guided educational promotion in Africa have not matched development requests founded on culturally-sensitive and ideologically appropriate models of theorisation and application. The blame has not only been the subjection of educational planning and delivery to foreign language policies but also the determination by successive leaderships in postcolonial times to uphold their loyalties towards these policies, thereby, relegating to the background the huge linguistic resources of the continent. The puzzle that continues to burden many minds today, therefore, is why Africa cannot craft its own policies and so liberate itself from the linguistic colonisation and mental enslavement perpetuated by current policies and practices. How do we explain that unlike other continents that have suffered the pangs of colonisation, Africa seems to be the only continent that is least prepared to adopt alternative approaches to cultivating its development? For how long will this situation persist in the continent? Indeed, one wonders whether Africa is aware that no country has ever achieved development by despising and so discarding its languages and cultures in favor of alien ones. Put differently, one wonders people of the continent of Africa can break out of the "fateful logic of the unassailable position of the colonial language" (Alexander, 1999: 3). Rather, what we witness today is that vibrant, promising and emerging economies today have defied the colonial yoke by ensuring that although they encourage the learning of foreign languages, their learning, the basis of modern socio-economic and political advanced are founded fundamentally their languages and cultural values. The case of Asian countries that share the same colonial history with Africa is glaring. Questions like the ones asked here, signal the dangers of foreign language promotion perpetuity on a continent that is in dire need of linguistic and educational reforms.

Quite often when issues of language policy have been debated in Africa, the focus has been on the inability of governments to propose appropriate frameworks for effective language planning theorisation and actual application. Accordingly, failures in the development and promotion of education based on the language of instruction have been attributed to the absence of strong political will and unpreparedness to officially endorse learning in mediums other than languages inherited from colonisation. In recent years, though, the focus seems to be shifting fairly quickly to new dimensions of complication and challenges. This current shift in language policy and planning discourses has highlighted a rather paradoxical situation whereby, despite marked advancements registered at individual country levels, actual application has continued to suffer thus raising concerns as to whether there is really need for policy changes at all on the continent. The shift has thus has tended to draw attention to formulation inadequacies and implementation insufficiencies. On a general note, policies on the continent are either not well-formulated or they are well-designed but are not properly implemented. As the situation stands, this problem can be perceived from several angles involving but not limited to: government's desire to maintain the status quo by ensuring that foreign languages continue to dominate learning at all levels, the unwillingness of parents and communities to adopt alternative educational models based on languages they consider as limited in the performance of functional roles in a society that is rapidly being transformed into a global village and in which language of limited diffusion have little or no space and the challenges involved in bringing indigenous African languages into the limelight of educational planning and delivery.

In this collection, we pool together a wide range of language policy and planning experiences from six countries in Africa. These are countries that have made some significant strides towards the establishment of African indigenous language-based policies. However, from experiences reported in the various contributions, it becomes clear that between language policy and its actual implementation, there exists a great variance (Prah, 1999: 543). In fact, what we gather from these experiences points to some kind of dilemma, indeed, a serious paradox. While in countries where appropriate multilingual policies have not yet been established, advocacy for such policies is rife, in those that have already adopted them the situation still leaves much to be desired – they have fallen short of ensuring the effective implementation of the policies. In these countries, a critical look at implementation leaves one with more questions than answers. Despite the presence of attractive policies, the educational system as well as all written communication in the public arena is still largely dominated by foreign language use with little or no official endeavor to usher in the required change. The very big question that we are tempted to ask here is: Why, despite all the expressed needs for contextually-relevant language policies and given the policy advancements observed, is effective language policy implementation so difficult to achieve? In other words, what is really holding us back from engaging in appropriate language policy and planning even when it is evident that governments are now more conscious of the benefits of alternative policies? The various contributions provide some clues to some of the intriguing peculiarities of language planning and policy at various country-levels.

Gabriel Mba reviews language policy and planning in Cameroon. In a journey through "the linguistic profusion" in Cameroon, coupled with a historical study of reflections that various stakeholders have had for its exploitation, he questions the different positions and actions regarding language policy and especially those with a say on the immense reservoir of mother tongues in the field of education in Cameroon. He observes that the linguistic complexity of the country has led stakeholders to engineer different language policy and management models based on their understanding of the situation, their expectations and felt needs. After briefly presenting language education enactments representing what is generally considered as Cameroonian language policy, he summarises the key policy orientations made by Cameroonian linguists. He thinks that the history of Cameroon's languages is yet to be written due to the difficulties encountered in implementing present policy orientations.

Blasius A. Chiatoh examines language policy developments against the background of mother tongue-based education application. He argues that the failure to implement mother tongue education has generally been blamed on the absence of appropriate policies especially with respect to the specification of goals and the definition of strategies and mechanisms of implementation. He questions the appropriateness of decrees, legal and constitutional frameworks as language policy and submits that rather than constituting policy in themselves, they actually only constitute language policy-related legislation which in view can appropriately be referred to as "expressions of intent". However, he concurs that despite the insufficiencies of current legislation, it does provide some important window of opportunity for government and educational stakeholders to initiate transformative change through the introduction of mother tongue-based education in Cameroon. Drawing from Bagmbose (1999: 23-28), he highlights the essential qualities of an ideal language planning model for Cameroon.

Beatrice L.L. Titanji's paper focuses on the more practical level of language planning and policy. Her contribution centres on the Mungaka experience of literacy promotion in Cameroon. She retraces the history of the development and promotion of Mungaka in education and evangelism notably the role of the Presbyterian Church in the colonial and postcolonial era (1800s-1970s). She argues that the successful spread and use of Mungaka as a language of education, literacy and evangelism provide evidence that a language policy that gives prominence to Cameroonian indigenous languages would enhance learning and subsequently accelerate development in the country.

In his chapter, Josephat Rugemalira argues that the Tanzanian experience in language policy and planning is not as unique and laudable as many scholars have been tempted to think. His submission is that the promotion of a single national language – Swahili, as a replacement of the language of the colonial masters – English is not a success story. In his opinion, the conflict observed in the three layers of the Tanzanian linguistic environment arises from two sources, namely, the purist tradition in linguistics and then the imbalanced economic relation between Tanzania and the Anglophone centre situated in Europe and America. He strongly argues that there are no guarantees in the long-term for Swahili as the national language to play its rightful role since the Tanzanian economy continue to be a negligible appendage of the powerful economies of the North.

Linda C. Nkamigbo in her paper presents an overview of language policy and planning in Nigeria. According to her, Nigeria's language policy recognises English and the three major languages – Hausa, Igbo and Yoruba as official languages. As such, government encourages their use in vital public domains such as education and legislation. However, the policy fails to address the fate of Nigerian minority languages. As contained in the Federal Government National Policy on Education (NPE), indigenous mother tongues are to be promoted in the first three years of primary schooling with English used subsequently in later stages. However, she regrets that policy is not being implemented as English remains the medium of instruction in a vast majority of Nigerian schools right from the first year of the nursery. According to her, the failure to implement the policy comes from the lack of political will on the part of government. She then discusses the benefits of mother tongues in education particularly in early childhood and recommends a National Policy on Education based on the principle of biliteracy.

Kathleen Heugh examines the South African experience in language policy and planning. She traces the history of language policy and planning over the last century. In her opinion, the marginalisation of Dutch (Afrikaans) speakers by British colonial policy after 1901 unavoidably had a huge impact on apartheid language policy during the second half of the 20th century, a situation that led to implementation of mother tongue education that was perceived by speakers of African languages as a mechanism for the advancement of separate and unequal development for these different groups of people. In her argument, the post-apartheid language policy adopted for the country, although founded on multilingualism, has defaulted towards an English monolingual paradigm for three main reasons namely; the legacy of apartheid, the lack of political will and deliberate misinterpretation of language policy by key official advisors.

In her paper, Atikonda A. Mtenje reviews the Malawian experience in language planning. She examines the development of language policies in Malawi from the colonial era to post-independence (a period marked by the one-party state) to the era of democracy with a focus on the dominance of Chichewa over other local languages in the one-state period. She then goes further to explain the declaration of the Malawian Ministry of Education authorising the inclusion or integration of local languages into early primary school learning (standards 1-4) and posits that despite some major strides made in this direction, the declaration is yet to enjoy government approval and implementation. Among the main challenges affecting policy, she cites improper planning, lack of political will, negative attitude of the elite towards African languages and the lack of sensitisation. At the end, she presents a number of outstanding lessons one could learn from the Malawian experience.

In the next chapter, Seyum Bekale attempts an overview of the Ethiopian experience in language policy and planning. Centering on the different historical epochs, he analyses the evolution of language policy in Ethiopia. The earliest historical period, the Pre-LP era, was marked by the development and spread of Ge'ez, then the language of the monarchs with other Ethiopian languages used in oral communication by native speakers until they were replaced by Amharic. As for the imperial and Derg periods, these saw the emergence of Amharic as the sole national official language within a one-nation-one-language state. This policy marginalised all the other languages of the country until recently with the official recognition of the country's linguistic plurality. On the whole, despite problems related to policy implementation, several Ethiopian languages now enjoy written development and are being used as languages of instruction and as official languages in decentralised localities as well as in the media.

Abdelrahim Hamid Mugaddam's presents an overview of language policy and planning in Sudan. He addresses the problem of language policy in two different historical periods, namely, the colonial period and the postcolonial period. Basing his discussions on the language of education, arabicisation of education and the status of indigenous Sudanese languages, he explores the efforts made by Sudan's successive governments to manage the use of languages in different domains. He tarries on what he refers to as "the prolonged debate on arabicisation" between both scholars and decision-makers in the North as well as in the South and concludes that so long as Arabic maintains its hegemony in the North with English gradually assuming a similar position in the South, indigenous languages will remain marginalised.

Blasius A. Chiatoh and Pius W. Akumbu come in with a proposal for a national language policy for Cameroon. Observing that 50 years after reunification of the two Cameroons (1961), and despite its linguistic diversity, Cameroon still operates an exoglossic language policy based on the promotion of English and French in education and other domains. Moving from the position that such a policy is neither integrative nor representative and so cannot fully respond to the needs of Cameroonians, they strongly advocate for a total overhaul of present educational practices based on the language of instruction. In the guise of providing guidelines on the procedures and ingredients for adoption of an appropriate language policy, they briefly present language as having vital economic, educational, cultural, political and ideological value. They then propose general and specific principles to be considered in language policy elaboration, the qualities of an appropriate policy as well as the steps in policy formulation. They conclude their submission with a fervent appeal for the diagnosis and treatment of language issues in Cameroon to be informed by scientific and inclusive approaches.

References
Alexander, N. 1999. African Renaissance Without African Languages? In N. Alexander (Ed.) *Language and Development in Africa, Social Dynamics*, Vol. 25. N° 1. pp. 1-12.
Bamgbose, A. 1999. African Language Development and Language Planning in N. Alexander (Ed.) *Language and Development in Africa, Social Dynamics*, Vol. 25. N° 1. pp. 13-30.
Obanya, P. 1999. Popular Fallacies on the Use of African Languages. In N. Alexander (Ed.) *Language and Development in Africa, Social Dynamics*, Vol. 25. N° 1.
Prah, K. K. 1999. The Postcolonial Elite and African Language Policies. In Leslie Limage (Ed.) Selected Papers from the World of the Language and Literacy Commission of the 10th World

Congress on Comparative Education Societies, Cape Town, 1998. Dakar: UNESCO/BREDA. pp. 543-553.

Ruiz, R. 1995. Language Planning Considerations in Indigenous Communities. *The Bilingual Research Journal*, Vol. 19, N° 1. pp. 71-81.

Trudell, B. 2008. Contesting the Default: The Impact of Local Language Choice for Learning. Paper presented at the UNESCO/UNU Conference on Language and Globalisation: Building on our Rich Heritage, Tokyo-Japan.

Wolff, H.E. 1999. Multilingualism, Modernisation and Mother Tongue: Promoting Democracy through Indigenous African Languages. In N. Alexander (Ed.) *Language and Development in Africa, Social Dynamics*, Vol. 25. N° 1.

The Cameroonian Situation

Chapter 1
An Overview of Language Policy and Planning in Cameroon
Gabriel Mba

> Overviewing a specific country's language policy and planning is an attempt to account for the various studies carried out in this domain and also a personal observation and understanding of the subject matter. This is the intention of the present communication that focuses on Cameroon, where the complex linguistic landscape of the country has brought the different stakeholders to engineer different language policies and management to suit their understanding of the issue as well as comply with their felt needs and expectations. This paper seeks to identify these policies and to determine how they have been implemented.

Introduction

Cameroon's multilingual landscape has been subject to many studies carried out with diversified aims and objectives using multidisciplinary approaches. According to Todd (2008), multilingual countries fall into three categories:
    a) Countries that were born multilingual,
    b) Countries that have become multilingual,
    c) Countries that have had multilingualism thrust upon it.

Cameroon is found in the first group as four distinct language families (Afro-Asiatic, Niger-Congo, Nilo-Saharan, and Indo-European) are present and actively managed by various language speakers. Studies on language treatment and management have been conducted individually or collectively expressing diverse points of view on how best the Cameroon government could take advantage of her linguistic resources to enhance her development initiatives. Hypothetical or theoretical language policies have been set up proposing different formulae that capture the bulk of languages according to the global trend of language issues, problems, and prospects and also according to specific fields of actions and activities where language matters.

As Khubchandani (2010: 67) rightly puts it as a concluding remark to a holistic approach to promoting lesser-used languages,

> It is necessary to bring a pluralistic vigour to policy making to ensure fair play in communication by nurturing cultural diversity (just as environmentalists show respect by nurturing bio-diversity). A new Communication order must successfully formulate a coherent policy regarding the rights of lesser-used languages that knits together complex pluralities and can contribute to the quality of communication in a changing society to ensure integral cultural development for all humankind.

The present paper is, therefore, a journey throughout "the linguistic profusion" in Cameroon, coupled with a historical study of reflections that various stakeholders have had for its exploitation. We will end this journey by questioning the different positions and deeds regarding language policy and especially those with a say on the immense reservoir of mother tongues in the field of education.

The Sociolinguistic Context of Cameroon
What a mess! This is a typical reaction one may have while contemplating the linguistic complexity of Cameroon, a triangle hidden in the gulf of Guinea, that nurses more than two hundred indigenous languages, two foreign official languages (French and English), two European languages inherited from its colonial history (German and Spanish), two other languages used for specific purposes, and rightly so, in the field of religious studies and practices (Greek and Latin) and now in-coming and quite attractive languages adopted for mobility, economic, commercial and/or prospective integrative reasons (Chinese, Korean, Italian, and Arabic).

French and English are both languages of administration, media, politics, education, diplomacy, and so forth. From a geographical point of view, the French language covers 3/4 of the country while English covers the remaining 1/4. In terms of administrative constituencies, French is the first official language of eight regions while English is that of two. Their use in the daily business of the administration and individuals is not balanced although the constitution claims that the two languages are of equal status. French is given far more consideration in state affairs than English. Official texts and decisions are first labelled in French and then translated into English. This linguistic puzzle has pushed Cameroonians in their desire of communication to adopt some language loyalties such as Pidgin English and what is termed "camfranglais" which combines aspects of both indigenous and official languages.

English, like French, is going through a structural nativisation (Nkemleke, 2008) as the English language proficiency of Cameroonians is declining from standard to what is called Cameroon English (Simo Bobda & Mbangwana, 1993).

Pidgin-English, largely used in the two officially English speaking regions and to some extent in the littoral and western regions, is a hybrid language constituted on the basis of English, French and some Cameroonian languages. It is reported that

> Long before Cameroon became a political entity following its annexation by the Germans in 1884, pidgin English had been in use along the Guinea Coast for several hundreds of years. By 1800 when the English intensified their commercial activities in the area, Pidgin English was firmly implanted along Cameroon's coast where it was the principal medium of commercial transactions. Its use was intensified and its uses diversified by the Baptists missionaries from London and Jamaica who founded mission stations in Bimbia, Douala and Victoria in 1841, 1854, and 1858 respectively. The opening of plantations by the Germans, following their annexation in 1884 brought together people from the Cameroon hinterland to whom Pidgin English was going to become a useful medium of communication. They used it in the plantations and later on carried it back to their areas of origin. Thus the language continued to spread" (Menang, 2006: 232)

From this assertion, it is obvious that Pidgin English settled even before all actual European languages in use in Cameroon, and the attachment that the Anglophone speaking population has with this language explains the implied identity and consciousness they feel it provides to them. This identity is confirmed by the fact that upon entering school, many children in the English speaking regions and cities have a relative mastery of Pidgin English and formal English comes later in their process of language learning. They resort much to pidgin for communication needs in and out of school. Many children have Pidgin English as their mother tongue at the expense of the mother tongue of their parents. In many cases Pidgin English is used in buying and selling, in religious teaching and worship, in home interaction, in out-group communication and in cultural expression. Furthermore, it is a usual practice even for highly educated Anglophones to switch constantly to pidgin in verbal interactions. That is why different processes that shape the structure of this language have been largely researched by linguists (Ngefack & Sala, 2006a & b; Simo Bobda & Wolf, 2003). Some writers have argued for its inclusion as a language of education, because of its long lasting settlement story, its vehicular nature and creolisation, yet others consider Pidgin English to be a bastardised language that should not be part of the school curriculum.

"Camfranglais", a coined means of communication that started as a distinctive register for university students and later on became their identity marker, has the image of a language largely based on the structures of the French language, with an enriched lexicon drawn from the English language and some Cameroonian indigenous languages. Lexically, words are borrowed from languages in contact in the Cameroonian context with the aim of breaking from the French language norms and by so doing, engineers identity markers that are pragmatically representative of the state of the new code and its speakers. Initially restricted to university students and stigmatised as a campus means of verbal interaction, especially in perfect relation with the oral practices of African oratory, "camfranglais" has spread as a vehicular language among youngsters. As a manifestation of language practices in urban contexts, many scholars have found it to be an interesting research domain that enhances human creativity in shaping and coding messages in the way that suits not only what they say but also the way they say it and fundamentally their proper identification from what has been voiced out (Simo-Souop, 2011; Biloa, 1999; Feussi, 2008; Ngo Ngok-Graux, 2007, Mba, 2011).

The preliminary inventory of the numerous indigenous languages of Cameroon gave an estimate of 239 living languages (Dieu et al, 1983). The methodology used to proceed to the numbering of languages was eclectic in nature as it capitalised on the classification framework proposed by renowned scholars in the domain (Greenberg, 1966; Guthrie, 1965). Thus, Cameroon was divided into nine zones of related languages through resemblances or genetic parenthood. Zone 1 and 2 represent Chadic languages of the Afro-Asiatic family, Zone 3 the Adamawa languages of the Niger-Congo family, Zone 4 Bantu languages, Zone 5 Bantu languages formerly called A50, A60 and A40 by Guthrie, Zone 6 Bantu coastal and hinterland languages from Limbe to Campo also known as A10, A20 and A30, Zone7 Benue-Congo languages that are not Bantu, Zone 8 Western Grassfields languages from Momo, Menchum and Ring groups, and Zone 9 Eastern Grassfields languages. Certain languages like Fulfulde, Pidgin, Kanuri and Ngambay could not fit in any of the zones for geographical, genetic or for both reasons. Kanuri and Ngambay are the sole representatives of the Nilo-Saharan languages while Fulfulde stands as the only West Atlantic language although the Niger-Kordofanian phylum is overwhelmingly represented in zones 3 to 9 (Dieu, 1983: 31).

Comparing Cameroon to Nigeria another multilingual country in Africa, Todd (2008: 4-5) remarks that each country has her own characteristics and consequently uniqueness when describing its multilingualism.

> Cameroon has much in common with Nigeria or Ghana or Sierra Leone:
> - Geographical position and bio-diversity
> - Historical and colonial links
> - Linguistic affinities in African languages, in the prestige of Arabic, the use of English and an English - derived pidgin or creole. Cameroon, however, has a smaller population than Nigeria and uses both French and English as official languages. These are fundamental distinctions that have social, cultural, educational and economic consequences.

Given this linguistic striking picture, it is obvious that numerous questions could be raised in relation with language standardisation issues, state language policy and implementation, people attitudes and representations towards the various languages, language choices in education, individual as well as group communication, language and identity maintenance and linguistic marketing.

Language Policy and Language Planning in Cameroon

Language policy is a conscious choice of a language or languages in relation to the social life of people while language planning is actually the implementation of language choices using the most convenient channels, empowering the different steps of the process, providing the necessary financial means and trained manpower and constantly assessing its effectiveness for instant reorientation. Individuals can have their own language policy as well as states may do. But here we do focus on an activity carried out by states or state institutions in order to cater for the citizenry.

Before independence, Cameroon experienced three different colonial administrations (German, British and French) with quite different languages policies. The initial use of Cameroonian languages alongside German as languages of communication was a strategic way to gain peoples' esteem and enforce German later. This policy is similar to the indirect rule system put in place by the British. The British language policy gave room to local languages and, in the education system, the two regions under their colonial administration were given a chance to use indigenous languages in the first four years of primary school and English in the last three. The education system was ecological in nature as African values were of some importance to British colonisers who felt that administrating people means having a good cognizance of their communities and practices. The French colonial masters had a contrasting policy known to be that of assimilation. French should by all means be the language of communication in all domains of public life and affairs and particularly in that of administration and education. All the necessary tools for such a "redemptive mission" should be set on motion. The colonial official Journal in 1924 published a law stipulating that.

> *Aucun livre ni brochure, aucun imprimé ni manuscrit étrangers à l'enseignement ne peuvent être introduits à l'école sans autorisation du commissaire de la République; La langue française est la seule en usage dans les écoles ; il est interdit aux maîtres de se servir avec leurs élèves des idiomes du pays* (J.O 1924: 175).

Obviously, it was the enactment of a monolingual language policy that has been reinforced after the 1944 Brazzaville conference which recommended once more that indigenous languages be discarded from the school system in all French colonies. Stumpf (1979: 42) has this to report on the decision:

> *L'enseignement doit être donné en langue française, l'emploi pédagogique des dialectes locaux parlés étant*

> *absolument interdit aussi bien dans les écoles privées que dans les écoles publiques.*

This other decision, consonant with the first one, was geared towards mission schools that opted for the use of indigenous languages as strategic tools for the mastery of the French language on the one hand and as language of Christian education on the other.

After independence, different successive language policies have been set up by government. The first constitution established in 1960 at the dawn of independence instituted a language policy solely based on the promotion of French and English in all sectors of social life notwithstanding the huge amount of local languages. It was a constitution focused on early bilingualism as a language problem was already felt by ruling authorities (Fonlon, 1969). The second constitution elaborated in 1972 went far beyond to establish more legal instruments in favour of a strong official bilingualism (French and English) and, consequently, adequate structures and institutions (creation of various linguistic centres for bilingual training, experimental bilingual high schools, internship language programmes for university students in France and Britain, etc) were put in place to render efficient the different measures taken. The third constitution of 1996 which is a revised version of that of 1972 has been more sensitive about the multilingual landscape of Cameroon by integrating dispositions that give a more positive image to local languages. It goes in the preamble of this constitution that local languages shall be preserved and protected. Some other specific enactments especially in the area of language education have taken place among which are:

- Law no 98/004 of 14 April 1998 on the orientation of education that promotes among other things the use of indigenous languages and cultures.
- Law no 98/003 of 8 January 1998 reorganising the ministry of culture that formerly creates a department for mother tongues.
- Decree no 2004/004 of January 2004 reorganising the then ministry of national education that creates pedagogic inspectorates for mother tongues which are presently operational.
- Law no 2004/018 of July 2004 on decentralisation transferring powers to local councils to implement programmes that will help to eradicate illiteracy and ensure a better management of educational infrastructure. It goes far

ahead to instruct local councils to cater for the promotion of national languages.
- Law no 2004/019 of July 2004 empowering regions to support the promotion of local languages through education and literacy.
- Decree no 2012/268 of 11 June 2012 organises the ministry of basic education and creates an inspectorate in charge of literacy, of non formal basic education and of the promotion of mother tongue education, as well as corresponding entities at regional, divisional and sub-divisional levels.

This sudden and positive move by government institutions and officials especially from 1996, is not in our sense a reappraisal of the importance of indigenous languages and a need for a more equitable education system and communicative needs of the citizenry; it is rather a push resulting from the efforts of local and international NGO's in the area of mother tongue based bilingual education and the international environment that is more supportive of multilingual education. The multilingual approach gives individuals to cater for their language using the various channels of education and literacy, and empowers each and every one to stand for the preservation and spread of his or her cultural and linguistic heritage. In Cameroon as in some other African states "language choice in education is a politics of persuasion rather than bargaining (Albaugh, 2007: 2)." But also the "bargaining strategy" has gone operational not only under the influence of international organisations like UNESCO but increasingly through the change in the former colonisers' attitude, as "governments concede language rights in education in order to gain the support or quiescence of language groups". France for example which stands as the former coloniser of a good number of African countries (including Cameroon) as Albaugh (2007: 2-3) puts it

> Suddenly decided to care about local languages because its leadership has been persuaded by a francophone group of scholars - an epistemic community - that learning initially in a local language helps a child to learn French.

This explains the ELAN (*Ecole et Langues en Afrique*) project tailored by the French government institutions to suit African governments. Is it an attempt to control how far individual governments can or must go in the teaching and effective use of indigenous languages in the school system and social life affairs or a deliberate attempt to assist African states in the management of their linguistic resources? Time will tell but one fact is clear - it is to Africans to support, finance and implement their language planning and policy having in mind the rights of individuals, the horizontal and vertical dimensions of social communications and their vision and prospects.

Scholars' Reflections on Hypothetical Language Policies for Cameroon

Key Cameroonian scholars in the field of language policy formulation and implementation (Ngijol, 1964, 1978; Bot Ba Njock, 1966; Towa, 1987; Fonlon, 1969; Chumbow, 1980, 1987; Tadadjeu, 1977; Tabi Manga, 2000) have proposed language planning models that could help to enhance the country's linguistic diversity. The planning models have evolved from bilingualism to trilingualism and from trilingualism to quadralingualism, giving room to local lesser-used languages to feature among identity revival issues that rescue language integrity in the arena where the widely used official languages dominate (Mba, 2006).

The official bilingual model has been the preoccupation of early language planners and scholars, with no reference to the numerous local languages. For them, a language policy that considers local languages is a source of national destruction as the unity of the country and that of the citizens should be built on foreign languages. Cameroonians were not yet ripe to talk about mother tongues as they were just starting to reconcile after independence wars, sufferings and hardship. The efforts of the first republic were more attentive to the decisions that could best reinforce this policy and see to it that Cameroonians become bilinguals. Published works assessing this policy observe, though, that if Cameroon was on paper recognised as a bilingual country, her citizens were not. The local languages that were carefully side lined, were revealed to be part of the reasons why the individual official languages were not mastered, as well as a significant factor in the failure of the exclusive foreign languages bilingual model. A need for a more global vision of language policies was in required.

Advocacy for a language policy that incorporates Cameroonian local languages started with Ngijol who in 1964, in the midst of the efforts for the promotion of official bilingualism, proposed that one mother tongue should be used at the national level. This will act as a unifying force and reduce the threat of tribalism. But, with time and reflecting about the difficulties of the implementation of such a policy, he went further (in 1987) to suggest the use of a number of national, provincial or regional languages. In fact he distinguishes in terms of status three different native tongues: minority mother tongues, provincial vehicular languages and national languages. A set of criteria were set up for each type and an indicative list of languages provided.

Bot Ba Njock (1966) just after Ngijol (1964) proposes a contrary linguistic policy where all mother tongues should be used in the early years of education. Considering the technical difficulties of implementing this policy (lack of trained linguists, low level of language development) he suggested the use of zonal languages resulting in the selection of one or more languages per region.

Towa (1987), having in mind Ngijol's first and second proposals, suggested a reconciling solution being the determination of a mother tongue at the level of the nation and a limited number of vehicular languages. These vehicular languages (twelve in number) will be used in schools and endowed with the status of national languages. All the remaining ones will serve the purpose of adult literacy and thus, will not run the risk of extinction.

Chumbow after some sound and positive criticisms mounted against the implementation of the bilingual state language policy (1980) presented in 1987 an ideal language planning for Africa following the canonical models. If language planning is an activity to be coordinated by a central agency or body it should be a model having three main components, the last one being integrated at each step: policy formulation, policy implementation, and evaluation. A redemptive language planning is the one that enhances the development of the state and that of individuals and groups. So all languages, official as native ones should be unequivocally given a clear status, be integrated in the planning, and means allocated for implementation and evaluation.

Tadadjeu's trilingualism (1977) later on reconceptualised as extensive trilingualism envisaged that Cameroonians of tomorrow will have the capacity to communicate in at least three languages among which one would certainly be a native Cameroonian language (preferably his or her mother tongue), the second being his or her first official language (French for Francophones and English for

Anglophones), and the third one would be for some a Cameroonian vehicular language and for others the second official language. If the three languages represent the desirable basic linguistic competences, the additional adjective (extensive) means that the number of languages one can judge useful and adequate to his or her needs are not limited. This will depend on individuals' linguistic needs and desires, on linguistic contexts and possibilities as well as institutional necessities. The extensive trilingualism theory has a twofold communicational linguistic dimension. The vertical dimension is fulfilled by native Cameroonian languages and ideally the mother tongue of a person while the horizontal one is materialised through official languages and native vehicular languages. This vision establishes the functional complementary relation among languages as specific domains of activities require certain specific languages. For example, traditional and cultural activities are best described by native Cameroonian languages than French or English. In the same vein, school activities may both be conducted in official and local languages. Cameroonians with two different mother tongues could refer to official languages or a local vehicular language they deem necessary and which they master to communicate. In the conception of the extensive trilingualism theory, there is a stable component based on three different languages and a variable component rooted on a non limited number of languages. It is up to an individual to build that capacity (that variable component) with regards to his or her local, regional, professional needs or administrative or institutional possibilities.

The quadrilingualism theory elaborated by Tabi Manga (2000) is based on a functional taxonomy of languages that are in use by citizens be they foreign or local. Local languages are given more consideration and their functional use and geographic area of communicational vitality and relevance are highlighted. Four language strata are designed:

a) Maternal languages used at the level of individual families and which could not stand education purposes because of their very limited geographical coverage.
b) Communitarian languages spoken within the limits of an administrative division but which, due to the important number of speakers could feature among languages having a national dimension.

c) Vehicular languages that go beyond their natural geographical area and are used regionally by speakers of some other languages as their regional lingua franca. These are languages which normally could be termed national languages and therefore have a national destiny.
d) Official languages (French and English) that are state and international languages widely used. They function as working languages in all aspects of national life.

Although this taxonomy recognises the importance of all native languages it reduce the scope of languages that could have an administrative or national destiny compared to the extensive trilingual model that was solely built on the communicative nature of languages without selecting some for school purposes.

Contributions of Local Language Standardisation Agencies, Applied Research and Programmes to the Building of Language Policy

Most of the transformations in government language policy and attitudes are due to field work largely carried out by local language agencies and time and often by applied linguists working in state institutions that are in favour of a comprehensive language chart.

In fact, individual local languages have men and women who are voluntarily involved in the description, writing, teaching and modernisation of their languages. This is easily perceived in their participation in projects launched by international language bodies like SIL Cameroon, Universities, research institutions, local NGOs like the National Association of Cameroon Language Committees (NACALCO), and the Cameroon Association for Bible Translation and Literacy (CABTAL).). Key programmes that have had an incidence on the government language policy are: *Projet de recherche operationelle pour l'enseignement des langues au Cameroun* (PROPELCA), Basic standardisation of all unwritten African Languages (BASAL), *Lexiques thématiques du Cameroun* (Cameroon thematic lexicon), Development of Cameroonian Languages (DELCAM) and Language Dynamics (DYLAN).

State research institutions and especially the defunct Institute of Human Sciences (ISH) through the centre of research and anthropological studies (CREA) has initiated some important programmes that resulted in producing the preliminary inventory of

Cameroonian languages, the studies on lexical expansion, on language dynamics, on language development and promotion.

Since its activities started in Cameroon in 1969, the Summer Institute of linguistic (today SIL Cameroon) has, apart from translating the word of God into local languages and training first hand and mature local language professionals (Discover Your Language project), has done a lot, providing the scientific description of many languages. Her involvement in experimental mother tongue teaching through PROPELCA and the Kom Experimental Mother Tongue Education Project (KEP) programmes has sealed her partnership with the Cameroon Ministries in charge of literacy and education and NACALCO.

The University of Yaoundé launched in 1978 the operational research project for language education in Cameroon on the basis of the trilingual planning model which has experimented not only the teaching of French and English in secondary schools but also that of French/English coupled with Cameroonian mother tongues in pre-primary, primary and secondary schools. The scientific community has satisfactorily benefited from the results of this experiment.

NACALCO, which is the federation of individual language associations (78 language members as of 2012), has gone a further step to reorganise these local bodies and create a high sense of commitment to the ideal of designing common projects and strategies in language development. That is why all language workers are being trained on the same modules and the same projects are conducted on a considerable number of languages, a cross fertilisation of individual experiences being the focus. Thus, some cardinal language projects have been undertaken to the benefit of the associations and languages of the federation. The PROPELCA project inherited from the University of Yaoundé 1 has been continued and generalised throughout the ten regions of the country. BASAL, established to provide writing systems for languages in need has so far given opportunity to eleven Cameroonian and two Ethiopian languages to tackle their written development. The strategy chosen is to build a body of young African linguists volunteering to stay in a community and work together with community members in order to initiate the description of the language, produce the first reference reading and writing material, train the local manpower and establish the first language committee. The adult literacy component of the NACALCO project consists in training literacy workers, assessing and helping ongoing literacy programmes and above all serve as a reference for professionals or would-be professionals such as university students. The Electronic rural school in African languages (ERELA) programme is geared towards introducing computer in the teaching/learning of Cameroonian languages in the rural areas. It is admitted that rural areas are weaned from the potentials of the computer in language related issues and the aim is to give opportunity to rural schools to match the teaching of mother tongues with the computer knowledge. NACALCO has partnered with SIL Cameroon in the PROPELCA and BASAL programmes.

CABTAL specialises in translation and literacy and has developed some expertise in the two fields. The literacy programmes are church related contrary to the ones initiated or supervised by NACALCO which are open to any component of the society. CABTAL produces not only church related documents in specific languages but also organises sessions for scripture in use in different communities.

Churches in Cameroon as elsewhere are powerful organisations in language matters. The church has been before and after independence a fabric of language use, contact, maintenance and preservation. Not only the word of God is translated but the scriptures are used for planned sermons as well as unplanned ones. All the languages present in the country are used according to the selected audience. That's why selective local vehicular languages or contact languages (Pidgin English, Fulfulde, Ewondo, Duala, Mungaka...) are sometimes favoured instead of English or French. In church practices, choirs do sing songs in diverse Cameroonian languages that are not the indigenous languages of the area, contributing thus to multiple language awareness and language peace. In some instances, when a sermon is given in one of the official languages, an instant translation is rendered in the main local language of the area. Sometimes, when need arises, some minority groups are taken apart after the church services for a thorough explanation of the sermon in their language, under the guidance of more experienced church workers. As concerns languages of education, churches are at the forefront of language education choices that automatically give a strong position to native languages. Teachers in mission schools are instructed to use mother tongues as a pedagogic tool when there is need and especially in rural areas. In the past some of the mission secondary schools have opted for the teaching of local languages (*Collège Liberman, Douala;*

Collège de la Retraite, Yaoundé; Saint Paul, Bafang; Maya, Kekem; Jeanne d'Arc, Nkongsamba, Séminaire de Mélong). Recently, beginning in 2010 the ministry of secondary education has been attempting to copy the example. Even the PROPELCA programme which has been so resourceful for applied linguistics and practical knowledge in Cameroon, had been the affair of catholic and protestant mission schools at its launching and experimental phases. The first language committees were church-based and the standardisation of numerous Cameroonian languages has benefited from the pastors' and priests' inputs. Similarly, most literacy programmes are initiated, controlled and supervised by churches. A whole department is sometimes dedicated to literacy and translation. This is the case with the following 16 language projects supported by churches: Karang, Duupa, Dugun, Kompana, Doyayo, Gbaya, Tikar, Dii, Samba, Kolbila, Pere, Mambila, Kwanja, Bum, Nizaa, and Vute. It is then evident that churches are playing a significant role in language policy building and essentially in policy implementation.

Critical Analysis of Language Policy and Implementation in Cameroon

A critical examination of the existing literature on the official bilingualism recognises that there was no better alternative than assuming the historical linguistic heritage of Cameroon. The language policy focusing on the colonial languages was a good one. Nevertheless, it is in the area of policy implementation that grievances were recorded. There is an urgent need to go beyond the linguistic juxtaposition of the two official languages in the school system, and in the administrative life, to a more integrative one that makes citizens effectively bilingual, thereby empowering them. Accordingly Mbangwana (2004: 24-25) has this to say:

> If being bilingual in Cameroon was demonstrated in many ways to be more rewarding and attractive, then people will see it as a plus, that is an added value [ ] Just give a hint to Cameroonians that in order to occupy certain top positions in the republic it requires that such holders of posts should be bilingual in English and French then you will see how concerned Cameroonians will be in trying to be bilingual.

Concretely, there is a long way to go in the evaluation of the policy. Implementation measures should be reassessed in order to constantly readjust the objectives in relation to the changing social environment and individual needs. Many enforcement measures for a more redemptive official bilingualism policy and especially in the framework of its implementation are actually in need. What of native Cameroonian languages?

An evaluation of the different proposals of language policy and planning involving Cameroonian languages has been made by Dunnigan (1989: 74) and many of her conclusions still hold today. Talking about the incomplete nature of Bot Ba Njock and Towa's proposals she states that,

> An ideal plan should describe the institution responsible for decision-making, the structure of the decision-making process and criteria upon which the decisions are based. The stage of evaluation is not an explicit part. Evaluation, which, logically, relates to the goals, is difficult for status decisions because the fulfilment of goals such as national unity cannot be measured in a concrete way.

There has been an evolution in the perception Chumbow and Tadadjeu had about language policy and planning. Though canonical models have to be followed in this enterprise, community social structures have to play a role. The centralised planning model should give way to a more decentralised one where policy decisions should be taken by government or any government-appointed institution but in line with the social structures that have a say in decision-making and that are more involved in implementation procedures. A top-down and down-top process will better enhance any language policy that addresses a multilingual and multicultural setting as it is the case of Cameroon.

The Unwritten Story of Language Policy and Language Planning in Cameroon

The language policy and planning story of Cameroon is yet to be written as what is apparently a policy is experiencing implementation difficulties linked to the hesitations of state workers on who fall the responsibility of building a coherent policy and a set of tools and package of strategies for implementation. I view the operational scheme adopted as a little bit prudent but not coherent enough. No clear decision is taken for instance in the area of education to stipulate the level of intervention of each individual language. Key questions are still waiting for adequate answers that will push the different language stakeholders to assume their duties properly. Among these questions the most evident ones are:

1) How is the use of French, English and mother tongues in basic education knitted together in the school programmes?
2) Which and where do local languages fit in the different classes of secondary education? Should all local languages get into the secondary education?
3) Are local languages media or subjects of education?
4) What is the whole picture of language learning/teaching in rural and urban settings?
5) How are institutions of learning, teaching and training prepared to do research and teaching?
6) How do we sensitise the citizens with regard to any clear policy and implementation strategies taken to go with?
7) What partnership is established among the various language policy making bodies and field practitioners?

These sample questions consider both the political will on policy making and implementation. The responses will throw more light on the government vision and effectively set the various institutions or people in charge on the good foot. Any attempt to slow down the responses to these questions is like a foot-dragging experience that hampers the collective efforts of various stakeholders. The dynamics of a language policy and planning rest on its capacity to be flexible and comprehensive enough to address the communicative and educational needs of the citizenry in a constantly changing society.

The laws on decentralisation that empower councils and regions to preserve and promote local languages in their specific constituencies seem to be a corner stone in the area of language planning and policy. Many indigenous, lesser-used Cameroonian languages will find favour in this context as their cultural weight will be reascertained. One of the striking setbacks in language maintenance, use, promotion and diffusion is the forgotten cultural weight of individual languages that affect language structures, shape the linguistic conscience of native users and especially intervenes in various speech acts. Performing a speech act is realising a choice of certain language patterns, of certain language constructions, words and formulae. The trend of globalisation where each and everyone is engaged has a positive effect on language contact and pluralistic communication but one wonders whether it has favoured the small languages not only in Africa but also in other remote areas of the other continents. A language policy and planning that will not send a helping hand to the above mentioned languages runs against the normal stream of language development and forcefully favours the extinction of part of the world's culture. Is this where the language use, practices and policies in Cameroon will lead us to? I can't provide for the time being a definitive answer but potentials exist to avoid such a situation.

Conclusion

Highlights of this paper have been on the sociolinguistic situation of Cameroon, on language planning, on Cameroonian scholars' hypothetical language policies, on the collaborative efforts of local language standardisation agencies, churches and applied research programmes, as well as the critical analysis of the implemented language policies . It goes clearly that the language policy and planning of the country is still to be built, and decentralisation if well conducted could really render visible a full functional image of the linguistic and cultural diversity of the country.

References

Albaugh, E. A. 2007. Language choice in education: A politics of persuasion. *Journal of Modern African Studies,* 45, 1 pp 1-32.

Biloa, E. 1999. *Bilinguisme officiel et communication linguistique au Cameroun,* New York: Peter Lang.

Bot Ba Njock, H. M. 1966. Le problème linguistique au Cameroun. *L'Afrique et l'Asie* ; 73 pp 3-13.

Chumbow, B. S. 1980. Language and Language Policy in Cameroon. In *An African Experiment in Nation Building: The Bilingual Cameroon Republic since Reunification,* Colorado, Boulder, pp 281-311.

Chumbow, B. S. 1987. Towards a language planning model for Africa. *Journal of West African Languages,* XVII, Vol. 1. pp 15-22.

Dieu M. et Renaud P. 1983. Atlas linguistique de l'Afrique centrale: situation linguistique en Afrique centrale, inventaire préliminaire, le Cameroun, ACCT/CERDOTOLA/DGRST, Paris, Yaoundé.

.Dunnigan, L. 1989. Mother tongue literacy in Cameroon: A linguistic planning perspective, maîtrise dissertation, University of Yaoundé.

Feussi, V. 2008. Le Camfranglais comme une construction socio-identitaire du «jeune» francophone au Cameroun». *Le français en Afrique* No. 23 pp 33-50.

Fonlon, B. 1969. The language problem in Cameroon. *Abbia*, 22, 5-40 (2) pp 131-162.

Greenberg, J. 1966. *The languages of Africa* (2nd edition 1966), Bloomington, Indiana, Indiana university research centre in Anthropology, folklore and Linguistics, The Hague: Mouton.

Guthrie, M. 1965. Language classification and African studies. In African affairs, a special issue to record the proceedings of the 1964 conference of the African studies Association of the United Kingdom, London Royal African society, pp 29-36.

Journal officiel de l'Etat du Cameroun, 1924.

Khubchandabni, L. M. 2010. Living together in a multilingual world: A holistic approach to promoting lesser-used languages. *Linguapax Review*, UNESCOCAT, Barcelona pp 59-71.

Menang, T. 2006. Pidgin English and the Anglophone identity in Cameroon. In Mbangwana, P. Kizitus, M. and Mbuh T. (Eds.), *Language, literature and identity*, Göttingen: Cuvillier Verlag, pp 227-235.

Mba, G. 2011. Langues de moindre diffusion et transmission intergénérationnelle en milieu plurilingue et pluriculturel. collection espaces discursifs, Paris: Harmattan, pp 139-154.

Mbangwana, P. 2004. Cameroon nationhood and official bilingualism: a linguistic juxtaposition. *RIALSS* no 1, PP 15-38.

Ngijol Ngijol, P. 1964. Nécessité d'une langue nationale. *Abbia*, 7 pp 83-99.

-----------. 1978. *Etude sur l'enseignement des langues et cultures nationales*. Yaoundé, Centre National d'Education.

Nkemleke, D. 2008. Frequency and use of modals in Cameroon English and application to language education. In Harrow, K. & Mpoche, K. (Eds.), *Language, literature and education in multicultural societies: Collaborative research on Africa*, pp 242-261.

Ngefack, A and Sala, B. 2006a. Cameroon Pidgin and Cameroon English at a confluence: areal investigation time. *English World-Wide*, 27, pp 217-227.

Ngefack, A and Sala, B. 2006b. What's happening to Cameroon Pidgin English? The depidginisation process in Cameroon Pidgin English. *PHIN* 36, pp 36-41.

Ngo Ngok-Graux, E. 2007. Les représentations du camfranglais chez les locuteurs de Douala et de Yaoundé. *Le français en Afrique* no 21, pp 219-227.

Simo-Souop, A. 2011. Quelques traits de fonctionnalisation du camfranglais. In Tsofack, B & Feussi, V (Ed.), *Langues et discours en contextes urbains au Cameroun: (dé)constructions - complexités,* pp 121-137.

Simo Bobda, A. and Mbangwana, P. 1993. An introduction to spoken English, Akoka, university of Ibadan.

Simo Bobda, A. & Wolf, H. G. 2003. Pidgin English in Cameroon in the new millennium. In Lucko, P, L. Peter and H.G. Wolf (Eds.), Studies in African varieties of English, Frankfurt, pp 101-117.

Stumpf, R. 1979. La politique linguistique au Cameroun de 1884 à 1960. Berne, Peter lang ,pp 157 (60 pages annexes).

Todd, L. 2008. Choices facing multicultural society with regard to language, literature and education. In Harrow, K. & Mpoche, K. (Eds.), *Language, literature and education in multicultural societies: Collaborative research on Africa,* pp 3-23.

Tabi-Manga, J. 2000. Les politiques linguistiques du Cameroun. Essai d'aménagement linguistique. Paris, Karthala.

Tadadjeu, M. 1977. A model for functional trilingual education planning in Africa, unpublished PhD Dissertation, University of South Carolina.

Towa, M. 1987. Vers la proposition des langues nationales : positions finales. *le Republicain*, 59 pp. 11-12.

Chapter 2
Cameroonian Languages in Education: Enabling or Disenabling Policies and Practices?
Blasius A. Chiatoh

The non-promotion of African mother tongues in education has been blamed on the absence of appropriate language policies especially at the level of specification of goals and the definition of implementation strategies and mechanisms. Yet, even in the absence of an elaborate policy, possibilities and opportunities quite often exist, which if fully exploited, could significantly enhance the presence of these languages in education. In Cameroon, like in many African countries, having a perfect language policy has been more of an illusion than a reality. In such a situation, total reliance on a perfect policy for promoting mother tongue-based education also means recognising the possibility of never achieving this goal at all.

Recently, Cameroon has witnessed progress in the direction of legislation in favour of mother tongue promotion. However, this legislation reveals major short-comings that make it appear more as 'a written expression of intent' than actual policy. Nevertheless; the opportunities contained therein are not negligible. While within non-governmental circles these opportunities are maximally exploited, within government circles, the inadequacies inherent in legislation have come to provide justification for inaction thus revealing the significant lack of government commitment to further language in education reforms based on mother tongues.

In this paper, I examine the relationship between policy, legislation and actual practices and argue that the present legislative framework notwithstanding, committed public investment by way of concrete language planning practices is still an agenda for the future. Present legislation remains largely a barrier rather than facilitator to successful mother tongue education in the country.

Introduction
Since reunification in 1961, the language policy question in Cameroon has occupied central stage in educational discourses both within the public and private circles. Regrettably, consensus is yet to be achieved on what actually constitutes an adequate language policy. Within government circles, policy has and continues to be perceived as the enactment of laws void of necessary ingredients for effective implementation such as overt definition of goals, phasing, resource allocation, and stakeholders, specification of implementation

strategies and mechanisms, and evaluation. Such limited perception and interpretation of policy leads to the formulation of pieces of legislation that can only appropriately be referred to as 'half-baked policy' or better still 'written expressions of intent'. In fact, the legislation passed over the years seems to be more of widow-dressing than a real commitment to resolve existing language, education and written communication problems in a highly multilingual Cameroon.

Despite the growth in national awareness of the need to integrate indigenous languages into national development efforts (see 1996 Constitution), careful analysis reveals deliberate political resolve to strangulate all potential forms of reforms thus casting doubts as to government's commitment to reverse the status quo. One wonders how and why government, although publicly supportive of the development of the country's languages soon becomes a stumbling block to the implementation of its own proposed reforms. In such a context, can one say with certainty that existing legislation is the product of genuine commitment to provide adequate solutions to the language problems affecting national life? Can one really count on government for any educational innovations based on language? Is government truly committed to sustainable social change built around the country's linguistic resources? Or are supposed reforms intended simply for the achievement of a monolithic political agenda?

A look at the country's current socio-political landscape points to the fact that what obtains at the level of educational policy and planning is a replica of the state of affairs elsewhere in the wider national community where it has become an unlegislated tradition to preach one doctrine in public and to practise its opposite in private. One is thus tempted to imagine that language in education reform does not really constitute a cherished ideal for government, which seems more determined to consolidate existing power relationships through the furthering of foreign language education. On this count, insights into the reform inertia that characterises the socio-economic and political life of the country become readily evident.

Disjuncture Between Policy and Legislation: A Necessary Specification

An important issue in debates on languages in education is that of policy. Although language policy is quite often conceived as synonymous to language planning, there is need sometimes to clearly differentiate between the two concepts (see also Seyum, this volume).

In this respect, it will be much safer to consider policy as decision-making on the choice of which language(s) should be used in which domains in society. Viewed from this perspective, policy involves addressing issues of the status (official or unofficial and/or otherwise) of languages within the nation. On its part, planning would involve the concrete measures undertaken to ensure the practical application of policy. Planning initiatives would include such activities as graphisation, standardisation and modernisation and renovation and terminology development (Hornberger, 2006: 27; Kaplan & Baldauf 1997, 38; Chilora, 2004: 10-17). But in Africa in general and in Cameroon in particular, the problem does not end with such specification since this may lead to other forms of interpretation and consequently, misunderstanding. Another dimension of the problem is whether or not policy and legislation mean one and the same thing. Here, we must observe that while it takes legislation to make policy, policy is not limited to legislation. Besides being legislation, policy goes further to make specifications on the goals and outcomes of legislation as well as the strategies and resources for its realisation. What we must emphasise, though, is the deliberative nature of policy (Eastman, 1983). By this we imply that it is the result of public discussions about language policy in terms of the best alternatives to the status quo (Djité, 2008: 57). Legislation on its part will refer to the legal frameworks or texts that focus on the use of language(s) in society. It could take the form of laws, constitutional provisions, decrees, etc. on how the language(s) of a nation are to be used. We can, therefore, say that while policy deals with consensual decisions on the use of languages in a nation, legislation is the concrete representation of these decisions in the form of written texts that transform these decisions into law. But as can be observed, some Cameroonians tend to equate legislation with policy and as a consequence, tend to overlook some of the important details involved, thereby, contributing to the implementation inertia observed in the country today.

Put differently, what policy is should be determined first and foremost from how explicitly set goals are defined and the correlation between these goals and real learning and written communication needs of the national polity. The more explicit goals are and reflective of reality, the higher the probability for effective policy implementation. Policy must go beyond texts of legislation to involve their actual application. The question which arises here is what this

reality is that must be reflected in policy goals, how it is to be determined and who has the responsibility of undertaking the task of determining. For us to understand these issues, we must address the following vital questions:
1) What are the real learning and written communication needs in Cameroon?
2) How are they determined?
3) Who determines them?
4) For what purposes?

A careful examination of these questions reveals that language lies at the centre of all the learning and communication problems in this country. First, important domains like education, mass media, legislation, and administration all function in foreign languages that a vast majority of the population neither understands nor speaks (Tadadjeu & Chiatoh, 2002: 3). In contrast, those who have access to the services generated by these domains constitute a very small fraction of the population. They constitute, indeed, the elite class made up of people who have succeeded somehow in the school system. Second, we realise that learning and communication needs in Cameroon are not properly diagnosed and so are wrongly defined. This is justified by the wrong choice of language in education and other areas of development planning. Children speak one language at home and yet a different language in the classroom, a situation that is psycho-pedagogically and culturally inappropriate and unacceptable. Third, we must acknowledge that so far, educational policy matters have been addressed almost exclusively from a non-scientific point of view especially with respect to the use of languages in education. Fourth and last, such an attitude has been adopted for purely political rather than educational reasons. Embracing languages other than the foreign official mediums as instruments of instruction has proven to be a too difficult commitment to undertake.

Our situation is thus one characterised by an acute language problem. Children learn in languages that in reality should be third and fourth languages to them. And talking about a language problem, Rubin (1983: 4) defines it in terms of language choice as follows:

> ... On the one hand, it is often defined in terms of language choice – the need to decide which variety/language will be used in certain sectors of the polity. An example of such problems might be what language to use as a medium of instruction in

education, or what language to use in mass communication, or what language to use in the legislature.

What this view suggests is that careful identification and definition of a language problem is the key to the adoption of an appropriate language policy in the nation. But even more important is the fact that the identification and definition of such a problem is based on very diligent analysis of the prevailing linguistic situation on the one hand and then the impact that the choice made is likely to have on the entire society on the other. This leads us to the second question which has to do with who determines the reality or the language problem. This question is extremely relevant in our context for two main reasons. First, government is generally insensitive towards grassroots voices in matters of policy formulation and implementation. Second, official policy is overly ambiguous and so gives room to multiple interpretations and speculation with regard to exact government intensions.

Another important consideration in the interpretation and definition of a language problem is the need for informed opinion. Although it is absolutely necessary to take into account the different opinions and aspirations of all within the national polity in the elaboration of a truly representative policy, the policy formulation process, after all, is not a free-for-all affair. Rather, it is preferable that language policy matters, owing to their extremely sensitive and delicate nature, be guided by attested expert knowledge. In other words, the diagnosis, identification and definition of a language problem should be left in the hands of experts, who alone, master the intricacies involved. The prioritisation of trained sensitivity in language policy matters, as opposed to general academic sensitivity, has the advantage that it potentially contributes to providing productive scientific orientation in the resolution of properly-identified language problems through well-informed and consensual decisions around the choice of language in controlling domains. Clearly, therefore, decision-making cannot be dissociated from informed opinion for two reasons: First, decision-making formalises policy through the processes of legislation and implementation. Second, language policy definition indirectly implies the definition of power relationships in the nation and usually the building and consolidation of such relationships is achieved at the detriment of the majority of the citizens. This becomes especially crucial in Cameroon where, in addition to a high level of linguistic complexity, we have a decision-making process that is reputed for undemocratic practices.

It is worthy to note that although prior scientific data on the prevailing sociolinguistic situation as well as proper analysis of language and communication needs are always indispensable in the adoption of appropriate language policy in multilingual settings, in Cameroon, despite its extreme linguistic fragmentation (over 250 mainly minority languages), decision-making is mostly motivated politically. The result is that there is always great dissonance between policy prescriptions and the actual implementation process. In a context like ours, therefore, while language planning tends to be equated with policy making alone, implementation tends to be treated with lack of seriousness or even downright levity (Bamgbose, 1999: 18).

Bilingual Policy, Monolingual Practice
From the foregoing, we understand that ideally, policy adoption in a nation must be in consonance with existing learning and communication needs. But in reality, this is not the case especially in Cameroon. A quick look at present legislation could lead to the misleading impression that language problems have been carefully taken care of, indeed, that learning in more than one language is already a living reality in the country. However, a closer look and a more critical analysis reveal quite the contrary. The point here is that more than a decade after the first-ever constitutional recognition of the need to promote Cameroonian national languages, not much has actually changed on the ground. If we consider that policy is meaningless until it produces concrete effect on the actual state of use of languages in the nation, we might not be wrong to conclude that so far, language policy reform in the country has been more of an illusion than a reality. Official bilingualism remains the ideal option within government circles while interest in mother tongue-based bilingualism is upheld mostly within research circles, and to a lesser extent among local communities. We observe, for instance, that although constitutionally, English and French enjoy equal status as official languages, in reality, there is a lot of inequality in the assignment of domains of use to these languages. French has and continues to enjoy a de facto supremacy (Chiatoh, 2006: 148; 2012: 10) over English in both public and private domains. Apart from a

few cases, most official documents and decisions appear exclusively in French (Chiatoh, 2012: 8-9) with occasional translations into English. From another perspective, despite recent attempts to promote official bilingualism in primary schools, most classrooms remain practically monolingual first because the teachers themselves are not bilingual or because while the first official language in each case continues to serve as the medium of instruction the second continues to be taught as a subject. As regards mother tongue-based bilingualism, it is important to note that since this does not yet enjoy government recognition, its promotion is still limited to a few experimental classroom situations.

On the whole, therefore, classes remain predominantly monolingual with both teachers and learners hardly ever capable of operating in more than one language, except perhaps, occasionally as happens when the teacher resorts to the use of the mother tongue to explain certain unfamiliar and complex notions (Chiatoh, 2010: 136). In urban areas, the situation contrasts sharply. Due to the metropolitan nature of the urban areas, children generally grow up speaking more than one language – usually an official language and a language of wider communication such as Cameroon Pidgin or Fulfulde and then sometimes the local language of the locality depending on the prestige (either political or artistic) it enjoys. An important phenomenon here is the emergence of a new generation of children who have as a mother tongue, a non-indigenous language. Experience demonstrates that in some localities of the country, some children, due to parental influence, grow up speaking only either English or Pidgin in the Anglophone section and just French in the Francophone section. If they have English as their mother tongue, then they are most likely to speak another language most especially Pidgin or to a limited extent French as the second language. But if on the other hand their mother tongue is a vehicular language such as Pidgin, then they will most likely speak some English or French (learnt either in school or from the general environment). However, in ordinary daily interactions, the average Cameroonian (literate or non-literate) speaks at least two to three languages, that is, the mother tongue, a vehicular language and/or a foreign official language. Officially, this picture suggests that although government explicitly recognises English-French bilingualism, it implicitly promotes the dominance of one official language over all the other languages. In the same way, although legislation provides for the promotion of national languages, these are yet to find their way into the classroom as more attention is placed on official language promotion. The bottom-line is, therefore, one in which each section of the country (Anglophone or Francophone) promotes mainly its first official language.

As obtains elsewhere, the language problem in Cameroon has to do mainly with choosing diligently from existing alternatives, the one that best suits the country's realities and development needs. If this is the case for development more generally, then it is even more so for education, given the core role this plays in laying the foundation for broad-based development. In this respect, Kaplan & Baldauf (1997: 31) think, and rightly so, that making such choices should not in any way disrupt the existing social order but rather should help to strengthen it while offering the opportunity for interaction with the outside world. While recognising the delicateness of making such choices particularly with regard to endogenous and exogenous languages, they caution:

> The choice of a national language(s) is not as simple as it seems on the surface since selection normally implies a choice among competing languages. Vernacular languages provide the opportunity to establish a common heritage, a common history, and to facilitate unity; on the other hand, exogenous languages often provide access to the external world. The choice of a language(s) ideally should result in the smallest possible disruption to the social structure, yet at the same time the decision should not isolate the polity from the outside world.

Although they focus primarily on the question of a national language(s), their argument is as valid for such a choice as it is for education. In other words, among other domains, the presence of a language problem in a nation is to be felt mostly in education, that is, in the classroom since the classroom symbolises the relevance, legitimacy, value and authenticity of languages in the nation.

Understanding Enabling and Disenabling Policy
Language policy issues tend to be extremely complicated to handle. Three reasons seem to account for this: One, everybody seems to have an opinion, rightly or wrongly so, on the choice of language in the country and, of course, all expressed opinions deserve consideration.

Two, it is difficult to achieve consensus on the exact length and breadth of a language problem. For instance, the problem of linguistic complexity is further compounded by the question of distinguishing between language and dialect. While some people think that they speak separate and autonomous languages, others believe that they are, in effect, speaking only different varieties of the same language thus the difficulty of determining the precise scope of a language problem. Three, it is difficult to achieve consensus on what is and what is not good policy. Whereas some are convinced that pieces of legislation alone are enough to be considered as language policy, there are those who believe that legislation without concrete implementation measures only amounts to window dressing. In my opinion, unless a policy is accompanied by appropriate implementation measures, it is not policy enough.

Accordingly, therefore, if there is any problem with language policy and planning in Africa in general and Cameroon in particular, it is precisely because, besides not being explicit in its specification of objectives, it suffers from very serious implementation deficits. It is these implementation deficits that render policy disenabling. However, we need some clarification as to the factors that constitute enabling policy. In his discussion of language planning and policies in Africa, Bamgbose (1999) underscores the fact that the existence of legislation in favour of national languages in education instils a sense of guilt in those who violate the norm. He goes further to underline that government's overarching position in the African context makes it mandatory that the first port of call in any effort at persuasion must be policy-makers in the government. Even more importantly, he proposes some conditions which he sees as underlying successful planning, and which summarily present here as follows:

1) The government must be convinced of the role of African languages in development;
2) Policies must be such as likely to raise the status of African languages;
3) Policies on development of African languages must be phased;
4) Implementation must be specified at the time of policy formulation;
5) Implementation is best entrusted to specialised agencies rather than to government;
6) Grassroots involvement and private initiatives in language development must be encouraged;

7) Negative attitudes to African languages must be combated through awareness campaigns;
8) For policies to succeed, they must be backed by a strong political will.

In the simplest terms, the above conditions suggest that language policy does not only consist of written texts (legislation) but that above all, it must in its formulation, show proof of a clear willingness on the part of adopters to readily enforce application. In this respect, it must exhibit clarity in its definition of goals, strategies, resources and mechanisms of implementation, follow up and evaluation. Taking the above eight points as a check-list for evaluating the appropriateness of policy, we can say that policy is only truly policy when it is inherently enabling, that is, when it provides maximal opportunity for large-scale implementation with the potential for guaranteeing speedy application. In this regard, a policy is enabling when its adequacy in terms of specification of objectives and effective implementation is assured. However, we must specify that for this adequacy to be truly ensured; policy goals should not only be explicitly outlined but also, policy articulation should be free of escape routes that make it practically impossible for implementation to easily take place. On the basis of this, therefore, a disenabling policy is one which lacks the necessary safety-valves for successful application as a result of fundamental weaknesses in its formulation such as half-hearted specification of goals and objectives and the absence of mechanisms for effective implementation and follow-up. Due to these insufficiencies, the policy is bound either to fail or to suffer enormous feet-dragging when it comes to implementation.

Analysis of language policy reforms in Cameroon: Enabling or disenabling?

If legislation alone were sufficient in bringing about education reforms, then the generalised promotion of national languages in Cameroon would be a reality today. From reunification there has been concern about language policy although significant reforms only actually started in 1996. But in practice, though, the use of Cameroonian languages in education was already being experimented since 1981 within the framework of the Operational Programme for

Language Education in Cameroon (Propelca). Between 1996 and today, the following important reforms have been realised:
- The constitution of February 1996, providing for the promotion of national languages as part of national cultures.
- Law N° 98/004 of 14 April 1998 on guidelines for organising education in Cameroon that provides among other things for the promotion of national languages.
- Decree N° 2002/004 of 4 January 2002 reorganising the Ministry of National Education that creates provincial pedagogic inspectorates for mother tongues.

Two other developments that recognise the importance of national languages in education are:
- Law N° 2004/018 of July 2004 on decentralisation that empowers local councils to implement programmes for the eradication of illiteracy and the management of education, section 3 of which provides for the promotion of national languages.
- Law N° 2004/019 of July 2004 empowering regions to undertake education and literacy supporting among other things, the realisation of the linguistic map of Cameroon, the promotion of national languages, participating in editing in national languages and the promotion of the audio-visual press in national languages.

These developments point to the fact that although government attaches importance to national languages in education, in reality, there is the absence of political will to enforce policy application and consequently to effect change based on the language in education issue. For one thing, every single legal disposition contains an escape clause (Bamgbose, 1999: 19) that permits government institutions not to undertake application. Let us consider some of these:

The constitution of 1996 recognises national languages as the sources of national cultures that deserve promotion. But inherent in this recognition is an outstanding "escape route" that significantly weakens the ability to enforce application. Article 3 of section one of the constitution makes it clear that the state shall "endeavour to protect and promote national languages" (p 8). While the constitution stipulates that the official languages of Cameroon shall be English and French, it is practically silent on the status of national languages. This is crucial since very few people would be prepared to invest in the promotion of languages that enjoy very little or no prestige at all within the national polity. Besides, neither in the constitution nor anywhere else is there a specific articulation on how precisely national languages should be promoted. With these inherent loopholes, there is no doubt that these constitutional provisions have remained a dead letter.

Law N° 98/004 of 14 April 1998 provides, among other things, for the promotion of national languages. But like the constitution, it falls short of defining the scope of promotion of these languages by not specifying their role in the educational system or in any other domain. Rather, it clearly states the need to institute official language (English-French) bilingualism as a factor of national unity and integration. What the law acknowledges, therefore, is the use of English and French as languages of instruction thus a suggestion that national languages can only be promoted as subjects or disciplines on the timetable. Again, we must admit that this is only speculation since there is no clear statement about this. If our speculation is anything to go by, then it means total disregard for the possibility of national languages serving as the mediums of instruction. Whatever the case, government's silence on the status of national languages in the classroom significantly reduces the potential for application as it seems to express more of a wish than a national obligation. In this way, the law encourages continuous domination of the school system by the foreign official languages especially given that the law formally admits that these foreign languages are instruments of unification and integration. The lapses observed in this law reflect the unwillingness and un-readiness of public education officials to embrace national languages. This indirectly paves the way for negative attitudes towards these languages leading to their rejection. When they are not rejected, their use is limited to informal teaching, that is, as disciplines that are not considered in promotion examinations from one class to the other.

Decree N° 2002/004 of 4 January 2002, creating Provincial Pedagogic Inspectorates (PPI) for mother tongues, fails to set up a neutral non-governmental monitoring and evaluation mechanism to oversee activities. Suggestions from researchers especially within the framework of the NACALCO Centre for Applied Linguistics on the importance of such a mechanism are yet to be adhered to. It is, therefore, a decree that sacrifices, a priori, effectiveness given that educational programmes are drawn up, harmonised and globally evaluated at the national level. While, it cannot be ignored that decentralisation in educational planning and implementation is a cherished ideal, it is also vital to note that the absence of a central monitoring mechanism makes of the provisions of this law, an affair only limited to the provinces and thus of no national import. Even then, the decree has remained essentially a red letter. Since its signature in 2002, it has never been applied.

Law N° 2004/019 of July 2004 empowering regions to undertake education and literacy in national languages, although more explicit than the other reforms, still does not establish the relationship between regions and educational institutions. It fails to define both the functions of these languages in education and the scope of regional involvement in the management of schools particularly with respect to influencing the choice of language in education. It is not clear whether or not regions have the latitude to adopt their specific language policies and if not, how effectively they can transform national policy into reality at the regional level in a country where the application of legislation, decrees and the constitution is still heavily controlled by the central administration.

All these legal frameworks share two key things in common. Firstly, they recognise the importance of national languages in development and secondly, they lack clarity in the specification of the precise scope of national language promotion. Nevertheless, the simple fact that the frameworks are there, coupled with their recognition of the relevance of shared responsibility between different arms of government (ministries, regions and councils), make of national languages, at least in writing, the pillars of educational development. But this, in typical Cameroonian style, is just as far as legislation can go. On the whole then each of the reforms only addresses in part the issue of language policy. Even when they are considered together, they still fail to elaborately address the major concerns of policy development in the country. This signals the absence of an elaborate language policy document accompanied by a clear definition of goals, strategies, mechanisms of implementation and evaluation and reporting that take into account all the languages of the nation without biases of any kind. In short, the above reforms do not in themselves constitute policy as it is mistakenly supposed in Cameroon. Rather, they form only a minor dimension of the major requirements for policy that is contextually relevant and practically applicable on a generalised scale.

The Connection Between Policy and Practice

As it is the case with language policy and practice, the relationship between policy and practice is inextricably interwoven so that we cannot successfully talk of one without talking about the other. Understandably, appropriate policy is most likely to lead to effective practice or implementation. Yet sometimes, it may be possible that practice fails to reflect policy appropriateness. Such is the case with experimental (research) programmes that aim at influencing policy. In Cameroon, where research does not inform policy and where policy has been reduced to pieces of disjointed pieces of legislation, that are never really implemented, it is no doubt that implementation activities are reduced to the barest minimum. Educational reforms are politically motivated and the choice of language in education favours foreign official languages in schooling because of the advantages that these languages offer in the maintenance of elite power relationships. Official language hegemony and elite power maintenance are ensured by the ministries of education (Basic, Secondary and Higher Education) and where necessary, by their external services (provincial and divisional delegations and inspectorates). As the structures directly involved in actual policy application, these services determine whether or not national languages are included in the educational system.

In the light of the above, some major clarifications deserve attention here. The first is that well before the beginning of reforms in 1996; language planning practices based on mother tongue education orientation were already being experimented within the framework of the Operational Research Programme for Language Education in Cameroon (Propelca). The programme, initiated by the University of Yaoundé, was instrumental in the adoption by the General Forum on Education (1995) of mother tongue education in the country. This led to the consideration of national languages by constitutional and other reforms from 1996 onwards. The second is that the Propelca experiment is today, primarily a private initiative, promoted by the National Association of Cameroonian Language Committees (NACALCO) through its Centre for Applied Linguistics (CLA). The third is that mother tongue-based language planning activities in Cameroon are undertaken solely by private institutions with little or no recognition or support from the state. The fourth and last clarification is that over the years, government has adopted a rather disenabling "laisser-faire" attitude by neither forbidding nor encouraging the presence of national languages in the classroom. In so far as teaching these languages has not interfered with the official programme, they have been tolerated. But what the ministries have done has been to sideline indigenous languages through the consolidation of English-French bilingualism in formal and non-formal circles particularly at the primary level where the mother tongue is most needed.

However, between 2000 and 2003, and with the support of UNICEF, government undertook an experimentation of the use of national languages within the framework of the promotion of accessible and quality education in some of the zones with the lowest enrolment rates in the country such as the East, Adamawa and North provinces with pilot schools in selected divisions. The programme focused on key areas of language promotion such as material production, personnel training and supervision. External services (Divisional and Sub-divisional Delegations and Inspectorates) of the then Ministry of National Education (MINEDUC) were charged with the supervision of the experiment. Conducted under the coordination of the NACALCO Centre for Applied Linguistics, the experiment offered an ideal opportunity for government to put into practice the various reforms. Regrettably, despite the encouraging impact of the experiment, it was suspended in 2003 and since then has neither been followed up nor evaluated. This leads us to wonder whether the experiment was really necessary in the first instance and whether Propelca results presented to the General Forum on Education in 1995 were not enough. By the way, if they were really deemed worthwhile, could this alone not form the basis for nation-wide application of the model? This experience demonstrates that policy reforms notwithstanding, government is not prepared to engage in committed educational reforms based on mother tongue education.

Also at the central level, one observes continuous measures to forestall the effective promotion of mother tongue based education reforms in Cameroon. In 2000, MINEDUC introduced the teaching of the second official language (OL2), that is, English for Francophones and French for Anglophones, in early primary education as part of its measures to reinforce and consolidate official bilingualism. This was followed by the introduction of national cultures with the aim of building competence in traditional Cameroonian values. Regrettably, no attention was paid to the role of indigenous languages as the most efficient tools of transmission of traditional values. Even at the level of content of national culture teaching, attention centred exclusively on the non-linguistic aspects such as local craft, songs, dances and cookery. One thus wonders how effectively traditional values can be properly transmitted through the exclusive use of non-indigenous mediums of communication. These two interventions, generally perceived as important innovations within official circles, reveal that in reality, official educational attitudes favour foreign languages at the expense of indigenous modes of communication. What we must not lose sight of here is that these interventions only help in watering down the relevance of national languages by shifting attention away from the main focus, which is systematic use of the mother tongue medium in education to different yet unreliable approaches of using foreign languages in the Cameroonian classroom. Clearly, attitudes of this nature only help to render ineffective existing policy on the promotion of national languages.

At the level of external services, that is, delegations and inspectorates of education, charged with grassroots implementation of reforms, there exists another important hindrance. Texts of application and institutional structures of policy application are not yet in place. As a result, educational authorities at this level are not anxious to promote national languages in education on the claims that without these texts of application they are not empowered with the practical modalities required in the application of legislation. Suffice it to say here that in Cameroon, laws cannot be implemented until texts of application have been elaborated. What is even more disturbing is that it usually takes many years, if not decades, for these texts to be elaborated. For instance, texts of application do not yet exist for any of the laws promulgated since 1998 and there is no indication that their elaboration will become a reality any time soon. We observe, therefore, that the practice of texts of application as a precondition for implementing legislation in general and educational policy reforms in particular, constitutes a serious disenabling factor in language policy development in the country. This clearly illustrates the fact that what we usually consider as language in education reforms in Cameroon is always actually window dressing, firstly because what we refer to as language policy in this country does not meet the requirements for policy in the real sense of the word (Chumbow, 1990: 288) and secondly, because there is demonstrated commitment to facilitate the implementation of existing legislation even if this is not satisfactory enough.

General Observations

If we consider enabling policy to consist of a clear definition of goals accompanied by strategies, resources and mechanisms of implementation, monitoring and evaluation, then it becomes clear that Cameroon does not possess a language policy. In this case, it would be proper to talk about disenabling policies by virtue of the absence of these qualities. In the same way, if enabling practices are taken to comprise official state-managed programmes, then one can readily conclude that language in education practices in Cameroon are disenabling. But if on the other hand, we consider enabling policies to involve all the reforms (as part of policy evolution) in the sense that they create some avenues for some positive evolution of educational innovation based on the language of education, especially in contrast to total rejection in the not too distant past, then it can be said that policy evolution in this country is to a certain extent enabling. Similarly, if enabling practices are taken to comprise all the activities, either promoted by government or non-governmental institutions as a result of an evolution in educational policy reforms based on language, then it can be affirmed that these practices are enabling at least at the private level. In this regard, the NACALCO experience with Propelca alongside other private experiments, by virtue of their impact at both the level of the local and national communities constitute concrete evidence of practices that can effectively be considered as enabling in the sense that they are capable of inspiring and guiding policy planning and management in the country.

If practices within public educational circles are not in consonance with present reforms, this is simply because some pertinent questions have not been adequately addressed in the reform formulation process. Some of these are:

1) Who designs the language in education policy in a nation? Is it a shared responsibility between partners and stakeholders or it is a sole proprietorship of the government?
2) What are the ingredients of an appropriate language in education policy? Is legislation sufficient to constitute policy?
3) Why does a multilingual, multicultural and an emerging country like Cameroon need educational innovation based on mother tongue-based language in instruction reforms?

What does it take to ensure effective implementation of language in education policy?

As far as enabling practices are concerned, an attempt to address these questions will certainly clear the air of some of the major misinterpretations that account for the deficiencies observed in policy content and implementation planning in this country. However, it is possible that enabling policy be accompanied by enabling practices or that both policy and practices are not sufficiently enabling as it is the case in Cameroon. Whatever the case may be, it is desirable that practices be enabling even in the presence of a disenabling policy since such practices have the potential to trigger reforms. Ideally, of course, policy should not only be enabling but also it should be accompanied by sufficiently enabling practices.

In the particular case of Cameroon, for policy formulation to be adequate and its implementation effective, some vital issues need to be taken into account prominent among which are:
1) The development and promotion of all Cameroonian national languages in formal and non-formal education;
2) The raising of local languages to the status of official languages and their effective use in all functions in mainstream oral and written local communication (education, administration, religion, etc.);
3) The production of quality pedagogic materials and other forms of written documentation in these languages to encourage fair competition between these national languages and foreign official languages;
4) Written communication competence in at least one national language should become a precondition for access to jobs at both local and national levels;
5) The training of trainers in mother tongue education should be compulsory at the primary, secondary and tertiary levels.

These and many other actions can potentially render language policy not only adequate but also practically applicable on a generalised scale. Further reflections in this respect, deriving from a frank and profound resolve to initiate change based on language in education reforms will certainly yield the best dividends.

Conclusion
Language policy reforms in Cameroon may project an enabling environment for the promotion of a balanced language policy but in reality, the content of the reforms and the accompanying practices

within the public sector reveal major lapses. I have examined the discrepancies between policy planning and implementation and concluded that the lack of government commitment accounts largely for the absence not only of appropriate policy but also of the implementation of the existing legislation as part of the evolution of policy development. My goal has been to highlight the fact that whatever the case, policy development in Cameroon is not yet a reality even if there are reforms and practices that should trigger interest in policy development and to demonstrate that meaningful social change in Cameroon can only be achieved through educational reforms based on the development of an appropriate language in education policy. This, in a sense, explains why MINEDUC undertook, some years back, to spearhead the elaboration of a comprehensive language policy for Cameroon with the support of the *Organisation Internationale de la Francophonie* (OIF). Regrettably, this lofty initiative died a natural death. This initiative needs to be revived as a matter of necessity and urgency.

References

Bamgbose, A. 1999. Language Development and Language Planning. In N. Alexander (Ed.) *Language and Development in Africa, Social Dynamics*, Vol. 25. N° 1. Centre for African Studies, University of Cape Town.

Biya, Paul. 1986. *Communal Liberalism.* McMillan Publishers.

Chiatoh, B. A. 2006. Language, Cultural Identity and the National Question in Cameroon. In Paul Mbangwana, Mpoche Kizitus and Mbu Tenno (Eds.). *Language Literature and Identity*, Cullivier Verlag Gottingen, pp. 144-152.

Chiatoh, B. A. 2010. De l'Oral à l'écrit en langue maternelle à l'école: implications pour préparer un enseignement bilingue/multilingue au Cameroun. In Komarek-Chatry, M (Ed.) *Professionaliser les enseignants de classes multilingues en Afrique*, Paris: L'Harmattan pp. 133-155.

Chiatoh, B. A. 2012. Official Bilingualism and the Construction of a Cameroonian National Identity: 50 Years of Experience. Unpublished paper.

Chilora, H. G. 2004. Corpus Planning Developments in Zimbabwe, ToTSA Working Paper, Cape Town: PRAESA

Chumbow, B. S. 1990. Language and Language Policy in Cameroon. In Kofele-Kale (Ed.) *An African Experiment in Nation Building:*

The Bilingual Cameroon Republic since Reunification, Westview Press pp. 281-311.

Desai, Z. 1999. Enabling Policies, Disabling Practices. In Limage (Ed.) *Comparative Perspectives on Language and Literacy*, Dakar: UNESCO Regional Office.

Djité, P. 2008. *The Sociolinguistics of Development in Africa*, Multilingual Matters.

Eastman, C. M. 1983. *Language Planning: An Introduction* Chandler & Sharp Publishers, Inc: University of Washington.

Hornberger, N.H. 2006. Frameworks and Models in Language Policy and Planning In Ricento Thomas (Ed.) *An Introduction to Language Policy: Theory and Method*, Malden: Blackwell Publishing.

Kaplan, R.B. & Baldauf, R.B., Jr. 1997. *Language Planning: From Practice to Theory* Multilingual Matters.

MINEDUC. 1998. Law N° 98/004 of 14 April 1998 Providing Guidelines for Education in Cameroon, Yaoundé: MINEDUC

MINEDUC. 2002. Law N° 2002/004 of 4 January 1998 Organising the Ministry of National Education, MINEDUC: Yaoundé

Republic of Cameroon. 1996. Constitution of the Republic of Cameroon, SOPECAM.

Rubin, J. 1983. Bilingual Education and language Planning. In Kennedy (Ed.) *Language Education and Language Planning*, George Allen and Unwin (Publishers) Ltd.

Tadadjeu, M. & Chiatoh, B.A. 2002. The Challenge of Satellite Communication in African Languages CLA: *African Journal of Applied Linguistics (AJAL)*, pp. 1-15.

Chapter 3
Literacy in Cameroon: The Case of Mungaka
Beatrice Lima Lebsia Titanji

From the late 1800s to the early 1970s Mungaka emerged as an indigenous Cameroonian language taught in schools and used widely for evangelism. The Bible translation into Mungaka was the first in the region and although the language was written using the German orthography, many native and non-native speakers learned to read and write in it. Mungaka remains a language of wider communication in the North West Region with most of the Presbyterian churches in the rural areas using the Mungaka hymnals and Bible. Many people who have learned this language continue to use it, especially among themselves as a secret code when need arises. The successful spread and use of Mungaka as a language of education, literacy, and evangelism provide evidence that a language policy for Cameroon that gives prominence to the development and use of indigenous Cameroonian languages would enhance learning and subsequently accelerate the development of the country.

Introduction

Cameroon is a multilingual country with about 250 national languages and two official languages, English and French. Cameroon finds herself in this panoply of languages where her people have to switch from varying mother tongues to foreign languages. The language of the Bali Nyonga people of Bali Subdivision, Mungaka, served as a lingua franca in the North West Region from late 1800 to the 1970s (Ndangam, 1972). Mungaka was initially used as the language of the church and as the missionaries spread Christianity, the use of the language as a lingua franca was also enhanced. Although it was somehow repressed as a result of the World Wars, it resurfaced just before the independence of Cameroon and continued to serve in a very strong way as the language of communication in the Presbyterian Church in Cameroon (PCC). At independence, the language policy that was instituted relegated national languages such as Mungaka to the background whereas English and French were promoted as official languages. The Government of Cameroon did not take the option of mother tongue education seriously until recently when national languages have been considered, in theory, as good enough for early education. The introduction, use, and spread of Mungaka as a language of education and literacy suggest that the use of national languages as media of instruction and/or school subjects will greatly improve on learning and development initiatives in Cameroon.

Mungaka is one of the early written national languages of Cameroon. Bali Nyonga has a population of about 50,000 people (Ethnologue, 2009). The language is named Bali, Munga'ka, Nga'ka, or Ngaaka (Titanji et al., 1988). It is spoken in the Bali Subdivision, Mezam Division of the North West Region of Cameroon. Bali Nyonga constitutes one of the many groups of Chamba origin found mostly in the North West Region. All other Chamba groups speak closely related varieties of Mubakoh. Bali Nyonga abandoned Mubakoh (their original language from the Adamawa) to speak Bati because during their migratory tours and military campaigns they settled temporarily among the Bati at Mom in the West Region of Cameroon. Although Mungaka is currently the language of only about 50,000 native speakers, it is understood and spoken far and wide by non-native speakers in the North West Region of Cameroon. The language was first written by German-Swiss missionaries of the Basel Mission who were welcomed and supported by Fon Galega I, and later by Fonyonga I. In 1889 Eugene Zintgraff arrived Bali Nyonga and spurred Galega I to ask for schools to be opened by the Basel Mission. When Galega I died in 1900 his son and successor Fonyonga I continued with the same policy and was himself interested in reading and writing Mungaka. After the preaching of the first sermon in a market place, the Fon asked for the first school to be built. Fonyonga I told the missionaries that they could only leave after due promises that other missionaries would come to Bali without delay to start work. He sent one of his sons with them to learn how to read and write.

Outside of Bali Nyonga, Mungaka has been and continues to be spoken in the North West Region as a language of wider communication. Several analysts (Ndangam, 1972; Lima, 1973; Nti, 1973) have variously referred to and described Mungaka as a lingua-franca, arguing that for long it has enjoyed and still enjoys the same status as Duala, Ewondo, Fulfulde and Pidgin-English which in their own rights are also lingua-francas. Nti posits the label 'Mungakaphone', an extrapolation of similar labels such as Anglophone, Francophone, Arabophone that are extensively current in the literature to refer to the role played by Mungaka in the North

West Region. According to him, Mungakaphone implies and includes non-native speakers from all areas where Mungaka was and is actively used. The term should thus be actually understood to include both native and non-native speakers who use Mungaka for communication.

Mungaka as a School Subject

Mungaka became a school subject in the late 1880s when the Fon of Bali, Galega I, showed interest in the Whiteman's education scheme which included reading and writing. He invited the first missionaries who had already started work in the South West and Littoral Regions to visit his Fondom. In 1906 the missionaries published a primer in Mungaka which was at once used in teaching in the newly established primary schools (Vernacular Schools). It should be noted that such primary schools were opened by the mission in Bafut and many other villages where the missionaries were stationed while Bali Nyonga served as their headquarters. Evangelism was in Mungaka and this explains why many educated North Westerners above sixty sometimes communicate intimately in Mungaka when they meet. Bali Nyonga served as the focal point where teachers learned how to read and write and were then sent to teach in neighbouring villages. The coming of the schools enhanced Christian evangelism and in 1908, 32 scholars were baptised as the first Christians in the Grassfields area. In 1909 the first three couples were married in church. Fonyonga I offered to pay teachers' allowances of 5 shillings each per month until the First World War interrupted the work. The war was a great blow to the work of the Mission. The school work was halted and the boarding schools where the Europeans taught were discontinued. After the war work on Mungaka continued and by 1933 the translation of the New Testament was completed. The entire Bible was available in Mungaka in July 1961. The Bible could be read in all the Basel Mission (later Presbyterian) churches in the North West and the gospel was preached in Mungaka to the delight of the new converts who flocked the churches as they could understand the language. This led to a new enthusiasm in the youths to learn and eventually teach Mungaka. The language therefore served as the official language in religious matters in the North West Region (the Grassfields Region of northwest Cameroon) just as Duala served in the Coastal Region. This was consonant with the philosophy of the

Church to operate in the peoples' own languages. This situation led to the intense use of Mungaka both as the language of Church affairs and, surprisingly, as a language of secular interactions. It is remarkable that some North Westerners who had learned the language and who now live in other regions of Cameroon still continue to use Mungaka as a unifying language/factor and for other personal transactions.

This enthusiasm led to the publication of the Mungaka dictionary in 1992. The dictionary was originally compiled by Rev. Georg Tischhauser in the nineteen thirties while he was in the service of the Basel Mission and living in Bafut (a neighbouring village to Bali Nyonga). Some of his informants were not native speakers of Mungaka with the result that non-Mungaka words and expressions found their way into the dictionary. In 1938, Reverend Johannes Stockle spent some weeks with the first compiler and was introduced to the Mungaka language. The present Fon of Bali-Nyonga, Dr. Ganyonga met Reverend Stockle who introduced himself and expressed his interest in Mungaka. The Fon, like his forefathers, was delighted to bring him into contact with village elders and certain knowledgeable native speakers who gave him the assistance he needed.

The team of six elders and many others who joined along the line contributed in many ways to make the work a success. In the course of the work all non-Mungaka words and expressions were removed from the dictionary. The book gives the cultural and traditional background of several expressions and is intended to serve as a reference work. According to Fon Ganyonga III (Stockle & Tischhauser, 1992) "Language functions as a vehicle of culture and since culture is dynamic, there are bound to be words and expressions which can only be understood within their historical contexts." In the foreword to the dictionary, the Fon expresses the wish that the book will not only enable native speakers to gain more semantic and grammatical clarity in their language but will go a long way to assist interested non-native speakers to learn Mungaka and ultimately promote better understanding - the basis of peaceful co-existence.

Evaluation of the Programme
The Mungaka language served a necessary purpose at the period it functioned as a language of education and literacy in the North West Region. That many of those who studied Mungaka continue to

proudly use it today points to its success during that period. Mungaka could only be compared to Duala that was used for similar purposes in the South West and the Littoral Regions. The relegation of national languages to the background gradually saw a decline in the use of Mungaka in the Church and schools since children had to study in English. Prior to independence was the blow from the two World Wars that saw three European countries; Germany, Britain and France scrambling for Cameroon in particular and Africa in general. The question of who was in control obviously took a toll on the new found literacy programme that was still taking roots. As Germany eventually bowed out (defeated in the First World War), the change in administration retarded the fast growth that was witnessed in the early years (1889-1910) when schools were opened and taught in Mungaka.

The Basel Mission returned in 1925 with great plans for the Grassfields with agricultural schools planned for Foumban, a crafts' training centre for Bali Nyonga and the spread of the gospel to the Adamawa region. Even though the Second World War came and thwarted most of the lofty plans, the missionaries were not deterred as Adolf Vielhauer and Rev. Wunderli reoccupied the Bali Station and got involved in literacy work. The German administration had tried to hinder the spread of the Bali language beyond its geographical boundary after an ammunition controversy. The arrival of Vielhauer saw a new spirit as he initiated the translation of the Bible in part and then as a whole for many languages of the Grassfields region. Work continued with the collection of short stories in 1915, revised in 1930, and the New Testament in 1933, revised in 1958. Vielhauer completed the Mungaka Bible in 1961 with the assistance of Rev. Elisha Ndifon; a native of Bali Nyonga who spent several years in Germany working with him. The Basel Mission had thus succeeded in their mission of bringing education to the natives in their own language. Part of the success of the programme can be seen in the fact that many people were happy to learn Mungaka and to use it and especially that those who learned it are still using it today when they have the opportunity.

It may be important to note that although Mungaka is not in current use in the literary scene of Cameroon in general and the North West Region in particular, the 1962 Constitution of the PCC states that Mungaka is one of the languages of the church alongside Duala, English and French.

How/why the Programme was Abandoned

Werner Keller (1960) observes that differences between the Grassfields chiefs about the use of Mungaka surfaced during the Second World War. However, no overt Church declarations were made to abolish the official use of Mungaka in schools and Church services. Many local church leaders, for purely pragmatic reasons, began to readjust to other local languages, English and Cameroon Pidgin English. In 1954, a new opposition arose against the use of Mungaka. The Provincial Education Officer sent a letter to the Basel Mission prohibiting the use and teaching of the Bali language outside the area of the Bali tribe. The Mission and the Church expressed their protests against the prohibition and stated in a resolution that Bali should be used in all the Infant Schools in the Grassfields. In 1955 both Bali and Duala were forbidden as the medium of instruction in Infants I and II. In 1956, the Board of Education in Buea decided that the vernacular could only be used as a medium of instruction in a region where at least two-thirds of the children speak it. On September 27th, 1958, the Government passed the following rule:

> "Although the mother tongue of children may be used to assist in introduction, English is to be the medium of instruction in Primary Schools and all the text books used are to be in English. Although there is to be no restriction in the use of Bali and Duala in religious instruction, these languages are not to be given any precedence over other mother tongues."(op.cit. 1960).

This ruling dealt a dead blow to the Presbyterian Church and to the Basel Mission. Though the situation seemed rather hopeless at the time, negotiations with the authorities concerned continued. It was hoped that the Government will reconsider its decision since the fate of Bali and Duala as written native languages was at stake. Nothing was done and has never been done with regard to the two languages as media for literacy.

After the completion of the Bible in 1961, literacy in Mungaka somewhat mellowed with the coming of independence and Government's rulings against the language. The language policy of the new Cameroonian administration did not encourage the use of national languages in any way. Meanwhile, the churches continued evangelism in Mungaka since the entire Presbyterian Church had trained teachers, evangelists and pastors for their congregations. The independence of Cameroon had two phases that impacted on the language situation. First, the French-speaking section celebrated independence in 1960 and called the country "La Republique du Cameroun." English-speaking Cameroon followed in 1961 and Cameroon became a federated state: Federal Republic of Cameroon. It was then that the new administration opted for a bilingual nation with English and French as official languages for administration and education.

This decision sidelined Mungaka as a language of literacy in the Grassfields region. Some churches continued using Mungaka for mission work but the future seemed bleak as young people were no longer enthusiastic and interested in learning a language that would not lead them to find jobs or have economic benefits. There was no pressing urge to study in Mungaka after the referendum of 1972 which reiterated the need for bilingualism in English and French by all and sundry. Bilingual Colleges such as the Bilingual Grammar School in Man'O War Bay were created to emphasise the new language policy. All of these led to the facing out and eventual abandonment of the programme.

Although the language suffered an artificial abandonment, its place in the church remains intact as sermons are still preached in the hinterlands in Mungaka and the song hymnal remains the one in use today. The hymnal was revised in 1982 and new tunes added to meet up with the renowned Church Hymnary in English used by the Presbyterian Church in Cameroon.

Lessons from the Programme
Several lessons can be learned from the Mungaka programme in favour of the use of national languages in education and literacy in Cameroon.
1. It proves that national languages can be used for literacy purposes.
2. Some national languages can serve as regional languages.
3. Cameroonians can learn to read and write in other languages if these were chosen as regional languages.
4. Basic literature can be developed in national languages.

Looking at the present dispensation, there are hopes in the horizon as government seems to be picking the pieces and encouraging people to go back to their roots. This has led some Bali Nyonga people to start writing in Mungaka using the new orthography (Titanji, personal communication). Previous work in the language had been done using the German orthography making it difficult for some learners. With the primers written in the new orthography, many people will be exposed to the stories and literacy could resume in the language in a region that had hitherto used Mungaka extensively. The children who will first learn to read and write Mungaka will find it easier to learn a new language (like English) because the vocabulary and sound system of the target language will not conflict with that of the L1. Policy makers thus have the task to accept or accelerate the introduction of national languages as languages of education/literacy in Cameroon.

Conclusion
The spread and use of Mungaka as a language of education and evangelism was fostered by the missionaries of the Basel Mission. Mungaka quickly became a lingua franca in the North West Region. The decline of Mungaka in the Church is only artificial as Mungaka choirs remain a dominant feature in the worship life of Christians of the Presbyterian Church in Cameroon. The Hallelujah Choirs Association is a case in point. This Choir Association groups people from all walks of life from all ethnic groups and villages of the English speaking Christians of the Presbyterian Church in Cameroon. The choristers sing essentially in Mungaka spiced with Meta (language of some parts of Moghamo Division, North West Region) choruses. They sometimes use other Cameroonian languages and English but Mungaka remains the main language. In the early days the choir was made up of purely Mungaka speaking people but today, it is made up of many ethnic groups in Cameroon and exists in several congregations of the Presbyterian Church. Today the choir numbers more than 5, 000 members singing in Mungaka.

The support that Mungaka received from the successive Bali Nyonga Fons serves as a lesson for local authorities to encourage and ensure that their indigenous languages are used in schools. The Mungaka experiment suggests that learning will be faster and more efficient in Cameroon if national languages were introduced and used in the school system either as languages of instruction or school subjects together with the official languages, English and French.

REFERENCES

Buea Archives Files. 1943. Bali Language. File 38.

Chilver, E.M. and Kaberry, P.M. 1966. Notes on the Pre-Colonial History and Ethnography of the Bamenda Grassfields. Ms.

Chilver, E. M. 1966. *Zintgraff's exploration in Bamenda, Adamawa and the Benue lands*, 1889-1892. Government Printing Press, Buea, Cameroon.

Chilver, E. M. 1967. Paramountcy and Protection in the Cameroons: the Bali and the Germans, 1889-1913. In Prosser Gifford and W.M. Roger Louis, Britain and Germany in Africa. *Imperial Rivalry and Colonial Rule*. New Haven and London.

Dah, Jonas N. 1983. Missionary Motivations and Methods: A critical examination of the Basel Mission in Cameroon 1886-1914. A Doctor of Theology Dissertation. Basel 1983.

Hallden, Erik. 1968. *The culture policy of the Basel Mission in Cameroon 1886- 1905*, Uppsala.

Lima, Adolf Sema. 1974. The Mungaka Language with special reference to its pronouns. Unpublished Dissertation. University of Leeds, England.

Mackey, Williams F. 1965. The description of Bilingualism. In Fishman, Joshua (Ed.), *Readings in the Sociology of Language*. Mouton, The Hague, Paris, 1972.

Malcolm, Green. 1982. *Through the Year in West Africa*, Batsford Academic and educational Ltd., London.

Ndangam, Augustine F. 1956. *Linguistic Survey of the Northern Bantu Borderland*, Vol. 1, O.U.P London.

Nti, David Foncham. 1973. A Phonological Comparison between some aspects of Mungaka (Bali) and English. Unpublished Dissertation, University of Yaoundé.

Schnellbach, Jorg. 1966. Church History notes to students, theological College Nyassosso.

Stockle, J. and Tischhauser, G. 1992. *Mungaka (Bali) Dictionary*. Cologne, Ruediger Koeppe Verlag.

Titanji et al. 1988. *An introduction to the study of Bali-Nyonga*. Stardust printers, Yaoundé.

Vielhauer, Adolf. 1944. Nu a ka n'dze Nkumu bun Kristo a. Basel Evangelical Mission.

Werner Keller. 1960. *A Survey of the General Development of the Presbyterian Church in Cameroon up to 1960*.

Experiences from Across Africa

Chapter 4
The Tanzanian Experience in Language Policy and Planning
Josephat Rugemalira

> This paper argues that the Tanzanian experience in language policy and planning is not as unique or laudable as most scholars have tended to imply–viz. That Tanzania has successfully promoted a national language, Swahili, to take over the functions of the language of the former colonial master - English. It shows that the conflict involved in the three layers of the linguistic environment in Tanzania is partly due to the purist tradition in linguistics, and partly due to the unequal economic relations between Tanzania and the Anglophone centre in Europe and America. The national language, it is argued, is not guaranteed, even in the long term, to assert its rightful role as long as the economy remains a negligible appendage of the powerful economies of the North.

Introduction

The Tanzanian experience is a typical case that illustrates how language policy and planning is a site of struggle - for cultural influence, economic dominance, and political control. The similarities with other African countries in this struggle are so obvious as to require little restating - a conflictual triglossic environment, with the ex-colonial language, English, at the top of the hierarchy, a regional lingua franca, Swahili, in the middle, and multiple local ethnic community languages[1] at the bottom of the heap (Rubagumya, 1991). Yet some of the battles lost or won and the methods employed are worth examining particularly because the Tanzanian case has been so often erroneously cited as a success story.

Similarities of the Tanzanian experience with multilingual situations outside the African continent go beyond the colonial factor; they revolve around the theoretical position that regards multilingualism as a curse, as inefficient and dysfunctional in the management of society:

> Wherever the language of the government and the law differs from that of the mass of the people, plans for

---

[1] There are 150 ethnic community languages (Atlasi ya Lugha za Tanzania 2009).

> economic, agricultural and industrial development are more difficult to make - because the basic research is hindered by the language barrier - and more difficult to put into effect. Linguistic diversity therefore acts as a brake on economic progress (Le Page, 1964:18).
>
> ..diversity of language impedes the nation's economic and educational progress as well as its unity (Le Page, 1964: 84).
>
> It is neither practicable nor desirable for the state to nurture and promote all languages spoken within its borders, as advocated by human-rights protagonists (Mkude, 2002: 76).

The official English only movement in the USA is a good example of the monolingualism school. In spite of the much-touted cultural melting pot image of the American dream, English is indeed regarded as the cement that binds the citizens together; all bilingual education programmes are in the final analysis assimilationist to the national language and culture. And for many people the monolingualism ideal is the original divine plan before the Babelian distortion through human pride[2]. Although the relatively recent international pronouncements in favour of multilingualism and cultural diversity provide ground for the counter-attack (World Conference on Linguistic Rights, 1996; UNITED NATIONS, 1997; UNESCO, 2001, 2003)[3], practice in the regional bodies shows that multilingualism is heavily under siege (Phillipson, 2009: 139). The UN declarations expressing concern about the future of the world's linguistic diversity and urging deliberate protection are themselves witness to this fact.

As we examine the case of the Tanzanian struggle for linguistic independence in this wider perspective, it will be important to determine the extent to which this national struggle has been swept

---

[2] In the Judeo-Christian scriptures the multiplicity of languages on earth originated from the failed plan of people to encroach on divine authority by building a tower to the heavens; God ruined these plans by making the people speak different languages and so be unable to work together on the project.

[3] Various international initiatives during the past fifteen years have sought to build a consensus to the effect that minority languages need not disappear; that they should not disappear; and that any language that is running out of speakers should be well-documented for the benefit of humanity. Languages need not disappear because humans are capable of mastering several languages very well and societies should be so organised as to accommodate multilingualism and multiculturalism. Nations are urged to foster "the learning of several languages from the earliest age" (UNESCO, 2001).

up into the global forces of neoliberalism (a.k.a. imperialism) and why multilingualism should fall victim to these forces. And since there are gloomy prognoses on the planet's linguistic diversity it may be worth reflecting on the tempting parallel being drawn, viz. that the world is headed towards the existence of one 'global' or 'international' language in the same way that Tanzania is headed towards one national language.

First, a brief background to the linguistic situation up to independence in 1961 is presented. This is followed by examining what appears to be language policy and planning activity, by looking at actual practice in government affairs, at the University of Dar es Salaam as a case study, and at the national language council set up to manage language affairs. The following section revisits the debate on the language of instruction and the final part discusses the challenges to the status quo and the future.

Historical Background and The Status Quo

The larger part of the territory that has evolved into present day Tanzania was first ruled by the Germans (1885-1919) before passing on to British hands after the First World War (1919-1961). The islands of Zanzibar and Pemba were ruled by the British throughout (1890-1963). So it was English rather than German that got entrenched as the language of power pitted against Swahili, the language of wider communication, and about 150 other ethnic community languages. This conflict was most visible in the decisions and practices regarding the language of government and education: While the Germans made considerable use of Swahili in administration and the education system, the British run an English administration and education system with only slight concessions to Swahili in both sectors (Rubagumya, 1990; Qorro, 2012).

One of the most significant steps in language planning was the establishment of the Inter-territorial Swahili Language Committee in 1930 to co-ordinate and harmonise the development and use of the language across the British East Africa territories of Tanganyika, Zanzibar, Kenya, and Uganda[4]. As will be discussed later, this constitutes the roots of the present Institute of Kiswahili Studies at the University of Dar es Salaam. So by the time of Tanganyika's

---

[4] The Tanzanian parliament recently ratified the protocol to (re-)establish a Swahili Commission for the East African Community (*Mwananchi*, 2 November 2012).

independence in 1961, and its union with Zanzibar to form Tanzania in 1964 the triglossic situation was already well-established. The post-independence experience - now already longer than the British occupation of Tanganyika - has witnessed only a mere tinkering with the establishment and arguably a strengthening of i) the position of English vis a vis that of Kiswahili, and ii) the position of Kiswahili vis-a-vis that of the ethnic community languages.

Manifestations of a Language Policy

By 'language policy' someone would normally expect a written statement by a governmental authority setting out the broad principles that will guide public behaviour in matters of language. The policy would give the desired direction of change in the use of the language resources available in the society and the strategies for effecting that change. The policy then becomes the basis for framing laws, regulations, and directives to determine action/practice. This applies to all sectors of public management, even in non-governmental organisations.

In the absence of an umbrella policy, everyday practice in the relevant sector/field may be guided by laws, rules, regulations and directives drawn from different sectors. These may produce contradictory actions depending on the wider context in which each such instrument was conceived and developed. For instance, the law for the licensing of mass media (radio, television, newspapers) may constrain the use of ethnic community languages even though the Bill of Rights in the constitution espouses the right to give and receive information. Or the law that controls the quality/standards of products and their safe use e.g. medicinal drugs, insecticides, machine tools, or food products, may limit itself to the use of an official language like English even if the consumers cannot understand instructions written in English.

Government Practice

At independence the first action of government in matters of language was to declare Swahili the national language and also official language in conjunction with English. It is arguable that the 'national language' title is empty of content when juxtaposed with the 'official language' title. It should go without saying that a national language is the official language of government and public affairs. If a national language shares its official position with a 'foreign' language then a justification for the situation ought to be provided in a language policy that also sets out the roadmap for the eventual removal of that foreign language from its usurped position. There has been no such policy in Tanzania.

A national language is understood as the medium that is accessible to a large section of the relevant nation mainly because it has cultural roots among the people of that nation and so it is the medium through which the members of that nation communicate with each other on a daily basis and get governed/ruled, i.e. it is the official language[5]. In this sense it is possible to conceive the existence of more than one national language to match the linguistic composition of the given society. It is also possible to conceive of a language that has cultural roots among a section of the people in a nation but it is not widely enough shared: this may be regarded as a community or regional language.

The effect of Swahili's status as a national language was to give it clout over the ethnic community languages; it systematically replaced them in several domains. The independence government abolished the traditional chiefs and thereby removed one public domain where ethnic community languages (ECL) might have found some use - namely the chief's local government. By giving prominence to the agenda of building a modern united nation with one national language, the ethnic community languages got painted in a negative light as forces of tribalism and traditionalism. Increasingly it became a matter of pride for the younger generation to speak Swahili rather than the ECL. Knowledge of Swahili would almost always be a sign that someone has been to school. In Swahili's own battles with English, government authorities would at various intervals issue directives to its functionaries not to use English "unnecessarily". But in the case of the ECLs voices to that effect would be confined to the domestic realm and would increasingly be ignored by the younger generation that was under various integrationist influences including i) universal primary education in the Swahili medium where speaking

---

[5] South African usage has sought to make a different distinction: there are eleven 'official languages' which are used in wider public contexts and in regional and central government affairs; then there are 'national languages' which are less significant in public life because they are spoken by smaller sections of the nation but have cultural / historical/ritual significance and deserve to be preserved (Constitution of South Africa, 1996).

an ECL is a punishable offence; ii) ujamaa/villagisation policies which could bring together people speaking different languages who might then find comfort in Swahili in this semi-urbanised environment; iii) secondary schools with a national catchment area, where pupils were deliberately transported across many regions away from home to get a "national education" in state (owned/nationalised) schools with non-fellow tribesmen; and iv) military service camps (National Service). These nationalising forces created an ethos that made it unpatriotic, almost subversive, to speak as an ECL. The population census questionnaire removed the question on ethnic identity, which from pre-independence practice to 1967 used to give an indirect picture of the languages in the country. A request to include a language question in the 2002 census was rejected:

> The Census Commissioner took the opportunity to make the point that Tanzania is past the stage of counting tribes and has made giant strides towards the creation of a homogeneous nation with one national language (Damas Mbogoro, personal communication). He maintained that any activity making reference to tribal languages is retrogressive in that regard (Muzale & Rugemalira, 2008: 9)

The 2012 census reaffirmed the suppression of the ECLs. A question[6] on literacy skills had the following options for the respondent to choose from: i) Kiswahili; ii) English; iii) Kiswahili & English; iv) other language; v) cannot read and write. A respondent who mentioned an ECL under option iv) was told that ECLs don't count as languages, that languages like Spanish and French were the intended choices[7].

The census is a potent policy and planning tool of course and the "literacy" question does really deserve further scrutiny. The question (No. 17 in the census short questionnaire) suggests that the intent is to indirectly obtain information on languages spoken (by people aged 4 years and above). The clerk who rejected an ECL as a possible answer must have gone beyond his/her belief because the census authorities give the impression that their interest was simply

---

[6] Je unajua kusoma na kuandika katika lugha ya Kiswahili, Kiingereza, Kiswahili na Kiingereza au lugha nyingine yoyote? (Can you read in Swahili, English, Swahili and English, or any other language).

[7] Dr. Amani Lusekelo's Nyakyusa was discounted. Dr. Abel Mreta was told that there is no provision for Asu (personal communication).

with literacy in English and Swahili and that there was no official list of "other languages". However, since it is clear that the census does not regard ECLs as languages it is possible that some people who said they could read and write an ECL would be categorised under option (v), viz. cannot read and write. It is also probable that the interpretation of the census results is going to be that most Tanzanians speak Swahili, the national language.

Other measures were more explicit in instituting curbs on the ECLs. The communications policy, laws and rules prohibit the use of ECLs in broadcasting.

> 15. Every free-to-air licensee shall-
> (a) ensure that only official languages, namely Kiswahili and English, are used for all broadcasts except where specific authorisation has been given to use non official languages (TCRA, 2005)

The election rules make it an offence to use 'divisive' language or a language other than Swahili in the campaigns (Tanzania, 2010b).

> Swahili shall be the only campaign language. Where Swahili is not understood and there is a necessity a candidate shall speak in Swahili while an interpreter interprets into the language spoken in the relevant area (section 2.1 k).

The code of conduct urges political parties and candidates to guard against tribalism, and all discrimination along gender, religious and racial lines (sections 2.1 d & 2.2 j). So even if there were no clause proclaiming Swahili the only campaign language, it would still be dangerous for a candidate to use an ECL because that would expose him/her to the charge of tribalism.

Although the 1976 Newpaper Act does not prohibit the use of ECLs in newspapers, the government has not registered any ECL newspaper since independence. This of course is partly accounted for by the fact that the Nyerere government controlled all mass media and private newspapers were first allowed in the 1990s under the liberalisation measures of the time. But the government's position against the use of ECLs in newspapers was made explicit by one government official:

> "Serikali imesema haitasajili magazeti yanayochapishwa katika lugha za makabila, kwa kuwa itakuwa ni kupanda mbegu za ukabila nchini na kuchochea migawanyiko. ...[Ingawa]sheria ya magazeti ya mwaka 1976 haizungumzi chochote

kuhusu usajili wa magazeti ya lugha za makabila […]kama usajili wa aina hiyo utaruhusiwa itakuwa vigumu kwa serikali kufuatilia habari zinazochapishwa katika magazeti ya aina hiyo kwa kuwa lugha zitakazotumika hazitaeleweka na wengi. Haitakuwa rahisi kwa serikali kufuatilia mabaya ambayo yanaweza kuchapishwa na magazeti ya aina hiyo kwenye makabila yanayohusika" (NIPASHE, 1999).

[The government will not register newspapers using tribal languages because this will sow seeds of tribalism and foment divisions...[Although] the 1976 newspaper act says nothing about newspapers using tribal languages, if such newspapers are allowed it will be difficult for the government to monitor what is published because the languages will not be understood my many people. It will be difficult for the government to keep track of bad things that could be published in such papers in the relevant tribes](my translation).

In this context one would be forgiven for thinking that the statements found in *Sera ya Utamaduni* (1997: 17) in favour of ECLs were inserted by mistake. The policy urges the research, conservation, and translation of ECLs; the need to produce dictionaries and grammars in ECLs; and the need to publish various materials in the ECLs. In any case the true intent of the pronouncements is stated: "The indigenous languages will continue to be used as a reservoir for the development of Swahili" (my translation)[8]. And although there are salaried Cultural Officers in the districts they do not work on the research and conservation of ECLs. Instead they contribute to the transformation of the local dances into hybrid forms using Swahili instead of ECLs and focusing on political messages that flatter the establishment - which ensures that the relevant dancing troupe can get favours from the government.

The measures discussed above in connection with the smothering of the ECLs were not part of a comprehensive language policy. Rather they were part of statecraft by the nationalist politicians who used Swahili as one of the tools for gaining control over the instruments of state or, as they would put it, 'cementing' the nation.

---

[8] "Lugha za asili zitaendelea kutumika kama hazina na chanzo cha kukuza Kiswahili." Tanzania (1997: 17).

Swahili also got considerable respectability to enable it to make some inroads into the domains of English. But on this front Swahili's fortunes have had a chequered career. In parliamentary debates Swahili essentially replaced English; but the bills have always been drafted and enacted in English even though the reading is of a **summary** version in Swahili. Similarly the rules and regulations that ministers draw up to facilitate the implementation of the laws are published in the government gazette in English. Government circulars are sometimes in English and sometimes in Swahili. Over the years there has been an attempt to provide Swahili translations to some key documents, notably the annual budget speeches, but not the acts of parliament. This spills over into the courts where proceedings are mainly in Swahili, but the records and the judgement are in English. So although the judge writes the judgement in English the public reading will be of a **summary** version in Swahili.

The relative strengths/constituencies of Swahili and English can be discerned in the division of turf. The nationalist mass movement associated with the independence struggle and socialism under TANU/ASP[9], and later with the successor party, CCM[10] has always been the bulwark for Swahili. Two examples of this base are more than symbolic of the Swahili movement. The first concerns the state controlled media. The party has published a daily paper, *Uhuru*, in Swahili since before independence (known as *Mamboleo* and later *Ngurumo*). The government published the *Nationalist* (later renamed *Daily News*). These were the only daily papers until the liberalisation moves of the mid 1990s - one in Swahili from the party, and the other in English from the government. The radio was also state controlled and had a small English section with restricted hours. The Swahili service was an effective tool of propaganda and played a significant role in the consolidation of the language in mass political activity and was under the effective control of party activists. Even after the liberalisation which saw the birth of private newspapers, radio stations and television channels, it was not until 2009 that the government launched a Swahili newspaper - *Habari Leo*!

The second example of the relative bases of the two languages comes from the constitutional process. The independence constitution was in English, of course. So was the 1965 Interim Constitution of the union between Tanganyika and Zanzibar, establishing the single-party

---

[9] TANU - Tanganyika African National Union; ASP - Afro Shiraz Party.
[10] CCM - Chama cha Mapinduzi (Revolution Party).

regime[11]. By the time of the unification of the two parties in 1977 the party was strong enough to not only draft its constitution in Swahili, but also the same party cadres took charge of the process which put in place the 1977 constitution of the united republic in Swahili. The gains on this score still hold ground today as the nation is in the midst of a constitutional review process. An attempt in late 2011 to backtrack by presenting the constitutional review process bill in English was thrown out of parliament after a public outcry opposing, in part, the use of English. The revised bill was drafted in Swahili and passed by parliament in early 2012 (Tanzania, 2012a). It is possible that if other laws were presented to the wider public for scrutiny as the constitutional review process bill was, some of these would draw enough public anger to force the government to write them in a language that the readers would understand.

As a workplace, government/public service is linguistically schizophrenic. Often the relevant agency has an English name following the legal instrument that established the relevant entity (e.g. Tanzania Revenue Authority; Energy, Water, and Utilities Regulatory Authority; Tanzania Communications Regulatory Authority; Tanzania Commission for Universities; Tanzania Ports Authority; Tanzania Electricity Supply Company; National Housing Corporation; Muhimbili National Hospital; Tanzania Roads Agency; National Institute for Medical Research; Capital Development Authority; National Social Security Fund). Most documents are in English and the people handling them struggle to understand them or to create new ones on old templates (see insert below from a government official issuing instructions regarding the 2012 census discussed earlier).

---

[11] In fact there were two parties, Tanganyika African National Union (TANU) on the mainland and Afro-Shiraz Party (ASP) in Zanzibar until their unification into Chama cha Mapinduzi (CCM) in 1977.

In oral communication they speak Swahili; in meetings they will sigh with relief if allowed to use Swahili and discussions will be animated and long. If English has to be used the discussions will be dominated

---

HALMASHAURI YA MANISPAA YA KINONDONI

OFISI YA SERIKALI YA MTAA WA OYSTER-BAY
S.L.P 105320, DAR ES SALAAM.
SIMU: Mob. +255 (0)713/753/787- 609717,
Rees: +255 (0) 22 2664519
Fax: 022 2664519, Email: serikaliyamtaaobay@yahoo.com

Kumb: Na. M/Kiti / O'bay / Br / 001493/12   Tarehe 25/08/2012

TO
THE ALL RESIDANCE AND
RENTER AT APARTMENT, HOTEL
AND OTHERS

REF: CENSER COUNTING PEOPLE 26 AUG 2012

Refer the above mentioned Subject

Remember the Government of Republic Union of Tanzania announce on 26.08.2012 is the day of counting people [censer] for all living visitors in Tanzania. This is legal order for Beural Statistics No: 1 of 2002.

Because for this day any people who sleep at your House, Hotel, or residence apartment on 26.08.2012 he or she must be accountable in this censer. Also all people must answer this Question from the Censer Officer.

ORDER
If your refuse to be countable or stop censer Officer to do the job of counting people from 26.08.2012and 7 days more its is criminal case, than you will be charged in the court and fine with sentenced in prison for 6 month. Then please give all assistance Censer Officer what he or she need

Thanks in advance.

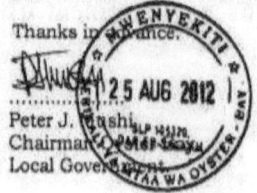

Peter J. Mashi
Chairman
Local Gove...

N.B   District Commissioner of Kinondoni

Hon: Mstahiki Meya – Municipal Council

Director of Kinondoni Municipal

Hon: Ward Registative Chancellor of Msasani

Ward Exacutive Officer of Msasani

by a few people and any daring dissenter has to apologise for using Swahili[12]. The surprising thing is that in virtually all of these situations there are no explicit rules mandating the use of one language or the other; rather it is the established tradition and/or the perceived high status of English which puts Swahili on the defensive.

The University of Dar es Salaam - A Case Study

The University of Dar es Salaam forms an interesting case study in this regard. When the university was established in the 1960s (initially as part of the University of East Africa) there was a languages and linguistics department that catered for English, French, and Swahili[13].

> When the Faculty of Arts and Social Science was inaugurated in July, 1964, there was no Department of Kiswahili. Instead, there was the Departments of Languages and Linguistics which offered courses in linguistics, French and English. Occasionally, some Kiswahili courses were taught as options, particularly in the second and third year.
>
> With the advent of the University of Dar es Salam on July 1, 1970, the Department of Kiswahili was born. It was a deliberate decision by the government that the national University had to have a department which would cater for the national languages. Hence the first take was in July, 1770

Maganga 1991: 7

A major reorganisation followed the dismemberment of the University of East Africa with each of the constituent colleges of Makerere, Nairobi and Dar es Salaam becoming independent universities. While Makerere and Nairobi formed/maintained

---

[12] A member of parliament claimed, during the parliamentary debate on the protocol to establish the Swahili Commission for the East African Community, that the reason for bad business contracts (e.g. in mining, procurement, management of enterprises) is failure of the government negotiators to understand the full intent of the contracts they commit the government to (MWANANCHI, November 2012). Would admission of ignorance ("with good intentions") be an acceptable defence in the face of a charge of corruption in these circumstances?

[13] Kozi yangu ya Fasihi ya Kiswahili niliianzisha mwaka 1968 katika Idara ya Language & Linguistics wakati John Woodhead alikuwa mkuu wa Idara. Na mwaka 1969, Mohamed Abdulaziz nami tukaanzisha BA Swahili & Linguistics katika idara hiyo hiyo. Wakati huo, BA English & Linguistics na French & Linguistics zilikuwa zipo tayari (Farouk Topan in a message to Saida Yahya-Othman on 22 October 2012). [I started my course on Swahili Literature in 1968 in the department of Language and Linguistics at a time when John Woodhead was Head of Department. And in 1969 Mohamed Abdulaziz and I started the BA Swahili and Linguistics in that same department. At that time BA English & Linguistics, and French and Linguistics had already been established]

departments of African languages and literature separate from the departments of English (language & literature), Dar es Salaam was determined to be innovative. For Swahili the university established a department, and also a research institute (Taasisi ya Uchunguzi wa Kiswahili)[14] - this being a carry-over from the colonial Inter-territorial Language Committee already mentioned. English was split into two branches: one branch formed the department of Literature while the other branch joined French to form a department of Foreign Languages and Linguistics (FLL).

The institutional structure of the university expressly refused to recognise the existence of ECLs. From 2001 a research project funded by Swedish SIDA has done considerable documentation work on the ECLs. The *Languages of Tanzania Project* is housed within the department of FLL. It has published over thirty books, mainly dictionaries, a few sketch grammars, collections of folk tales, four volumes of occasional papers in linguistics, and the *Atlasi ya Lugha za Tanzania*[15]. Debates within the project team have occasionally shown the tension of two perspectives about research on ECLs. The first perspective is that the central mission of this work is to document and, in this way, promote the ECLs for possible expanded domains of use by the respective communities:

> ...the project researchers framed the objectives in linguistic terms – language atlas production, documentation of grammar and vocabulary, and how these may inform linguistic theory, as well as broader considerations of preserving a people's cultural heritage. But someone at SIDA added something more appealing to a non-linguistic decision making audience, i.e. "It may also provide basic knowledge to issues related to school enrolment, extension services etc." In SIDA's analysis of "relations between research programmes and SIDA's development strategy" this project was slotted under two sectors: i) "Education – knowledge valuable to understanding of local languages and their relation to the education system"; ii) "Legal security – knowledge valuable to understanding of local languages and access to the legal system for the poor" (Rugemalira, 2011: 11-12).

---

[14] The department of Kiswahili and the Institute of Kiswahili Research eventually merged in 2009 to form the Institute of Kiswahili Studies (Taasisi ya Taaluma za Kiswahili).
[15] Tanzania language atlas.

The second perspective is that the ECLs are endangered and so need to be quickly documented and archived for posterity. Because researchers are racing against time they ought to start work on the most endangered, i.e. those that have the least number of speakers and are not being transmitted to offspring (Legere, 2002). In this perspective there is no future for ECLs. As projects come and go, the flurry of activity on ECLs under this project may eventually die as it is unlikely that local resources could be made available for continued research, and unthinkable that a teaching programme for these languages can ever develop at the University of Dar es Salaam.

An important appendage to the department of FLL is the Communication Skills Unit (CSU) created in 1978 in order to address the widely felt staff dissatisfaction with proficiency levels in English among the student population. As noted in Rugemalira (1990: 105) the CSU was not a new type of outfit in African university settings. Rather it was a familiar organ fabricated in the hope that it could tackle a fundamental problem, viz. the use of a foreign language in the educational institutions of a nation. The architects of the CSU designed for credit 'study skills' courses for the majority of the student body and were at pains to avoid calling them remedial grammar courses. The remedial programme that they designed for a smaller 'at risk' segment was eventually phased out as the general student enrolment rose and attendance/diligence at a non-credit course became difficult to enforce. The CSU course was in effect the extension of English language courses to tertiary level, the authorities having noted that the teaching at the lower levels had been inadequate and ineffective. The theoretical assumption here is that more teaching (more time) will result in better results.

The CSU model has been uncritically extended to all tertiary institutions (for certificate, diploma and degree courses) in the country given the preeminent position that the University of Dar es Salaam has historically occupied. It is arguable that the formula proposed by the CSU for tackling the 'language problem' was faulty from the beginning because it assumed that most students did not need to be taught English, but only study skills in order to adjust to the academic environment of the university. But even if they had designed a formula for teaching English they would have encountered several problems:

    i) Negative learner attitudes - why does anyone want to teach me more English when I did that in primary and secondary school?

Surely there are other things to learn at university! This is the fate that befell the remedial grammar component of the CSU programme.

ii) The fossilisation factor - bad teaching and learning over the years has fixed a certain interlanguage in the learner so that no remedial work will undo the damage.

iii) Cost effectiveness - the small classes of the late 1970s and 1980s (with students not exceeding 30 per group) were eventually replaced by large classes in the 1990s and the new millennium. Now a single lecturer typically has a class of up to 800 students (delivering three lectures per week) and cannot organise seminar groups for practice sessions. For the early student/instructor ratio to be maintained the university would have had to hire hundreds of lecturers just for this programme alone. In terms of cost it would be more effective if such resources were directed at the lower levels of school in order to make the language teaching there more effective.

The language problem has not gone away of course and the CSU dilemma[16] has become even more acute. University authorities have been prodding CSU staff to constitute themselves into a centre or institute of communication studies in order to more effectively tackle the worsening problem. Msuya's (2011) doctoral study found that the CSU courses have had no appreciable impact on the English proficiency levels of the students in spite of the students' felt need for a course that would help in this regard. The feeling among staff is that the university is not the place to tackle the English language problems of the students it admits. Two proposals have been advanced from staff: One is to set up a strict admission policy that would disqualify candidates without an adequate proficiency in English. The mere mention of this would raise hell from the population - that a Tanzanian can be denied admission to a university education because of failing an English examination, and this, 50 years after independence! The alternative is to set up a full year of English study before embarking on university courses - just in the same way as students going to China or Russia spend a year studying the language of the country before they start working on their degree courses. This

---

[16] This dilemma is captured by Msuya (2011: 11) in these words: "There are ... contending views among academicians about what communication skills courses seek to achieve... academic literacy, [or to improve] students' poor level of general proficiency in English language"

alternative may not be politically explosive, but its cost implications would call for a re-planning of the ELT regime in general. It might, for instance, require that the teaching of English starts later - in secondary school - and so concentrate the resources on a smaller front for effect.

The Institute of Kiswahili Studies (IKS) has a respectable track record of research and teaching and has been a pioneer in the use of Swahili as LOI in a university context. For many years this was confined to the undergraduate level. In 2009 however the use of Kiswahili in the M.A. programme - for teaching and writing the dissertation - was approved by the university senate.

From the administrative angle the experience of the IKS raises issues of language attitudes within academia. As would be expected IKS has been on the forefront to promote the use of Swahili in university administration and has had to struggle to make the point that they have a right to prepare meeting documents in Swahili and speak the language in university meetings. Recently the senate rejected the proposal for establishing a taught PhD programme from the institute and directed, among other matters, that the authors provide a glossary for the benefit of senate members who do not understand what they regard as difficult Swahili vocabulary. The feeling of the Institute Director was that this is unfairly frustrating their efforts; that what the honourable senators find incomprehensible is standard technical terminology in linguistics and literature, noting that he, as a language specialist, does not demand that documents from the Engineering and Sciences departments provide a glossary for their own technical terms[17].

Like other public organisations, the university does not have explicit rules on what languages to use but relies on tradition or established practice - which is the inherited British university system run in English. After Swahili was declared a national/official language it found its way into some of the official organs of the university. The most prominent is the Workers' Council - a rather superfluous organ imposed on public organisations during the populist/socialist phase of single party rule. With many members being non-academic (administrative) staff it was necessary that it conducts its business in Swahili rather than English. Similarly there is a separate committee for recruitment and promotion of academic as

---

[17] Dr. Aldin Mutembei, personal communication.

opposed to administrative staff; the former conducts its business in English while the latter works in Swahili. Accordingly documents that come to the Disciplinary Committee may be in English or Swahili depending on the type of staff member being put on the defensive. Most other university organs (academic departments, colleges and schools, University Senate, and University Council) normally conduct their business in English and the institutional message is very clear, that Swahili is for the lower ranks of the university staff.

On the whole then, government business is transacted and recorded in English. Whereas in the 1960s and 1970s pro-Swahili elements in government did attempt to enforce the use of the language in government communication these elements became noticeably weaker day by day from 1980s. Legere (2010) notes an increasing tendency on the part of the elite (including members of parliament) to code switch from Swahili into English or to just throw an English word into one's speech in order to show off. The websites of many government and parastatal agencies use only English and do not attempt to address the audience that does not understand English.

The National Swahili Council
The pre-eminent institution established by the government for promoting Swahili is the National Swahili Council - better known by its Swahili acronym, BAKITA[18] - established by an act of parliament in 1967. As a language academy conceived in the purist tradition the mandate of such an organ is problematic. As an administrative arm of government for formulating and implementing language policy, the potential impact is unlimited. Viewed as a research, development and publishing body, it would be difficult to distinguish it from the university institute already discussed.

BAKITA does try to play the role of language police as guardian of the purity of the Swahili language[19]. Where it may be able to get in the way of a writer or publisher involves the publication of school materials if these must seek approval from the Ministry of Education. Approval cannot be granted before BAKITA is satisfied with the Swahili standards in the relevant materials. But the council does not have any influence on any other materials that can be

---

[18] Baraza la Kiswahili la Taifa.
[19] "Kuhimiza matumizi fasaha ya lugha ya Kiswahili na kuzuia upotoshaji wake" [To encourage the correct use of Swahili and curb its corrruption] www.bakita.go.tz

published and sold without government approval - general books, novels, newspapers, radio and television broadcasts, etc. It would be unfortunate if BAKITA were to claim power to censor/edit such works. It would probably throw away more than half of the materials coming out of these channels, including the ever changing slang forms in the tabloids and FM radio talk shows. Could they regulate individual performance by, for example, banning code-switching in public speaking - e.g. parliament, radio and TV broadcasting? If they could, would it be legitimate use of government powers?

BAKITA might want to follow the lead of its French counterpart[20] in an aggressive regulation campaign regarding the domains of use of the national language. One possible area to tackle could be the language of product labels and packaging, as well as product manuals. A regulation that required all products produced locally for the domestic market to use Swahili or both Swahili and English would have as its rationale the protection of consumers by providing instructions in a comprehensible language. This could then be extended gradually to also cover imported products. If this got to cover IT hardware and software it would be a forward looking measure with tremendous potential in an area where local talent is considerably shackled by beliefs about the inadequacy of Swahili (cf. Halvorsen, 2010: 133)[21]. Similar regulatory activism might cover the government departments and parastatal organisations that produce documents in English only; this could then be extended to tackle private organisations/companies that work only in English, including the business names which are predominantly in English. A regulation could force them to adopt a bilingual policy. The council has not attempted to take on this regulatory role yet.

The research and development role has been most articulated in the activities of the council probably because of the collaboration and influence of the academics from the University of Dar es Salaam Institute of Kiswahili Studies. Their virtually permanent association with BAKITA as researchers, governing board members, chairpersons, and even currently one of them as executive secretary of BAKITA, has blurred the line between the functions of the council

---

[20] Academie Française
[21] "The production of Kiswahili academic and scholarly internet content is of great importance. It is argued, however, that participation through Kiswahili in the ICT era is inhibited and undermined by remnants of the colonial system, including the language policy" (Halvorsen, 2010: 133)

and the institute. While the council was very active in the coining of technical terms in the 1970s and 1980s, it is the university institute that has been consistent in producing dictionaries of all types (monolingual, bilingual, subject specific), as well as textbooks and general books. Indeed it is arguable that BAKITA was superfluous from the very beginning; that the language research and development functions could and have been well taken care of by the academic institute at the university, while the regulatory role could have been performed by a competent and willing body of civil servants in the appropriate ministry[22].

The Language of Instruction (LOI) Debate

In no other sector has language policy and planning been most agonisingly felt and contested than in education. And yet for some people it would appear that there has not been [perhaps there cannot be] a proper debate because the contestants do not have a common perception of what the issues are, or what the national education agenda should be.

The status quo on LOI is that in public schools, Swahili is used from nursery school to Primary Seven. Then there is a switch to English from Secondary One through University. In a few private primary schools (catering for less than 2% of the total primary school enrolment) English is used right from nursery school. The Swahili gain into English turf got established in the early post-independence years but is now in serious danger of being reversed. Some of the arguments or argument gaps in this debate, and the related decisions (or lack thereof) are quite astonishing. For instance, Criper and & Dodd (1984) found that English was no longer an effective LOI; but they went on to recommend that the government should issue an unambiguous circular reaffirming the continued use of English as LOI, in return for British aid. A similar consultancy report tied to foreign aid trod the same path as Criper & Dodd more than twenty years later: the consultants recommended the reintroduction of English as LOI in Zanzibar primary schools even though they acknowledged the low levels of proficiency in English[23]. And on the

---

[22] There has always been a director of culture and a desk officer in charge of language matters in government structure.
[23] See the discussion in Brock-Utne (2012: 14-15) of the recommendations of the MoEVT/University of Bristol report.

mainland, the drafter of the revised Education and Training Policy (Tanzania, 2009) may have been taking dictation from those consultants in Zanzibar, except where he/she ignores research findings on English proficiency levels in the school system:

> Various researches have shown that a person understands subject content well if learning is done in a language they understand well, and even better if it is in the first language. Experience from a greater part of the world shows that different communities/societies use their own languages to get knowledge and various skills and that foreign languages are taught for communication purposes. Students at the secondary school level master Swahili and English better than other languages. In order to enable the students to understand various concepts well the languages which are most commonly used in the country shall be used in accessing knowledge and various skills in school.
> Objective: to consolidate the use of Swahili and English in order to enable students to learn efficiently and fulfill social needs.
> Statement: The LOI at secondary school level shall be English. (Tanzania 2009, section 5.6.3; my translation)

The author of this passage knows that it is not true that Tanzanian students have a good command of English. So why does he/she disregard and twist the truth? And even if it were true that the learners have a good command of both Swahili and English, why does the policy statement pick out only English as LOI, immediately after conceding the need to use "languages that are most commonly used in the country."

The facts regarding the state of English in Tanzanian schools are quite clear - that proficiency levels are too low for the language to function as an effective language of instruction (Mlama & Materu, 1978; Criper & Dodd, 1984; Roy-Campbell & Qorro, 1997; Rubagumya et al., 1999; Qorro, 2008[24]). From this observation many people have argued that it makes pedagogical sense to use a language that both learners and teachers have better mastery of, which happens to be Swahili. In opposition to this a strong English lobby has

---

[24] Qorro 2008 provides an excellent review of the literature on this subject in Tanzania.

managed to keep English as LOI and even regain some lost ground for the language.

There are three broad beliefs that constitute the foundation of the English camp so that genuine discussion in favour of Swahili is impeded. The first is the belief that English is *the* international language of science and technology, that all one needs in order to access that science is to learn English; that to attempt to teach and do science using other languages is like re-inventing the wheel since English is 'already there'[25]. It follows from this basic ideological stance that knowledge of English is an essential (the most important) component of being educated. A curriculum without English is inconceivable.

The second belief is that the best way to teach and learn English is by making the language the medium of teaching all other subjects in school. Relegating the language to the status of mere subject will result in no mastery and worse still it will lead to the wiping out of the language from the country (which God forbid) because there will be no incentive for students to make an effort to learn it.

The third belief revolves around the neo-liberal agenda of promoting a 'free market' for goods and services globally. English is seen as a good that is freely available for pick-up at the market prices then prevailing. The government is prodded to open up the primary school market [but not the post-primary levels] further so that both private and public schools can choose to use English as LOI. In this regard an attempt by the Dar es Salaam City authorities to introduce English as LOI in the city's schools was blocked by central government in 1998[26]. But ten years later the unrelenting prodding of

---

[25] Clive Criper, personal communication, 1984.

[26] cf. Rugemalira (2001): "In the current context, the new private primary schools seem to be lending weight to the pro-English camp. Available information indicates that no private school that relies on fees can survive unless it uses English as the medium of instruction. Parents will simply not send their children to a Swahili medium private school. They generally will not tolerate any suggestions regarding code-mixing within the school, maintaining that any room allowed for use of Kiswahili will destroy the 'fledgling efforts at mastering English'.

There are three dangers in this development. The first is that, alongside cost, the language of school will increasingly become a segregating factor in society, which will undermine the foundations of a cohesive nation. This will become more so if quality education, whether by coincidence or design, is seen to be associated with English medium schools. The second danger is that because of the disproportionate significance attached by society, to mastery of the English language, wider educational objectives might be sacrificed

the English forces was beginning to produce results. As already noted, the Zanzibar authorities decided to reinstate English as LOI for some subjects starting with fifth grade in government schools, but implementation of this decision has apparently been delayed for lack of teachers. And Mainland Tanzania is poised to follow suit (Brock-Utne, 2012: 14-16)[27].

Plans and policies regarding what languages to teach in the schools, and when, have understandably been a reflection of the LOI issue. Swahili, besides being the LOI in primary school, is also a compulsory subject up to Secondary Four level. It forms one of the subjects in the advanced level combinations and there is now a degree in Swahili at the universities of Dar es Salaam and Dodoma. The policies in place do not acknowledge the problems that children face in their first few years of schooling since the majority do not have Swahili as their home language. Research has shown that a significant section of the pupil population does experience transition problems in learning in a language that is not spoken at home[28]. Indeed, as already

---

as schools scramble to demonstrate to anxious parents how fast they can get their pupils to speak English fluently. This fear is not without foundation. Anecdotal evidence suggests that parents' comments about the quality of the new schools invariably assign special weight to achievement in the English language. The third danger is that the government may seek a shortcut to the problems besetting the education sector by declaring English the medium of instruction from the primary school level. This would seem to give every school child an equal opportunity to *learn* English while at the same time deflecting public attention from the urgent need to make substantial investment in education. A few years back the Dar es Salaam City Commission attempted to do just that – reintroducing English as the language of instruction in the city's schools. At that time the move was blocked from the Ministry of Education (EAST AFRICAN, 1998)".

[27] The Minister for Education and Vocational Training has been quoted as saying that a return to English as LOI in government primary schools is imminent:

The government is planning to introduce English as a medium of instruction from Standard Three in a bid to raise the confidence of Tanzanian job seekers in the East African common market. Education and Vocational Training minister Shukuru Kawambwa said recently that the poor background in English language made Tanzanians fear East African job market. 'Tanzanian education is not inferior as people think. The problem we face is poor background in English language, we are going to make sure that in three years English will be the medium of instruction'. *The Citizen*, 21 October 2010.

[28] For instance, Mapunda (2010: 210) found that children in rural schools where Swahili is not the community language were placed at a disadvantage compared to their counterparts in schools where Swahili was the children's home language. In the rural schools "teachers stigmatise responses provided in the ECL. This stigma impacts pupils negatively as most decide not to attempt (withdrawal from participating). This in the long run is likely to have the effect of making learners look down upon their own cultural values in favour of the school's.... Similarly, because of the policy directives, teachers unquestioningly use only

noted, school practices proscribe the use of the ECL even in non-classroom activities[29]. But Swahili is a real second language in Tanzanian communities that do not have it as first/mother tongue, and most people, particularly those who complete primary school, do develop a respectable level of receptive knowledge. Still it is arguable that deficiencies in the education system (poor teaching, lack of facilities and materials, bad curriculum emphasis e.g. the absence of an articulated reading programme) are responsible for poor levels in Swahili proficiency. For instance, a report by a non-governmental organisation claimed that Kenyan pupils outperformed their Tanzanian counterparts in Swahili literacy tasks (cf. Uwezo, 2011).

When to start teaching English in school has been changing, back and forth. The table below provides a summary of the constant changes (Qorro, 2012: 52-4).

Year	English as subject	English as LOI	Remarks
1920	Primary Five	Primary Seven	Beginning of British rule. School system: years 1-4 lower primary; 5-8 middle /upper primary school.
1958	Primary Three		'The earlier the better' argument was a winner
1960		Primary Five	
1965		Secondary One	Swahili declared LOI for nursery & primary school, teacher training and adult literacy campaign. School system: 7 years for primary school
1970	Primary One		
1980	Primary Three		
1995	Nursery School		"Kiswahili and English shall be compulsory subjects for all students from pre-primary to Ordinary Level secondary education." MOEC 1995: 52 Liberalisation re-opened the door for *private* English medium pre-primary and primary schools

Table 1: ELT and English as LOI swings in the Tanzanian curriculum

---

Kiswahili even when pupils cannot make any significant progress. This trivialises and or inhibits the learning process."

[29] In English medium schools ECLs and Swahili are prohibited by 'Speak English' rules and humiliating sanctions are imposed as part of school quality assurance policies.

The general trend apparent in the table above is the progressive push of ELT to the very early years of school. It would be interesting to study the comparative efficiency of the two pedagogical positions: one, that learners should acquire an unshakable foundation of literacy in the first (one) language before being introduced to literacy in another language, as opposed to two, that all other factors remaining equal, the simultaneous introduction of literacy skills in different languages is unproblematic[30]. Of course in the Tanzanian case, all factors are not equal; in particular for most urban learners, oral proficiency in Swahili is nearly perfect at ages 4-6, while it is nil in English. For most rural children proficiency in Swahili is nil when they enter school.

On what other languages to incorporate in the school curriculum, there has been very little initiative. The introduction of French at the university and a few secondary schools in the 1960s was driven by foreign policy concerns. The Ministry of Foreign Affairs needed diplomatic personnel who would be able to use French. For many years the degree programme with French at the University of Dar es Salaam was combined with either teaching or international relations. The programme has remained extremely small because the recruitment base consists of only a few secondary schools. Even the recent introduction of a French option in the primary school curriculum may not change the situation soon partly because there are very few teachers, and partly because Tanzania is a keenly contested anglophone backyard[31].

Arabic is on the Zanzibar school curriculum but it is not a prominent subject, being taught in only a few schools. The attempt to introduce Spanish did not last may be because it was based on Cuban assistance. Chinese is yet to get an entry into the university system despite the aggressive moves of Chinese institutions. In general there has not been any serious planning for a place for several foreign languages in the school curriculum. Viewed in the wider context, this is a general planning failure partly caused by the manpower approach to educational planning - only educate enough people to fill the

---

[30] See Rugemalira (2005) for a discussion of this issue.
[31] In neighbouring Rwanda, which together with Burundi joined the East African Community in 2007, French has lost its privileged position after English was declared the main official language in 2008 (Rosendal, 2011). The ruling Rwanda Patriotic Front (RPF) is controlled by former refugees who grew up in Tanzania and Uganda and were educated in the English system in those countries.

positions available in the formal economy (all of which was state controlled until the liberalisation of the 1990s).

Attitudes and policies regarding bilingualism and code-switching in the education system are steeped in the purist, 'monolingualism good bilingualism bad' tradition. This has often stood in the way of ingenious approaches to the language question in the curriculum. So even though researchers (Mlama & Materu, 1978; Criper & Dodd, 1984; Brock-Utne, 2004) have noted that any thread of learning still available in the schools is attributable to the illegal use of Swahili - from secondary to tertiary levels, official policies/regulations still preach the complete separation of the two languages. A correct answer in an examination will not be marked at all if it is written in Swahili, and any code-switching will be penalised. Methods that would employ Swahili in explaining/giving instructions in an English language lesson are prohibited. Yet this is standard practice in many foreign language learning textbooks.

Lwaitama and Rugemalira (1990: 38) note a speculation that the reluctance on the part of government to allow the use of Swahili as LOI might be due to the fear that "a switch to Kiswahili would remove a formidable barrier to secondary education and would thus open the floodgates for universal secondary education, a demand the government would not be able to meet". By 2006 the floodgates could not be firmly held in position any longer: the politicians abandoned the incremental plans of the education ministry bureaucrats and ordered the establishment of a secondary school in every ward. Table 2 shows the dramatic contrast between the 1980s dismal transition rates from primary to secondary school with the expansions of the new millennium. In the first five years of the eighties decade, a total of less than 100,000 students were admitted into secondary school, in a country with a population of more than twenty million[32] at the time. Twenty years later the transition rate was over 20%, having risen from an average of 4%; but the absolute figures were still incredibly low. In 2002, when the population was counted at 35 million, only 107,282 students got admission into secondary school (both public and private). The admission figure of 2004 is more than double the 2002 figure. The annual admissions from 2006 to 2009 are more than four times the 2002 figure, and about 54% of the primary seven class.

---

[32] Population census figures for 1978 and 1988 were 17 million and 23 million respectively.

Year	Primary Seven Leavers	Secondary One Intake	Percentage
1981-1985	2311003	99709	4.3
1986	380096	27430	7.2
2000	389746	84709	21.7
2001	444903	99752	22.4
2002	493504	107282	21.7
2003	490018	147490	30.1
2004	499241	180239	36.1
2005	493946	243359	49.3
2006	664263	448448	67.5
2007	773553	438901	56.7
2008	1017865	524784	51.6
2009	999070	438827	43.9

Table 2: Primary to Secondary School Transition Rates (Source: Tanzania, 2010a)

The expansions in the primary school level had to spill over into the secondary level: "There has been an increase in total enrolment (Form 1- 6) by 143% from 675,672 students in 2006 to 1,638,699 pupils in 2010" (Tanzania 2010a,Table 4.1).

But this partial and sudden opening of the floodgates into secondary education created another challenge. Most of these new ward schools have no facilities or personnel - the most visible symbol is a building, with inadequate teachers, furniture, books, and other materials. The massive failure rates in the Secondary Four examinations in 2011 were shocking but not unexpected as the trend shows a declining performance over the past five years[33]. The shock and frustration of parents and students fed into an increasing sense of class divisions: wealthier families have access to good quality private primary and secondary schools, with English as LOI right from kindergarten; the poor majority are stuck in a mediocre government system that even those who run it do not believe in.

The metaphor of the floodgates is meant to focus attention on an important policy issue, viz. whether mass education can be effective through a foreign language. Trappes-Lomax (1990) answered this question in the negative, suggesting that it might be too costly to muster the requisite resources, and not practicable because of certain attitudes and habits that hinder the smooth mastery of any

---

[33] The percentage of candidates scoring in the passing divisions I-III has declined every year from 2007 to 2011 (36.6, 27.31, 17.91, 11.59, 10.05). See Tanzania (2012b).

foreign language. To appreciate the seriousness of the issue, consider the rates of success of learning foreign languages even in the most widely acclaimed cases of the Nordic countries. It is arguable that the majority of the population that does not go beyond the secondary school (perhaps even some of those who go to university) does not have mastery of a foreign language sufficient for the individual to pursue studies of other subjects in that foreign language. Or imagine this scenario: A British government report noted that many pupils aged 14 to 16 "cannot use foreign languages independently and spontaneously and lack the confidence to write or speak fluently at any length". In one in eight schools inspected in 2002-3 achievement was "unsatisfactory" in this area (BBC, 2004). If a consultant from France or Germany, or even a British consultant or politician, were to suggest that the best way to make British children learn French effectively is to use French in teaching all subjects in the entire school system, people might think the consultant was only making a joke. In the USA it is not the case that students, even at high school level have mastery over a foreign language and can use it to learn subject content in college. In short, the point of the argument is that low achievement rates in the English language in the Tanzanian school system are not merely a result of incompetent teachers but evidence of declining standards in education: in *any* foreign language learning programme there are individual and system factors that will constrain the achievement rates.

There are two lines that the government appears to be trying out as a palliative: the first is to extend English as LOI to the public primary schools and in this way soothe the poor in the belief that now their children can compete on an equal footing because they have access to English[34]. A draft revised version of the Education and Training Policy - ETP (Tanzania, 2009) documents this line of attack. Table 3 presents the 1995 version parallel to the 2009 revisions (translation of the 2009 version from the Swahili original is mine).

---

[34] The parallel Srilanka experience is really close: with independence (1940s) progressive policies brought in the use of native languages (Tamil and Sinhala) in all schools and public funding for the whole system, to replace the pre-independence dual system of private English medium schools and public and rural local language schools. Liberalisation of the economy around 2002 re-introduced the dual system both in medium and ownership. English as LOI begins at grade 6; ... the public schools are free but underfunded; schools may choose English as LOI; it is argued that this move will serve equity by making the language available to the poor in the 'free' government schools (Lindberg & Narman, 2005: 320)

Education and Training Policy 1995		Education and Training Policy 2009 (draft 1)	
Section	Statement	Section	Statement
5.2.3	The medium of instruction in pre-primary schools shall be Kiswahili, and English shall be a compulsory subject.	5.4.1	The languages of instruction in pre-primary schools shall be Kiswahili and English. Kiswahili and English shall be taught as subjects.
5.3.7	The medium of instruction in primary schools shall be Kiswahili, and English shall be a compulsory subject.	5.5.2	The languages of instruction at primary school level shall be Kiswahili and English.
5.4.9	The medium of instruction for secondary education shall continue to be English except for the teaching of other approved languages and Kiswahili shall be a compulsory subject up to Ordinary Level.	5.6.3	The language of instruction at secondary school level shall be English.

Table 3: ETP revisions in LOI policy

Note that the revisions open the door for a return of English as LOI in the lower levels but keep the door firmly closed against Swahili to also become LOI at secondary school level. Of course the public will soon realise that there are no teachers to bring this English to the masses. At the time of writing (November 2012) there are unconfirmed reports that the attempts to push English as LOI further down the education system is being halted for now and the revised Education and Training Policy will reflect the 1995 position on this issue[35].

The second line of government action is an attempt to fix fees in the private schools so that more poor people can afford their

---

[35] Martha Qorro, personal communication.

services[36]. Here too if the schools are starved of necessary resources quality cannot be guaranteed and there will not be any difference with the public schools. Also the private education section is much smaller than the public one; at the primary level it caters for under 2% of the total primary school enrolment. The 2010 enrolment in non-government primary schools was 152,279 out of a grand total of 8,419,305. At the secondary level the private share was 14% in 2010 (with 237,369 students in private schools out of a total of 1,638,699).

Conclusion: The Present and The Future
The state, by its nature, is inimical to individual freedoms and differences and is bent on imposing uniformity and central control of the citizens in the most efficient manner. From this perspective, multilingualism is bad. Yet the true democratic ethos requires the accommodation of differences rather than a simple dictatorship of the majority, let alone the imposition of the wishes of a powerful minority. In this perspective the suppression of the ECLs in Tanzania is as inexcusable as the continued holding back of Swahili in the face of English.

Still, even linguists may make language description and plan language development by suppressing some speech varieties in the process. The appropriate term is unification/harmonisation of dialects and orthographies of course[37]. In the Tanzanian case the influence of Swahili on conventions for writing the ECLs has been considerable. Will future generations - maybe five hundred years hence - be grateful to Nyerere and his followers for promoting Kiswahili at the expense of the ECLs?[38] Even in the sphere of religion where direct government intervention is limited, there have been clear signals of the decline of ECL use. The SIL laments the non-use of religious

---

[36] Some people have even suggested that the private English medium schools should be abolished as a way of leveling the field. And if Kiswahili becomes LOI at secondary level then there should not be room for English as LOI schools at all. For such people the central question is not LOI (and the debate is irrelevant), it is the class divisions between rich and poor.

[37] For a good example see the current initiative by CASAS at unification of orthographic conventions of African languages (Prah, 2002).

[38] Note how the descendants of the British empire builders are enjoying the fruits of their ancestors' labours that put English on a pedestal as the language of international politics, science and technology.

literature in the ECLs even where such literature is available in abundance[39].

In the 1980s pro-Swahili activists and scholars could comfortably state that it was a matter of time before Swahili would be declared the LOI in the Tanzanian school system: Lwaitama & Rugemalira (1990: 41) refer to "the inevitable change of media."[40] There was a feeling, even among pro-English stalwarts, that Swahili was an unstoppable avalanche sweeping over the face of Tanzania in a similar manner that English was sweeping over the face of the planet[41]. Twenty years later Brock-Utne (2010: 92, 96) expressed similar optimism in spite of the evidence tilting heavily in favour of English. What is the basis for such optimism? Brock-Utne pins her hopes on the possibility of a few currently marginal thinkers gathering momentum and becoming sufficiently influential to have their views accepted as common knowledge - even when experience has amply demonstrated that academics have had no influence on the decisions regarding LOI as their research findings have been largely disregarded.

> ... apart from the political elite and international donor agencies such as the British Council and the World Bank, other stakeholders in the LOI policy-making process have had limited influence on the articulation and implementation of existing LOI policies (Galabawa, 2004: 35)
>
> My involvement at language policy level for over a decade and a half has taught me that technical experts can try to influence the process, but their success really depends on the amount of influence they have on the political actors. This is indeed a sobering thought for academics who might think that their research findings are so self-evident that political actors do not need to be persuaded to adopt them (Desai, 2006: 110)

---

[39] "There are many languages in Uganda and Tanzania with Scriptures available in them, but it is a challenge to discern exactly why they are not being used"(Liz Thomson of SIL, personal communication 2010).

[40] The Presidential Commission on Education had proposed 1985 as the year to start the change in Secondary One and that would proceed up annually and reach the university with the 1992 intake (Tanzania, 1982).

[41] This feeling is captured in Nyerere's statement that "Kiingereza ni Kiswahili cha dunia" [English is the Swahili of the world] (*Mzalendo*, October 1984).

Such optimism needs to be tempered with an appropriate time-frame. In the short and medium term - over a period of up to fifty years, it may be difficult to envision the final triumph of Swahili over its nemesis. In the long term, (maybe over a century or two), Swahili may eventually become the national language it is destined to be and permeate every domain of use in Tanzanian society. Many of the opponents of Swahili as LOI - and African languages in general - would be prepared to live with that prognosis comfortably, saying the time is not ripe, the languages are not ready. A comparison can easily be made with the rise of English and the other European languages: that for them to emerge from under the dominance of Latin it took several centuries *and* structural changes in the economies and polities, including a major religious revolt that gave rise to the protestant churches![42]

The European comparison is disconcerting because there is no guarantee that the course of development of Tanzania's economy and political fortunes will strengthen Swahili, let alone the other ECLs. If the political economy continues to be a negligible appendage of the global economy under the control of a few powerful multinational organisations and superpowers (super-economies) then Swahili may not have a chance to become a language of power[43]. In this regard it is not clear that the pro-Swahili forces will be able to get a strong language clause empowering Swahili entrenched in the new constitution now being formulated. And even if such a clause is successfully negotiated it would not guarantee a bright future for the language, if the South African experience is anything to go by.

References

Assefa, Taye, Severine Rugumamu, & Abdel Ahmed. 2001. *Globalisation, Democracy, and development in Africa:*

---

[42] The translation of the Bible into German and English by the protestant rebels was a significant component of the structural revolution that would wring power from a few religious and secular aristocrats and into the hands of a widening merchant and craftsman populace.

[43] The 1980s vision of the World Bank required the Third World to focus its resources to primary education and leave tertiary education to economies that have a comparative advantage in providing it. This model is now bearing fruit to those with comparative advantage indeed: "...the collapse of the Indian university system has turned countries like Australia into sellers of tertiary education for overseas students from privileged backgrounds of India" (Ribeiro, 2010: 43). In China and Russia English medium Universities are setting up shop to cash in on the income from those, local and foreign, that are able to pay.

challenges and prospects. Addis Ababa: Organisation for Social Science Research in Eastern and Southern Africa (OSSREA).

Atlasi ya Lugha za Tanzania. 2009. Dar es Salaam: Mradi wa Lugha za Tanzania, Chuo Kikuu cha Dar es Salaam.

British Broadcasting Corporation (BBC). 2004. 'Fewer pupils' studying languages.

Brock-Utne, Birgit. 2004. English as the language of instruction or destruction - how do teachers and students in Tanzania cope? In Brock-Utne, Birgit, Zubeida Desai, & Martha Qorro, (Eds.), *Researching the language of instruction in Tanzania and South Africa*. Cape Town: African Minds. pp 57-84.

Brock-Utne, Birgit. 2012. Understanding what the teacher is saying in Kiswahili and English medium primary schools in Tanzania. in Qorro, Martha, Zubeida Desai, & Birgit Brock-Utne (Eds.), *Language of instruction: a key to understanding what the teacher is saying*. Dar es Salaam: KAD Associates.

Brock-Utne, Birgit, Zubeida Desai, & Martha Qorro, (Eds.). 2004. *Researching the language of instruction in Tanzania and South Africa*. Cape Town: African Minds.

Brock-Utne, Birgit, Zubeida Desai, & Martha Qorro, (Eds.). 2005. *LOITASA research in progress*. Dar es Salaam: KAD Associates.

Criper, Clive & William Dodd. 1984. *Report on the teaching of English and its use as a medium of instruction in Tanzania*. Dar es Salaam: British Council.

Desai, Zubeida. 2006. Reflections on LOITASA Project in South Africa - three years later. In Birgit Brock-Utne, Zubeida Desai, & Martha Qorro (Eds.), *Focus on fresh data on the language of instruction debate in Tanzania and South Africa*. Cape Town: African Minds pp 102 -112.

Desai, Zubeida, Martha Qorro, & Birgit Brock-Utne (Eds.). 2010. *Educational challenges in multilingual societies: LOITASA phase two research*. Cape Town: African Minds.

Le Page, R. 1964. *The national language question: linguistic problems of newly independent states*. London: OUP.

Galabawa, J.C. 2004. Salient policy issues in the choice of language of instruction (LOI) in Tanzania. In Desai et al. op. cit. pp 25-41.

Halvorsen, Torril. 2012. ICT-language and participation by the Tanzanian academia: a case study of the University of Dar es Salaam. In Qorro et al. *Language of instruction: a key to understanding what the teacher is saying.* Dar es Salaam: KAD Associates.

Kiango, John 2005. The search for a language of instruction: what should guide our choice? A look at South-East Asia. In Brock-Utne et al. op.cit. pp 293 - 306.

Legere, Karsten. 2002. The languages of Tanzania project: background, resources and perspectives. *Africa & Asia. Goteborg working papers on Asian and African languages and literatures.* No.2 pp 163-186.

Legere, Karsten. 2010. Swahili vs. English in Tanzania and the political discourse. *Studies of the Department of African Languages and Cultures,* No 44. University of Goteborg.

Lindberg, Jonas, & Anders Norman. 2005. Special situation of language and education in Srilanka - from self-reliance to neo-liberalism. In Brock-Utne, Birgit et al. 2005. op. cit. pp 307 - 324.

Lwaitama, Azaveli and Josephat Rugemalira. 1990. The English language support project in Tanzania. In Rubagumya (Ed.), *Language in education in Africa: a Tanzanian perspective.* Clevedon: Multilingual Matters. pp 36-53.

Maganga, Clement. 1991. A history of the department of Kiswahili, University of Dar es Salaam. *Swahili language and society.* pp 7-11.

Mapunda, Gastor. 2010. A study of the early literacy classroom interaction through Kiswahili: Cases of Ruvuma and Coast regions. Ph.D. Thesis. University of Dar es Salaam.

Mkude, Daniel. 2002. Minority languages and democratisation in the SADC region: the case of Tanzania. In Karsten Legere & Sandra Fitchat (Eds.), *Talking Freedom: Language and democratisation in the SADC region.* Windhoek: Gamsberg Macmillan Publishers pp 67-76.

Mlama, Penina & Mey Materu. 1978. Haja ya kutumia Kiswahili kufundishia elimu ya juu. Research report commissioned by BAKITA, Dar es Salaam.

Ministry of Education and Culture (MOEC). 1995. *Education and training policy.* Dar es Salaam.

Msuya, Erasmus. 2011. Communications skills course relevance and effectiveness at the University of Dar es Salaam. Ph.D. Thesis. University of Dar es Salaam.

Muzale & Rugemalira. 2008. Researching and documenting the languages of Tanzania. *Language documentation and conservation*. Vol. 2, No. 1, pp 68-108.

NIPASHE. 1999. Dar es Salaam.

Phillipson, Robert. 2009. *Some partner languages are more equal than others. Forum international de Bamako sur le multilinguisme. Actes du forum*. Bamako: ACALAN.

Prah, Kwesi. 2002. *Writing African: the harmonisation of orthographic conventions of African languages*. CASAS book series No. 25. Cape Town: CASAS.

Qorro, Martha. 2008. A review of the literature on the language of instruction research in Tanzania. In Qorro et al. pp 27-59.

Qorro, Martha, Zubeida Desai, & Birgit Brock-Utne (Eds.). 2008. *LOITASA: Reflecting on phase I and entering phase II*. Dar es Salaam: E & D Vision Publishing.

Qorro, Martha, Zubeida Desai, & Birgit Brock-Utne (Eds.). 2012. *Language of instruction: a key to understanding what the teacher is saying*. Dar es Salaam: KAD Associates

Qorro, Martha. 2012. Investing in English language teaching from the early grades in Tanzania primary schools: implications for the proposed education and training policy. In Qorro, Martha et al. (Eds.) pp 52-69.

Ribeiro, Fernando Rosa. 2010. Complexities of language and multilingualism in post-colonial predicaments. In *Education challenges in multilingual societies. LOITASA phase two research*. Cape Town: African Minds.

Rosendal, Tove. 2011. *Linguistic landshapes: a comparison of official and non-official language management in Rwanda and Uganda, focusing on the position of African languages*. Koln: Rudiger Koppe Verlag.

Roy-Campbell, Zaline & Martha Qorro. 1997. *The language crisis in Tanzania: the myth of English vs education*. Dar es Salaam: Mkuki na Nyota.

Rubagumya, Casmir (Ed.). 1990. *Language in education in Africa: a Tanzanian perspective*. Clevedon: Multilingual Matters.

Rubagumya, Casmir. 1991. Language promotion for educational purposes: the example of Tanzania. *International review of education*, 37:1 pp 67-87.

Rubagumya, Casmir, Kathyrin Jones, & Hermas Mwansoko. 1999. Language for learning and teaching in Tanzania. Unpublished (British) Overseas Development Administration research report.

Rugemalira, Josephat. 1990. The Communication Skills Unit and the language problem at the University of Dar es Salaam. In Rubagumya (Ed.), *Language in education in Africa: a Tanzanian perspective*. Clevedon: Multilingual Matters. Pp 105-122.

Rugemalira, Josephat. 2001. Private education and self-reliance in Tanzania. In Taye Assefa, Severine Rugumamu, & Abdel Ahmed (Eds.), *Globalisation, democracy and development in Africa: challenges and prospects*. Addis Ababa : Organisation for Social Science Research in Eastern and Southern Africa.

Rugemalira, Josephat. 2005. Theoretical and practical challenges in a Tanzanian English medium primary school. *Africa & Asia* 5:66 – 84.

Rugemalira, Josephat. 2011. Relevance and research capacity in the humanities. Paper presented at the inter-university conference on creating futures with research partnerships: $24^{th} - 25^{th}$ May 2011. University of Dar es Salaam. ms.

South Africa. 1996. *Constitution of South Africa*.

Tanzania. 1982. *Mfumo wa Elimu ya Tanzania 1981-2000: Ripoti na mapendekezo ya tume ya rais ya elimu*. Dar es Salaam.

Tanzania. 1995. *Education and Training Policy*. Dar es Salaam: Ministry of Education and Vocational Training.

Tanzania. 1997. *Sera ya utamaduni*. Dar es Salaam: Wizara ya Elimu na Utamaduni.

Tanzania. 2009. *Education and Training Policy*. Revised version - Draft 1. Dar es Salaam: Ministry of Education and Vocational Training.

Tanzania. 2010a. *Basic Education Statistics in Tanzania (BEST)*. Dar es Salaam: Ministry of Education and Vocational Training.

Tanzania. 2010b.*Maadili ya uchaguzi kwa ajili ya uchaguzi wa rais, wabunge na madiwani ya mwaka 2010*. Dar es Salaam: Tume ya Taifa ya Uchaguzi.

Tanzania. 2012a. *Sheria ya mabadiliko ya katiba*. Dar es Salaam.

Tanzania. 2012b. *Certificate of secondary education examination (csee) - 2011 report and analysis of the results.* Dar es Salaam: Ministry of Education and Vocational Training.

Tanzania Communications Regulatory Authority (TCRA). 2005. *The broadcasting services (content) Regulations.*

Trappes-Lomax. 1990. Can a foreign language be a national medium? In Rubagumya (Ed.), *Language in education in Africa: a Tanzanian perspective.* Clevedon: Multilingual Matters.

UNESCO, 2001. *Universal Declaration of Cultural Diversity.* Paris.

UNESCO, 2003. Convention for the Safeguarding of the Intangible Cultural Heritage. Paris.

Uwezo. 2011. *Are our children learning? Numeracy and literacy across East Africa.* Nairobi.

World Conference on Linguistic Rights, 1996. *Universal Declaration on Linguistic Rights.* New York.

United Nations, 1997. *Declaration on the Rights of Persons Belonging to National or Ethnic, Religious and Linguistic Minorities.* New York.

Chapter 5
An Overview of Language Policy and Planning in Nigeria
Linda Chinelo Nkamigbo

>This paper discusses status language planning and language policy in Nigeria. It observes that the exoglossic linguistic situation exists in the country. The language policy in Nigeria recognises English and three major languages – Hausa, Igbo, and Yoruba (referred to as WAZOBIA). So, policy makers encourage their usage through education or legislation without promoting the policy of minority languages. The language policy in Nigeria is evident in the Federal Government National Policy on Education (NPE). The NPE formulates the use of the mother tongue in the first three years of a child's primary education and subsequent use of English in the later stage. But this policy has not been implemented since English is the medium of instruction in a vast majority of Nigerian schools right from the first year in nursery school. The non-implementation of the NPE is as a result of lack of political will by government. The paper therefore recommends the reformulation of the NPE on the principle of biliteracy with priority given to mother tongue education. The paper also discusses the issue of the mother tongue in primary education pointing out its importance in early childhood education.

Introduction

Exoglossic situation is found in Nigeria, a linguistically heterogeneous nation. In Nigeria, a good number of languages are tied to different ethnic groupings with exception of a few languages that have gained wider currency as lingua francas within the regions. The ex-colonial language, English, is retained as the official language while three major languages, Hausa, Igbo, and Yoruba, are granted regional official status. In terms of language policy, the Type A Policy is adopted by choosing the language of the ex-colonial masters. The Type A Policy, according to Fishman (1971) cited in Agbedo (2000), is adopted in nation-states where the ruling elite has come to a conclusion that there is no available Great Tradition which can be drawn upon to unite the nation. Fishman goes further to explain that a Great Tradition is the assumed existence of a set of cultural features – law, government, religion, history – which is shared by the nation and can serve to integrate the members of a state into a cohesive body. In Nigeria, English is chosen over and above all other local languages such as Hausa, Igbo and Yoruba. Also, the educational policy stresses the importance of English to the detriment of the local languages.

Language Policy in Nigeria
The policy statement concerning language policy in Nigeria is contained in the *Federal Government National Policy on Education* (NPE) enunciated in 1977 and revised in 1987, 1995 and 2004. Among other things, the multilingual language policy seems to accord well with the logic of the Nigerian language situation described by Emenanjo (1998:4) as "...a multilingual and multicultural mosaic with some 400 odd languages: 3 demolects (Hausa, Igbo, and Yoruba); 12 choralects, 3 exolects (English, French, and Arabic of which, English is official), and the remaining other 'local' 'small group' languages..."

Specific provisions of the policy as observed by Agbedo (2000) recognise the special position of English as an exoglossic official language; Hausa, Igbo, and Yoruba as L_1 and L_2 and as potential indigenous lingua francas; the equality of all ethnic groups and their languages and the use of all languages in the nursery and 'junior' primary school education as well as in adult education. Olaofe (1990:51) sees the National Language Policy as a well-written document that is quite beautiful on paper. He goes further to assert that it caters for English as a language of inter-ethnic/international communication, the major and minor languages in the states, and the multi-ethnic/multilingual nature of the country. However, the policy has not yielded the desired result largely due to what Ojo (1998) cited in Agbedo (1998) feels is "...the yawning gap between policy formulation and policy implementation".

The problem of policy implementation tends to constitute the crux of dialectal disputations among scholars. To some, (cf. Chumbow, 1990; Jubril, 1990) the implementation problem stems largely from the obvious inconsistencies of the policy while the other argument is that the trilingual policy is impracticable in a multilingual Nigeria that has been trying unsuccessfully to simulate a delicate balance between inherently antagonistic ethnic nationalities. We argue that the non-implementation of the NPE is as a result of lack of political will by government.

The principle and practice of the national policy on education
The National Policy on Education (1979) which marginalises minority languages in education is, essentially *colonial*, out of tune with contemporary democratic zeitgeist, a flagrant violation of UNESCO report on The Use of Vernacular Languages in Education (1953), the UN Draft Declaration on the Rights of the Child (1988) and of the Principles for Indigenous Rights (1989), has only undergone *cosmetic* revisions (1981, 1995, 2004).

The situation of the mother tongue in education is far from ideal in Nigeria (cf. Shaibu, 2004). The National Policy on Education (1981) states that "Government will see to it that the medium of instruction in the primary school is initially the mother tongue or the language of the immediate community and at a later stage, English".

Prior to this policy, the importance of vernacular in education was first acknowledged in Nigeria in the 1925 memorandum on Education in British colonial territories. On this note, Fafunwa, Macauley and Sokoya (1989) observe, "Thus for the first time in the history of western education in Nigeria, the colonial government officially approved the use of mother tongue in education". This approval resulted in the active use of mother tongue as both a medium of instruction and as a subject in primary education. The NPE stipulation appears to be a vague one since every state in Nigeria does what it deems fit and the government does not state how it will 'see to it' that the mother tongue is used in early stages of a child's education.

Private schools, which outnumber public schools in Nigeria, do not adhere to the NPE stipulation. English is the medium of instruction in Private schools at all levels of education. Eme and Nkamigbo (2009) prove this using Onitsha in southeast Nigeria. The situation is the same in many other places. It is only in public schools where the three major languages are spoken that one can find the implementation of the NPE stipulation. Junaidu (2008) also observes that there is an appreciable degree of implementation of the stipulation in areas where some main languages such as Ebira, Edo, Efik, Ibibio and Izon are spoken. This is because the languages have received some attention in the development of metalanguages.

Primary Education
Primary education, according to the National Policy on Education (1981: 12), is "the education given in an institution for children aged

normally six years to eleven years". The general objectives of primary education as stated by the policy are as follows:
a. the inculcation of permanent literacy and numeracy, and the ability to communicate effectively;
b. the laying of a sound basis for scientific and reflective thinking.
c. citizenship education as a basis for effective partnership in and contribution to the life of the society;
d. character and moral training and the development of sound attitudes;
e. developing in the child the ability to adapt to his changing environment;
f. giving the child opportunities for developing manipulative skills that will enable him to function effectively in the society within the limits of his capacity;
g. Providing basic tools for further educational advancement, including preparation for trades and crafts of the locality.

On the use of the mother tongue in primary education
The mother tongue plays a vital role in education of the child, especially in the early years. In Nigeria, the *Ife-Six-Year-Yoruba-Primary-Project* corroborates this. Fafunwa et al. (1989) aligns with this notion thus, "…the first twelve years are very crucial in a child's development. It is during this period that attitudes and aptitudes are developed. It is also during this period that the child needs to be cared for diligently in terms of his mental, emotional and social development".

On starting school, the Nigerian child is faced with the situation of a confused linguistic state because he will be taught in a new language which is quite different from the one he has grown up with. This poses a big problem to the child. Fafunwa et al. comment, "… a child, if helped to lay the foundation of his future development in his own mother tongue, will likely be in a position to build upon it in later years in another language".

Towards a Solution
Given the seemingly intractable nature of Nigeria's language problems, a set of proposals has been advanced concerning the adoption of a functional national language policy. The proposals illustrate two distinct approaches – multilingual and unilingual to the

problems. Multilingual favours the adoption of the major languages while unilingual favours the adoption of only one national language. While the multilingual approach (cf. Simpson, 1978; Osaji, 1979; Olagoke, 1982) represents one variety of the attempt to streamline the current trilingual policy, the unilingual approach rejects all the proposals cast within the mould of WAZOBIA theoretical framework.

There is also the status quo approach which favours the retention of English as Nigeria's lingua franca. Perhaps, it was in recognition of the disparities that characterised the literature on solutions to Nigeria's language problems that Bamgbose (1976) identifies three policy options for Nigeria. These include (i) the status quo approach which will retain English as a lingua franca, (ii) the gradualist approach that involves planned multilingualism until one language evolves as a lingua franca and, (iii) the radical approach which calls for an immediate policy decision in favour of a particular language, one that will be taught in all states in addition to the major language of states and English. Bamgbose went further to posit that if the language of national integration is one which unites the various ethnic nationalities as well as the elite and the masses, that language is yet to be found in Nigeria and an essential prerequisite to finding it is a firm decision on one of the three policy options.

Interestingly, the current timid and flat-footed national language policy is the result of a policy decision already taken in favour of the status quo option. The so-called trilingual language policy which pretends to accord official status to a number of indigenous languages and priority attention to their development has turned out to be merely cosmetic and hypocritical as most Nigerian languages have hardly survived the overbearing heat of the English language often regarded by the 'ignorant' ruling elite and policy makers as 'Nigeria's lingua franca par excellence'.

It may seem reasonable to concede that Nigeria has not been lacking in glowing statutory provisions and institutional arrangements geared towards developing local languages. For instance, the former NERC (Nigerian Educational Research Council) now NERDC (Nigerian Educational Research Development Council) has produced curricular for the primary, junior and senior secondary schools in Hausa, Igbo, and Yoruba; Braille orthographies in Hausa, Igbo, and Yoruba; and funded metalanguage projects in Hausa, Igbo, and Yoruba. The National Language Centre (now renamed Language Development Centre) has equally produced four manuals of Nigerian languages covering twenty languages, a quadrilingual dictionary on legislative terminologies (in English, Hausa, Igbo, and Yoruba); primary science terminology in Hausa, Igbo, and Yoruba; harmonised L_1 and L_2 syllabuses for Hausa, Igbo, and Yoruba in Colleges of Education. The National Institute for Nigerian Languages has also been established presumably to train teachers in local languages and research into different aspects of Nigerian languages. Although laudable, these measures, according to Essien (1998:10), "...have come too little too late... and therefore fall short of the tremendous and sustained efforts, energies, and commitment that European governments put to develop their own languages to cope with the linguistic needs of their own respective societies...." The foregoing perhaps explains the unfortunate situation whereby English has remained the *dominant* language of the country, one defined by Essien (1996) as "... a language in a multilingual setting which, regardless of size, usually invests its speakers not only with a full panoply of uses that signify a standard language but also with prestige, self-confidence and power ...."

The grave implications which the prevailing linguistic situation for the indigenous languages and Nigeria's overall national development struggle have been variously discussed (cf. Simpson, 1978; Essien, 1998). The essential strands of the argument point somewhat gloomily to the fact that Nigeria's timid language policy and the blind glorification of the English language by the ruling class have conspired to undermine the local languages and rob them of their utilitarian values in all-important national development drive. In this connection, Agbedo (1998b) examined the concept of exclusion and showed how the efficacy of language as an instrument of exclusion has been used by the *milieu dirigeants* to exclude the vast majority of Nigerians from participating in the overall national development process. Given the maniacal tenacity with which the powerful minority in charge of the socio-economic and political management of the nation holds on to the primacy of language, Oyelaran (1990:27) laments that the ruling minority is devising newer ways of marginalising the non-literate majority, better methods of stripping their language of all values and of all roles in disseminating to Nigerians requisite information about the affairs of the nation.

As a way forward in this circumstance, the popular opinion appears to be on the side of the ideological imperative which requires that a truly independent, sovereign development-oriented Nigeria adopts a more realistic language policy that breaks clean with the language(s) imposed by erstwhile slave masters and vigorously sustained by today's neo-colonialists. This seems to be the most viable alternative since no nation, notes Oyelaran, has had a breakthrough through the instrumentality of an alien language. Not to heed this warning, continues Oyelaran, can only mean continued stripping of the people of Nigeria to a slave nation, satellite to any nation in whose language the minority controllers process information to the enrichment of their paymasters.

In the light of the fact that he who controls language controls history and perhaps destiny (cf. Allen, 1976) and given that English is by all intents and purposes, "a reinforcing agent of the British values and ways of life" (cf. Essien, 1995b), Agbedo (1999:5) enjoins Nigeria and other African nations where development is being carried out in what Fishman (1971) refers to as 'official exoglossic language' to develop with the language(s) rooted in the socio-cultural heritage, tradition and collective consciousness of the people as obtained in European, American, Australian and South East Asian nations. Agbedo concludes that this is imperative if African nations hope to cope with the challenges of the new millennium.

Recommendations

We borrow a leaf from Noah (2003) to recommend that the NPE be reformulated on the principle of biliteracy with priority given to mother tongue education, and English as an ancillary medium. In other words, we propose a policy that will be minority language-friendly. This will offer every child the opportunity to receive instructions in his/her mother tongue throughout the primary level of education.

The mother tongue will facilitate the learning of the second language, English. Bamgbose (1992) acknowledges this fact when he comments:

> Our multilingual approach should continue to accord serious attention to the indigenous languages as media of primary education, without sacrificing the need for a language of wider communication such as English.

Multilingual policy is highly recommended as this will involve the positive contribution of every linguistic group in Nigeria towards national development.

On this note, Noah (2003) asserts:

For any language reform to make sense to ethnolinguistic minorities, it has to be accompanied or better still preceded by parallel thematic changes in the socio-economic structures and political ideologies because linguistic marginalisation is largely *symptomatic* of a more general, deep-rooted discriminatory use of power which now manifests through demonic revenue sharing formula, socio-political marginalisation, economic destabilisation and near ethnic cleansing, especially, as it affects the Niger-Delta minorities.

References
Agbedo, C. U. 1998a. National language policy in Nigeria revisited. *Nsukka Journal of Humanities.* 9, 70-85.
Agbedo, C. U. 1998b. Language as instrument of exclusion: Implications for democratisation process in Nigeria. In *Proceedings from the International Conference on American Pragmatism: Implications for Democratisation Process in Nigeria.* University of Nigeria Nsukka, 4-5 November, 1998.
Agbedo, C. U. 1999. African languages and national development in the new millennium. Paper presented at the Against All Odds International Conference and Festival, Asmara, Eritrea, 11-17 January, 2000.
Agbedo, C. U. 2000. *General linguistics: An introductory reader.* Nsukka: ACE Resources Konsult.
Allen, J. V. 1976. Aba riots or Igbo Women war?: Ideology, stratification and the invincibility of women. In Hakin, N.J. and E. G. Bay (Eds.), *Women in Africa.* California: Stanford University Press.
Bamgbose, A. 1976. Language in national integration: Nigeria as a case study. 12th West African Languages Congress, University of Ife, Ile-Ife.
Bamgbose, A. 1992. Speaking in tongues: Implications of multilingualism for language policy in Nigeria. Nigerian National Merit Award Winner's Lecture, Kaduna.
Chumbow, B. S. 1990. The place of mother tongue in the national policy on education. In Emenanjo, E. N. (Ed.),

Multilingualism, minority languages and language policy in Nigeria. Agbor: Central Books Limited, 61-72.

Eme, C. A. and Nkamigbo, L. C. 2009. Asusu di ka ngwa oru ndi Igbo ji anabata mgbanwe ngwa ngwa: Ndi bi n'Otu-Onicha mgbakwasi ukwu. *Jonal Mmuta Igbo.* 4, 1-5.

Emenanjo, E.N. 1998. Towards a pragmatic language policy for Nigeria: Hindsight as foresight in the education domain. A mimeograph.

Essien, O. 1995b. Education and the mother tongue. *CASIL.* 9(2), 155-168.

Essien, O. 1996. Code-switching and code-mixing in Nigeria: A study of the phenomena among some ethnic groups. A paper presented at a departmental seminar, Department of Linguistics, University of Ghana, Legon.

Essien, O. 1998. National development, language and language policy in Nigeria. Lead paper presented at the 16th Annual Conference of the Linguistic Association of Nigeria.

Fafunwa, A. B., Macauley, J. L. and Sokoya, J. A. F. 1989. Education in mother tongue: The Ife Primary Education Research Project. Ibadan: University Press Limited.

Federal Government of Nigeria. 1977. *National Policy on Education* (NPE). Lagos: NERC Press.

Federal Government of Nigeria. 1979. *National Policy on Education* (NPE). Lagos: NERC Press.

Federal Government of Nigeria. 1981. *National Policy on Education* (NPE). Lagos: NERDC Press.

Federal Government of Nigeria. 1987. *National Policy on Education* (NPE). Lagos: NERDC Press.

Federal Government of Nigeria. 1995. *National Policy on Education* (NPE). Lagos: NERDC Press.

Federal Government of Nigeria. 2004. *National Policy on Education* (NPE). Lagos: NERDC Press.

Fishman, J.I. 1971. *Sociolinguistics: A brief introduction.* Rowley: Newbury House.

Jubril, M.M. 1990. Minority languages and lingua francas in Nigerian education. In Emenanjo, E.N. (Ed.), *Multilingualism, minority languages and language policy in Nigeria.* Agbor: Central Books Limited, 109-117.

Junaidu, I. 2008. Language policy, planning and management: An appraisal of the Nigerian situation. A paper presented at the

22nd Annual Conference of the Linguistic Association of Nigeria.

Noah, P. 2003. Education and minority language: The Nigerian dimension. In Ndimele, O-M. (Ed.), *Four decades in the study of languages and linguistics in Nigeria: A festschrift for Kay Williamson*. Aba: National Institute for Nigerian Languages. 173-182.

Olagoke, D. O. 1982. Choosing a national language for Nigeria. *Journal of the Linguistic Association of Nigeria*, 1, 197-206.

Olaofe, I. A. 1990. The relevance of linguistic teaching and learning to the implementation of the national language policy. In Emenanjo, E.N. (Ed.), *Multilingualism, minority languages and language policy in Nigeria*. Agbor: Central Books Limited, 50-60.

Osaji, B. 1979. *Language survey in Nigeria*. Quebec: International Centre for Research on Bilingualism.

Oyelaran, O. O. 1990. Language, marginalisation and national development in Nigeria. In Emenanjo, E.N. (Ed.), *Multilingualism, minority languages and language policy in Nigeria*. Agbor: Central Books Limited, 20-30.

Shaibu, V.A. 2004. Primary education in the mother tongue in Nigeria: Problems and prospects. In Ndimele, O-M. (Ed.), *The linguistic paradise: A festschrift for E. Nolue Emenanjo*. Port Harcourt: Emhai printing Press. 357-364.

Simpson, E. 1978. *Babel: Perspectives for Nigeria*. Quebec: International Centre for Research on Bilingualism.

UNESCO. 1953. *The Use of Vernacular Languages in Education*. Paris: UNESCO.

UNESCO. 1988. UN Draft Declaration on the Rights of the Child. New York.

UNESCO. 1989. UN Draft Declaration on the Principles for Indigenous Rights. New York.

Chapter 6
The South African Experience in Language Policy and Planning
Kathleen Heugh

The discussion in this chapter traces the history of language policy and planning in South Africa over the last century. British colonial language policy after 1901 marginalised speakers of Dutch (Afrikaans) in ways which were to impact on apartheid language policy and planning during the second half of the 20th century. This led to the implementation of 'mother tongue' education which was interpreted by speakers of African languages as a mechanism to advance separate and unequal development. Post-apartheid language policy, although based on the principle of 'multilingualism' has defaulted towards an English monolingual paradigm. This is even though South Africa had the advantage of learning from the experiences of post-colonial language policy elsewhere in Africa. The explanation given here is that it is a result of a coincidence of three factors: the legacy of apartheid, lack of political will, and (deliberate) misinterpretation of language policy by key advisors to government.

Introduction
Every country in sub-Saharan Africa has its own colonial history in which at least one European language was introduced and layered over an existing linguistic ecology. In each case, the pre-colonial ecology was characterised by a network of diverse multilingual practices. This layering over existing language practices has resulted in disruptive changes to the balance of power amongst language communities. Change resulted in an unequal arrangement between the exogenous language used for vertical political and administrative control, and the distribution and co-existence of many endogenous languages and their speakers. In this paper, the discussion takes a historical view of language policy changes in South Africa, where the effect on the linguistic ecology is most evident in relation to student achievement in the South African education system. Owing to the legacy of 'apartheid' (a political system based on segregation), it is necessary to provide a brief history of language policy from the early 20th century, in order to show how two parallel post-colonial debates emerged in South Africa over the last 100 years. One of these was to lead towards 'apartheid' language policy, and the other led to political resistance against this policy. For many people in Africa, post-

apartheid language policy (i.e. from 1994 onwards) seemed to offer much promise of restoring the balance within the pre-colonial linguistic ecology, and also facilitating democratic access to the linguistic resources of the contemporary world. In hindsight, one can now recognise where theoretical errors and political interests have taken language policy, planning and practices in a direction which achieves neither of the much hoped for changes. It is also evident that the prospects of language policy and planning were over-estimated by both linguists and ideologues committed to restoring a balance in the linguistic ecology.

Language, Identity and the Emergence of Two Nationalisms
This country has gone through at least two attempts at 'decolonisation'. The first was marked by the outbreak of war in 1899 between the Boer Republics and the British Colonial administration of different parts of South Africa. The second occurred at the end of 'apartheid' nearly 100 years later. By the late 19th century, although Britain had control over the Cape Colony and Natal, it sought political and economic control over the rich goldfields in the Boer-held Transvaal and Orange Free State Republics. The war, known as the Anglo-Boer War (also, the South African War) between 1899 and 1901, and British atrocities against Boer women and children, were to leave an indelible imprint on what was to become Afrikaner identity. After the British 'won' the war, the administrator, Lord Alfred Milner declared an English-only policy for the education of Boer children. What little education was offered African children was provided in missionary schools and these generally used between four and six years of 'mother-tongue' medium education followed by a switch to English medium. Amongst African communities, the switch to English medium for upper primary and secondary education created a hierarchical impression of English as the language of the educated person. The deliberate attempt to 'Anglicise' the defeated Boers, meanwhile, struck at the heart of the defeated community which harboured resentment against atrocities of the war, and served to strengthen an ethnolinguistic identity for Dutch-speaking people. Dutch had been creolising since the late 17th century (Roberge, 2002). This creole, now known as Afrikaans, replaced Dutch as the second official language of the Union of South Africa in 1925. It was this history which fostered Afrikaner identity and Afrikaner nationalism. Through a negotiated settlement between the Boers and the British

resulting in the Union of South Africa by 1910, the right of Boer children to receive education in Dutch was restored. However, the psychological background to this *taalstryd* (language struggle) was to continue for generations.

African communities were left out of the negotiated settlement between the British and the Boers in the 1910 agreement, and political resistance began to emerge in ways which alarmed the Boers. By 1912, amongst African communities, and many of those of mixed backgrounds, English came to be viewed as the language of the educated person, and also as the language which represented liberation and access to the world and all of its symbolic and material capital (cf. Bourdieu, 1991). Given that British colonialism had introduced separate development in Natal, and had excluded African participation in the negotiations for a semi-independent Union of South Africa, it is surprising that English should have been regarded so favourably by African people.

By the early 20th century missionary linguists realised that their work in transcribing African languages for purposes of evangelisation and early primary education had interfered with the linguistic ecology of the country. Often missionary groups transcribed the same or closely related languages using different orthographic conventions. They also created divisions where perhaps there were none, and conflated languages which may have been different. Various attempts to 'standardise' orthographies and approaches were made between 1906 and 1920 but these were not successful. A new generation of linguists, Gerard Lestrade, Clement Doke and Archibald Tucker, took up the discussions about standardising the orthographies of African languages in the 1930s (e.g. Msimang, 1992; Cluver, 1996). As the growth of Afrikaner nationalism was advancing through the 1930s and 1940s, so too was the emergence of African nationalism.

Discussions of National Unity and Standardisation of African Languages in The 1940s and 1950s

The proposals for the standardisation of orthographies within various language clusters, as recommended by Doke and Lestrade in the 1930s, and taken forward in the combined Zulu/Xhosa Language Committee and the Sotho Language Committee, between 1947 and 1957, were also picked up and given more public political attention by Jacob Nhlapo, a scholar, lawyer and journalist who was deeply rooted in liberal resistance politics of The New African Movement and the African National Congress (ANC). Nhlapo's concern arose not so much from a linguistic or literary concern, but rather with one focussed towards the socio-political unity and empowerment of African peoples. He understood linguistic diversity to be an obstacle: 'too many tongues stop us going forward' (Nhlapo, 1944: 4). For Nhlapo, a reduction of linguistic diversity through unification or standardisation of the Nguni and Sotho clusters of languages would assist social and political cohesion.

Like other key figures within the African politics, Nhlapo, also had particular views regarding the role of English. He suggested that the international and regional status of English were already overwhelmingly significant in South Africa: 'to most African scholars English is education, and education is English' (Nhlapo, 1944: 11).

Multilingual Education During Apartheid: Segregation vs. Language Rights

Since approximately 72% of people in South Africa at the time were of African origin, and about 10% of people were regarded as first language speakers of English, speakers of Afrikaans therefore formed a minority when the National Party (representing Afrikaner nationalists) came to power in 1948.

National Party thinkers were concerned firstly with ensuring that English would never again threaten Afrikaner identity. It was this concern which led to a conceptualisation of a political system based on 'separate development', and the ethnolinguistic separation of communities. An additional layer of influence was an ideological position inherited from the British colonial administration's attempts to confine certain African communities to particular localities. For example, in Natal, speakers of Zulu were supposed to live in an area known as 'Zululand'. Partly the idea that people could be contained to geographic zones and treated differently was influenced by the fascist debates in Spain and Germany during the 1930s. The system which emerged, 'apartheid', was established through various administrative arms of government, so that every government authority was established to deal with African people in terms of their ethnolinguistic backgrounds. Other distinctions were made for speakers of English and Afrikaans. Afrikaans-speaking people of mixed European, African, Khoe, San, South-East Asian or other descent, were designated 'Coloured'.

Apartheid education - Phase 1:

'Grand Apartheid' was established through separate ethnolinguistically defined education systems, particularly through legislation known as the Bantu Education Act of 1953. The principle of 'divide and rule' was supported through the principle of language rights. Each group (in theory) was to have the right to self-determination and own language education. Partly this was a residue of resistance to the post-Boer War Anglicisation policy of the British, and thus self-interest. By chance it also coincided with the *Report on the Use of Vernacular Languages in Education* (UNESCO, 1953) favouring primary education in the mother tongue.

Separate education departments, for each linguistic group, were established in different geographic regions of the country. Parallel education systems were established to replicate one another, except in two aspects. Material resources were unevenly allocated: most to the systems providing for 'White' English and Afrikaans speakers, less to those providing for 'Coloured' and Indian schools, and least to those providing for African language speakers. Government took control of the language committees established earlier and reversed the process towards harmonisation of the Nguni and Sotho clusters respectively. The committees were divided so that the 'Zulu/Xhosa Language Committee' was divided into two, and the 'Sotho Language Committee' was divided into three (North Sotho, South Sotho and Tswana). Other committees were later added for Venda, Tsonga, Swati and Ndebele. Msimang (1992) was later to call this the 'balkanisation' of African languages. Each language committee had the responsibility for developing terminology to be used in the translation of textbooks for eight years of primary school. Although it was widely believed by those outside of government that school books were 'dumbed down' for African children and that they were to receive an impoverished curriculum, there were two factors which made this difficult. Firstly, the language committee linguists included native speakers of African languages as well as other university-based linguists. These were persons of integrity, members of speech communities themselves and scholars. None of these had any interest in developing cognitively impoverished terminology for schools (see also Msimang, 1992; Satyo, personal communication 2001; Mahlalela-Thusi & Heugh, 2010). The translators similarly included home language speakers of African languages, and they had neither the interest nor inclination simultaneously to translate and 'dumb down' school books. Even if they had wanted to, this process would have been extremely difficult to accomplish across multiple language versions with language committees, translators and the text editors located in dispersed settings. The co-ordination of such an exercise was simply not logistically possible.

Archival research on African language provision during apartheid in 2001 and 2002 revealed that although the researchers assumed that they would find evidence of reduced cognitive load in the school textbooks between 1955 and 1976, they did not. Contrary to the expectations, this study of a cross-section of school textbooks (mathematics; nature study, i.e. biology; health education; social studies, i.e. history and geography) found only that materials were translated and sometimes further explicated in African languages. No evidence was found of truncated or cognitively impaired textbook versions in any of the African languages of this period. Secondly, the terminology lists developed during the apartheid era for use in textbooks and by teachers of African children were submitted through the Pan South African Language Board (PANSALB) to the post-apartheid terminologists within the Department of Arts and Culture (DAC), in 2000. The findings of DAC terminographers was that, with a few exceptions, they found no ideological or conceptual objections to the terminology lists. They did suggest that in some cases, the terminology needed to be updated (Manentsa, 2001, personal communication; Mahlalela-Thusi & Heugh, 2010).

Between 1955 and 1975, amongst African students there was a steady improvement in the achievement in literacy and numeracy which accompanied the provision of eight years of mother tongue medium education (MTE). Both English and Afrikaans were also taught as second languages (as subjects) by well-trained teachers and competent speakers of these languages during this period. In the ninth year of school, students were expected to switch to learning through the two second languages, Afrikaans and English. This system was not seriously implemented until 1976 when an attempt to force implementation led to a student-led protest in SOWETO, a large township on the outskirts of Johannesburg. Several students were killed by police and the reverberations across the country were so severe that government was forced to retract its language education policy. However, it needs to be emphasised that the policy of eight years of MTE resourced with terminological development, textbook production, competent teacher education and competent teaching of English, resulted in a school-leaving pass rate of 83.7% for African students by 1976. This is the highest pass rate ever achieved in the country by African students.

Apartheid Education – Phase 2
Resistance towards what was known as Bantu Education was on four grounds: enforced use of Afrikaans medium in secondary for mathematics, prolonged use of MTE for eight years, limited provision of secondary education, and a perceived reluctance to encourage proficiency in English. Government backed down by reducing eight years of MTE to four years; dropping of Afrikaans medium for some subjects in secondary, and *de facto* agreement that students might switch to English medium in Grade 5.

This change of policy and its ramifications have not always been understood by critics of apartheid. Corresponding with the reduction of MTE to four years after the SOWETO uprising, the school exit pass rate declined steadily to 73.5% in 1979, and to 44% by 1992 (Heugh, 1999: 187). There are several factors to consider, one being that the number of students enrolled in upper secondary increased significantly during the same period; and during the 1980s, owing to on-going civil unrest, students frequently boycotted school. Nevertheless, these declining achievement data correspond with Macdonald's findings for students who switched from MTE at the end of Grade 4 (with a vocabulary in English of about 500 words) to English medium from Grade 5, where the curriculum demands required a corpus of at least 7,000 lexical items in English. Macdonald found that subsequent to 1976, students in Grade 5 experienced such difficulty with understanding their schoolwork that this resulted in serious 'failure' to pass Grade 5 followed by significant attrition ('drop-out') from the system after Grade 5 (Macdonald, 1990).

The halving of the pass rate at the end of secondary school by the mid-1980s probably suited the government more than did the higher pass rates of the earlier phase, although there is no evidence that government directly planned this. Unfortunately, because political oppression had brought about a culture of suspicion, the poor educational outcomes of the second phase of apartheid are conflated with the principle of MTE in the first phase prior to 1976. It was only in retrospect and through a historical tracing of student achievement that the different educational outcomes of the two phases of apartheid have become evident. Most government officials and advisors continue to conflate the two periods and link MTE to poor educational outcomes in the 1980s and early 1990s (e.g. Taylor & Vinjevold, 1999; Fleisch, 2008).

Prefiguring Post-Apartheid Language Policy
Political repression, imprisonment of political leaders resistant to apartheid drove many debates underground between the 1960s and the late 1980s. While the language issue was a key issue of the student revolt in SOWETO in 1976, it received little attention from within the ANC subsequent to this. In some radical groupings in the Cape Town area, 'the language question' was mostly conceptualised as relating to how English would emerge as the language of liberation in a post-apartheid period. By the mid-1980s, Neville Alexander proposed the establishment of a National English Language Project to promote the idea of English as a 'linking language' or lingua franca for South Africa. In the internal wing of the ANC, people referred to 'People's English', a democratised form of English, rather than the 'highbrow' difficult to access variety of English. Language was not discussed in terms of 'language policy' until a discussion of language medium policy in post-colonial countries elsewhere in Africa (Heugh, 1987). This was the first time that the history and lessons of decisions taken in other African countries were considered in South Africa. The study drew attention to findings of the failure of English-mainly education in other post-colonial African countries to deliver educational expectations. It also drew attention to an alternative discourse in which English was viewed as an agent of neo-colonialism in the work of Ngugi wa Thiong'o (1981). After discussions with Heugh during 1986, Alexander reframed the National English Language Project, and it was established in 1987 as the National Language Project (NLP). During a study visit to the USA in 1988 Heugh came across two seminal papers in the Journal of West African Languages (Chumbow, 1987; Bamgbose, 1987) which were to have great significance for post-apartheid language policy development. From within the NLP, and later from within the Project for the Study of Alternative Education in South Africa (PRAESA), that Alexander and Heugh worked on different areas of language policy proposals, both influenced by Chumbow and Bamgbose (e.g. Alexander, 1989; Heugh, 1995a; Alexander & Heugh, 1999).

For Alexander, the language question was one aspect of a larger political concern for post-apartheid national unity. Having established the NLP, he left the language policy research and interventions to project staff while he turned his attention to his leadership of the Cape Action League and later the Workers' Organisation for Socialist Action (WOSA), small political parties to the left of the ANC. Alexander's interest in language policy until the 1994 elections focused on a reanimation of Nhlapo's proposal for the standardisation of the Nguni and Sotho languages. Just as Nhlapo's proposals were met with disapproval from within the ANC, Alexander, found that his suggestions were rejected by a range of stakeholders, including those sympathetic to the ANC. Linguists who were native speakers of South African languages and whose life work had been devoted to lexicography, terminology and translation, objected to what they understood to be linguistic engineering and attempts to reduce linguistic diversity. Nevertheless, the NLP convened a conference to debate the standardisation of African languages in 1991. It was at this conference that Alexander suggested that in the post-apartheid South Africa there should be a 'National Language (or Languages) Institute', similar to the Central Institute of Indian Languages, in Mysore, India. This proposal was successful and the new constitution (RSA 1996) made provision for a Pan South African Language Board (PANSALB), much along these lines.

From late 1992 onwards, Alexander and Heugh worked on language policy from the Project for the Study of Alternative Education in South Africa (PRAESA), based at the University of Cape Town. Alexander was simultaneously preparing himself to stand for election, as head of WOSA, in the first democratic elections to be held in South Africa in 1994. Heugh was asked to draft language policy proposals for most of the political parties to the left and right of the ANC and to write submissions, on behalf of the NLP and PRAESA, to the constitutional negotiators between 1993 and 1995.

An Interim Constitution was agreed to in 1993, and elections held in April the following year. A group of ANC language educators, under the leadership of Zubeida Desai, drew on Heugh's research on bilingual and multilingual education in their recommendations for ANC language education policy. After a resounding victory for the ANC in April 1994, Alexander returned to work at PRAESA, concerned at this time with primary school curriculum proposals rather than language policy. Shortly after the elections, Heugh was requested to convene a Language Policy Workshop for the new Minister of Constitutional Affairs. This was in order to 'fast track' the language provisions of the Interim Constitution. This workshop highlighted the need to establish the Pan South African Language Board (PANSALB), tasked in the constitution to monitor government implementation of language policy. At this workshop the need to translate language policy into a workable language plan was identified and Alexander was put forward as a key figure in this enterprise (Heugh, 1995b).

Within months, the Minister of Arts, Culture, Science and Technology (ACST) appointed Alexander to head a Language Plan Task Group (LANGTAG) to flesh out the implications of a language plan for the country. The LANGTAG Report (DACST 1996) was submitted to the Minister in less than a year. A fundamental flaw of this process was that it was a plan in the absence of a clearly articulated language policy, and it was a plan based on the assumption that a clear policy would emerge either in the finalisation of the constitution or in separate legislation. However, the final Constitution (RSA, 1996) did not include a clear language policy. Rather it included a set of principles to be included in policy.

By 1996, the Pan South African Language Board (PANSALB) had been established, with eleven members appointed by the Senate after an exhaustive national consultative process. While the linguists and educators on PANSALB believed that their role was to oversee government's language policy, government had other plans.

Unfortunately, government has never passed legislation regarding language policy at the national level. While a National Language Policy Framework (DAC, 2002) (a process in which Alexander participated) was accepted by parliament in 2002, it took another nine years before parliament accepted a National Languages Bill in October 2011 (Minister of Arts and Culture, 2011) in which government undertook to spell out national language policy within another 18 months (i.e. by March 2013). At the time of writing, this has not yet happened.

PANSALB was eventually rendered ineffectual for at least three reasons. Firstly, government gradually removed the power of this body to monitor government's articulation and delivery of policy. Secondly, the Department of Arts and Culture controlled the board's finances, budget and staffing appointments. Thirdly, pressure was exerted by senior officials for the Board to interpret the constitution's clauses on multilingualism to mean a multiplication of separate parallel sub-structures, for example, separate lexicography units, and separate language committees. Instead of supporting the horizontal development of multilingualism in the country, what happened was a replication of the apartheid language structures based on separatism (see: Heugh, 2003; Makoni, 2003).

Language Education Policy

While developments in national language policy failed to materialise, language education policy did emerge from a combination of debates, initiated from within the NLP, followed in the National Education Policy Initiative (NEPI, 1992), then in the ANC Education Desk's proposals for education prior to the 1994 elections, proposals to the various stakeholders on behalf of the NLP and PRAESA (see also Heugh et al., 1995); and in the LANGTAG Report (DACST, 1996). Alexander was also asked by the Department of Education to oversee the drafting of the language education policy. Because he was fully occupied with both LANGTAG and PANSALB, he handed this task to Gerda de Klerk, formerly of the NLP and then of PRAESA. She based the draft on research discussed in, *Multilingual Education for South Africa* (Heugh et al., 1995). The language in education policy for schools was adopted in 1997 (DoE, 1997a). Obviously, there are significant differences between the draft policy and the bureaucratic editing and subsequent changes. Nevertheless, the policy was based on the principle of additive multilingualism, i.e. using the student's mother tongue or home language, and retaining this as a medium of instruction for as long as possible (at least six to eight years) while a second and third language were to be added in the schooling context. As is the case in all policy documents, the nuances get lost in the translation. So, recognition that many students are already bilingual or multilingual by the time they reach school is lost in the policy document and reference to the additional languages for the purposes of formal education results in frequent misinterpretations of the policy.

Unfortunately, language education policy was treated as if it were separate from rather than integral to the new curriculum between 1995 and 1997. This has resulted in a disjuncture between language education policy and how it is interpreted in the curriculum. Even after three attempts at curriculum renewal in the country (DoE,

1997b; DoE, 2002; and Dada et al., 2009) the additive multilingual education policy is mistranslated in the curriculum documents as three years (at most) of home language (mother tongue) medium education for speakers of African languages, followed by a switch to English medium from the fourth grade. Speakers of English and Afrikaans (shrinking minorities now totalling 20% of students) receive home language education throughout the schooling process. Because of the association of apartheid period education with discriminatory practices, all resources held, by the national DoE, in African languages (terminology lists and textbooks) were destroyed (Moyane, 2002, personal communication; Mahlalela-Thusi & Heugh, 2010).

Despite promising research based initiatives (e.g. Desai, 2010), government has not made any serious attempts to implement an education policy in which African languages and multilingualism are taken seriously. Instead, there is a trajectory towards one language, English, as quickly as possible (see also: du Plessis, 2003; Plüddemann et al., 2004). Ironically, the implementation of current policy has come to be much closer to that envisaged in the Anglicisation policy of the British colonial office in 1901.

Literacy
The curriculum documents and new teacher education programmes provide very little guidance for how literacy or language teachers should ensure that students can read and write beyond early simple narrative texts by the end of the third grade. There is no practical guidance in how to translate 'the whole language approach' to literacy in naïve proposals (e.g. Bloch, 2006) for early literacy development towards increasingly complex reading and writing required from Grade 4 onwards. Complex texts across the curriculum from Grade 4 onwards require knowledge of a wider range of genres, especially expository texts including syntax employed in 'cause and effect', comparative, and hypothetical text. (See also Macdonald, 2002; Pretorius, 2002.)

Teacher education programmes, even for literacy teachers, simply avoided the practical application of how one was supposed to teach reading and writing (Reeves et al., 2008). Given that all the materials in African languages produced prior to 1994 had been destroyed, new reading materials had to be produced. This has given rise to a host of additional concerns. The new materials have been expensive. Teachers are reluctant to allow students to take them home and make them grubby. Often the books are simply locked up in a classroom cupboard, seldom used. Secondly, since all of the pre-1994 materials in African languages were destroyed, government officials complain that there are insufficient reading resources to facilitate literacy in African languages.

Student achievement declined after the changes from 1976 onwards, but this declined even further after the curriculum changes introduced in 1997. Every system-wide assessment of student achievement, particularly in relation to literacy and numeracy involving students from Grade 3 to Grade 9 conducted by the Department of Education since 1997 shows that the majority of South African students do not achieve even at the basic level, and that they lag behind the achievement of students in most other African countries (e.g. Prinsloo & Kanjee, 2005; DoE, 2005; Mothibeli, 2005; Reddy, 2006; Howie et al., 2008; Moloi & Chetty, 2011).

Arguments Against Implementation of Multilingual Education
Government officials repeatedly claim that most African parents and students do not support mother tongue or extended bilingual education in the school system, and this claim is repeated in texts intended to inform educational change (e.g. Taylor & Vinjevold, 1999). Yet, as Setati (2008) and others have pointed out, there is little documented evidence to support this claim beyond the aspirational middle class contexts of the larger urban centres. The only significant data at hand is that from the Pan South African Language Board's *National Sociolinguistic Survey* (PANSALB, 2000) in which, much to the surprise of many, 88% of South Africans over the age of 15 support both strong mother tongue education and strong teaching of English as a second language, not only through the school system, but also in higher education (Table 25D, PANSALB, 2000:125). Only 12% support English-only or English-mainly, including the 9% of English speakers at the time of the survey. Nevertheless, anecdotal reports that the majority of people in the country want English-only, or English-mainly, education are encouraged by government officials and first language speakers of English in influential positions (e.g. Taylor & Vinjevold, 1999; Ridge, 2000; Murray, 2002).

Research which delves beneath the surface-level appearances (de Klerk, 2002) shows, however, that while urban parents may claim a preference for English medium education, this is because English serves as a proxy for the best-resourced educational opportunities for children. It is more about access to better trained teachers and schools which are functional, rather than a rejection of the home or community language. The independent and English medium schools which formerly catered for 'White' middle class children, remain the best resourced in the country, and these are therefore the most desirable schools.

Poor achievement in reading and numeracy are used by some to advance reasons why it is probably best to default to reading educational materials in English. Critics of multilingual education focus on the 'failure' of multilingualism to deliver achievement in literacy: 'not all South African educational researchers have been convinced that learning in the "wrong language" is a crucial factor in poor achievement' (Fleisch, 2008: 113).

What such critics fail to understand is that since the new curriculum was introduced in 1997, literacy in whichever language is not being taught well, and is under-resourced (Reeves et al., 2008; Howie et al., 2008). This has to do with what Abadzi (2006) refers to as naïve dependency on constructivist curriculum which assumes well-resourced Western contexts, as well as those weak attempts at offering alternative approaches to teaching literacy in schools (Heugh, 2009). Several studies demonstrate disturbing failure of the system to ensure that students learn to read and write at all (e.g. Heugh et al., 2007; Howie et al., 2008; Reeves et al., 2008). The language and literacy question is connected, but the reason for the failure of children across all sectors of the system is not because of multilingual education, it is because of poor teaching of reading and writing through no fault of the teachers. Multilingual education is simply not being implemented and new approaches to literacy based on vague notions of 'whole language' have not been demonstrated to teachers in practical ways. This is a reflection of misguided advice and failure by government to grasp the needs of the majority of students in an African country. Multilingual education cannot (should not) be used to account for student failure if it is not being implemented.

Structural and Other Resources
The country is fortunate to have considerable linguistic expertise in African languages and the institutions to facilitate multiple activities. What has been lacking is government commitment to have this work

systematically encouraged. The Pan South African Language Board (PANSALB) has sub-structures established for the purpose of language development activities including lexicographic development. The government agency, Department of Arts and Culture has various language units, including for terminology development. These, have the capacity to resource the national department but disagreement between government departments from 1999 onwards has prevented co-operation. There are also considerable resources and training programmes in translation and interpreting (e.g. at the University of the Free State). Thus translation of materials should not be problematic.

The most serious area of skills-shortage is in regard to university-trained educators equipped to teach or develop new materials in African languages. Despite the terms of the Constitution and enabling education policy, the malaise in school education and lack of interest in building on existing resources in African languages has had consequences for departments of African languages, with rapidly declining numbers of students since the mid-1990s. Two notable exceptions are imaginative programmes in African languages at the University of Limpopo and Rhodes University.

A direct focus on teacher education was developed by The Project for Alternative Education in South Africa (PRAESA) based at the University of Cape Town (UCT) and offered as an in-service programme for teachers, the Advanced Certificate in Education (Multilingual) between 1997 and 2001. UCT was expected to take over the management of this programme in 2002, but because government did not appear to support multilingual education, the university decided to discontinue the programme. PRAESA then piloted a Training of Trainers of Multilingual Education in Southern Africa (TOTSA) for government officials and university educators between 2002 and 2005. Participants from all over Africa engaged with this programme, offered as a double-exit Post-Graduate Certificate and / or a Master of Education degree. Again it was intended that UCT would take over this programme, but it did not owing to lack of government interest.

Conclusion

Although linguistic diversity and multilingualism have been defining features of South African constitutions and education policy for more than 100 years, language rights and multilingualism have been misused, both during apartheid and in post-apartheid South Africa, in order to enhance structural inequality. Political change during the 1990s introduced the principles of linguistic equality alongside language rights and these were intended to be interpreted through legislation and policy which would provide the structural support of multilingualism, particularly in education. Despite promising beginnings, the enduring nature of colonial habitus has resulted in a set of disjointed partial attempts to establish language policy. Firstly, the constitutional principles supportive of multilingualism have not been translated into a coherent set of language policy legislation, and government has clearly dragged its heels. Although a Report of the Language Plan Task Group was submitted to government (DACST, 1996), and eventually a National Language Policy Framework was accepted (DAC, 2002), it was another nine years before a National Languages Bill (Minister of Arts and Culture, 2011) was made public. This Bill, however, merely stipulates that government is still to define the national language policy. Secondly, although a Pan South African Language Board was established in 1996 to monitor government language policy, it has become a 'white elephant' since government has thus far refused to enact policy. Thirdly, while education is the one area in which language policy has been spelt out, this too has been rendered ineffective, since the curriculum documentation shows consistent misinterpretations of the policy over a period of fifteen years. Instead of a multilingual education system, and despite nearly twenty years of costly curriculum changes and system-wide assessment, the majority of students are expected to use English as the medium for education. This is even though neither they nor most of their teachers have the necessary literacy and language proficiency to navigate the curriculum through English.

A flip-side to the focus on English as the medium of instruction in the curriculum has been neglect of and even destruction of the resources and expertise developed in the use of South African languages prior to 1994. Since 1994 there has been a decline in the number of university students studying African languages, there has been a neglect of training teachers through and in the African languages, there has been a neglect of training teachers to teach reading and writing in either the home language or in English (Reeves et al., 2008), and there have been serious inefficiencies in the state-run terminology development, and translation services. Instead of paying sufficient attention to the lessons from elsewhere in Africa, post-apartheid language policy, is characterised by failure to commit to an explicit policy supportive of multilingualism, while an implicit 'default to English' practice has taken a grip of every arm of government. This and its consequences are most obvious in education where the practice has exacerbated educational inequity between those who have to study through a language that they do not sufficiently understand and those few speakers of English and Afrikaans who continue to have mother tongue education. This inequity and the evidence of the most appalling underachievement of most school students is possibly far beyond any other country of the continent. The gravest error has been unrealistic expectations that government would articulate new language policy to enhance opportunities for civil society. To borrow from Bamgbose (1987), language planning undertaken by government in South Africa over the last twenty years has been a clear example of 'when language planning is not planning'.

References

Abadzi, H. 2006. *Efficient Learning for the Poor. Insights from the Frontier of Cognitive Neuroscience. Directions in Development.* Washington: World Bank.

Alexander, N. 1989. *Language Policy and National Unity in South Africa/Azania.* Cape Town: Buchu Books.

Alexander, N. and Heugh, K. 1999. Language policy in the new South Africa. In A. Zegeye and R. Kriger (Eds.), *Cultural change and development in South Africa. Special issue*, 1998-99, *Culturelink*, 9-33.

Bamgbose, Ayo. 1987. When is language planning not planning? *The Journal of West African Languages*, 7(1), 6-14.

Bloch, C. 2006. Theory and Strategy of Early Literacy in Contemporary Africa with Special Reference to South Africa. Summary paper of PhD Thesis. Retrieved from http://www.unioldenburg.de/zsn/download/CaroleBloch.pdf

Bourdieu, P. 1991. *Language and Symbolic Power.* Cambridge: Polity Press.

Chumbow, B. S. 1987. Towards a language planning model for Africa. *The Journal of West African Languages*, 7(1), 15-22.

Cluver, A. D. d. V. 1996. *Language Development in South Africa: A LANGTAG Report.* Pretoria: DACST.

Dada, F., Dipholo, T., Hoadley, U., Khembo, E., Muller, S & Volmink, J. 2009. *Report of the Task Team for the Review of the Implementation of the National Curriculum Statement. Final Report, October.* Pretoria: DBE.

De Klerk, V. 2002. Language issues in our schools: Whose voice counts? Part 1: The parents speak. *Perspectives in Education,* 20(1):1-14.

Department of Arts and Culture (DAC). 2002. *National Language Policy Framework.* Pretoria: DAC.

Department of Arts, Culture, Science and Technology (DACST). 1996. *The Language Plan Task Group Report.* Pretoria: DACST.

Department of Education (DoE). 1997a. *Language in education policy.* Pretoria: Department of Education.

Department of Education (DoE). 1997b. *Curriculum 2005. Lifelong learning for the 21st Century.* Pretoria: Department of Education.

Department of Education (DoE). 2002. *Revised National Curriculum Statement Grades R-9 (Schools). Languages English - Home Language.* Pretoria: Department of Education.

Department of Education (DoE). (2005). Grade 6 Intermediate Phase Systemic Evaluation Report. Pretoria: Department of Education.

Desai, Z. 2010. Reflections on the LOITASA Project in South Africa: three years later. In B. Brock-Utne, Z. Desai, M. Qorro and A. Pitman (Eds.), *Language of Instruction in Tanzania and South Africa – Highlights from a Project* (pp. 207-213). Rotterdam, Boston and Taipei: Sense Publishers.207-213.

Du Plessis, T. 2003. Multilingualism and language-in-education policy in South Africa – a historical overview. In P. Cuvelier, T. du Plessis & L. Teck (Eds.), *Multilingualism, Education and Social Integration. Studies in Language Policy in South Africa* (pp. 99-119). Pretoria: Van Schaik.

Fleisch, B. 2008. *Primary Education in Crisis: Why South African Schoolchildren Underachieve in Reading and Mathematics.* Cape Town: Juta and Co. Ltd.

Heugh, K. 1987. Underlying ideologies of language medium policies in multilingual societies with particular reference to Southern Africa. M. Phil Dissertation (unpublished). Cape Town: University of Cape Town.

Heugh, K. 1995a. Disabling and enabling: implications of language policy trends in South Africa. In R. Mesthrie (Ed.), *Language and social history: Studies in South African sociolinguistics* (pp. 329-350). Cape Town: David Philip.

Heugh, K. 1995b. Comments on the language policy clauses in the Constitution of South Africa. *Proceedings of the workshop: Constitutional Rights: Language*, Ministry of Constitutional Development, Cape Town, 16 February.

Heugh, K. 1999. Languages, development and reconstructing education in South Africa. *International Journal of Educational Development, 19*, 301-313.

Heugh, K. 2003. Can authoritarian separatism give way to language rights? *Current Issues in Language Planning* 4(2), 126-145.

Heugh, K. 2009. Into the cauldron: an interplay of indigenous and globalised knowledge with strong and weak notions of literacy and language education in Ethiopia and South Africa. *Language Matters, Studies in the languages of Africa, 40* (2), 166-189.

Heugh, K., Siegrühn, A. and Plüddemann, P. (Eds.), 1995. *Multilingual education for South Africa*. Johannesburg: Heinemann.

Howie, S., Venter, E. and Van Staden, S. 2008. The effect of multilingual policies on performance and progression in reading literacy in South African primary schools. *Educational Research and Evaluation: An International Journal on Theory and Practice*, 14(6): 551-560.

Manentsa, N. 2001. Personal Communication, 31 March.

Macdonald, C. 1990. *Crossing the threshold into Standard Three. Main report of the Threshold Project*. Pretoria: Human Sciences Research Council.

Macdonald, C. 2002. 'Are the children still swimming up the waterfall? A look at literacy development in the new curriculum' *Language Matters, 33*, 111-141.

Mahlalela-Thusi, B. and Heugh, K. 2010. Terminology and School Books in Southern African Languages. Aren't there any? In B. Brock-Utne, Z. Desai, M. Qorro & A. Pitman (Eds.), *Language of Instruction in Tanzania and South Africa – Highlights from a Project* (pp.113-131). Rotterdam, Boston and Taipei: Sense Publishers.

Makoni, S. 2003. From misinvention to disinvention of language: multilingualism and the South African Constitution. In S. Makoni, G Smitherman, A Ball and A. K. Spears (Eds.), *Black Linguistics: Language, Society and Politics in Africa and the Americas* (pp. 132-153). New York: Routledge.

Minister of Arts and Culture. 2011. South African Languages Bill [B23-2011]. October 2011. Cape Town: Department of Arts and Culture.

Moloi, M. and Chetty, M. 2011. *SACMEQ III. Trends in Achievement Levels of Grade 6 Pupils in South Africa. Policy Brief No. 1 (June 2011).* Southern and Eastern Africa Consortium for Monitoring Educational Quality. Retrieved from www.sacmeq.org.

Mothibeli, A. 2005. Cross-country achievement results from the SCAMEQ 11 Project – 2000 to 2002. A quantitative analysis of education systems in Southern and Eastern Africa. *Edusource Data News*, 49, October. Johannesburg: The Education Foundation Trust.

Moyane, L. 2002. Personal Communication.

Msimang, C., T. 1992. *African Languages and Language Planning in South Africa. The Nhlapo-Alexander Notion of Harmonisation Revisited.* Pretoria: Bard Publishers.

Murray, S. 2002. Language issues in South African education: an overview. In Mesthrie, R. (Ed.), *Language in South Africa* (pp. 434-448). Cambridge, New York, Melbourne, Cape Town: CUP.

NEPI. 1992. *Language: Report of the National Education Policy Investigation (NEPI) Language Research Group.* Cape Town: Oxford University Press and National Education Co-ordinating Committee.

Nhlapo, Jacob. 1944. *Bantu Babel: will the Bantu languages live? The Sixpenny Library, No. 4.* Cape Town: The African Bookman.

PANSALB. 2000. *Language use and language interaction in South Africa: A national sociolinguistic survey.* Pretoria: Pan South African Language Board.

Plüddemann, P., Braam, D., October, M., & Wababa, Z. 2004. Dual-medium and parallel-medium schooling in the Western Cape: from default to design. *Occasional Papers, No. 17.* Cape Town: PRAESA, University of Cape Town.

Pretorius, E. 2002. Reading ability and academic performance in South Africa. Are we fiddling while Rome is burning? *Language Matters, 33*, 169-196.

Prinsloo, C.H. and Kanjee, A. 2005. *Improving learning in South African schools: The Quality Learning Project (QLP) summative evaluation (2000 to 2004) technical report*. Pretoria: HSRC.

Reeves, C., Heugh, K., Prinsloo, C.H., Macdonald, C., Netshitangani, T., Alidou, H., Diedericks, G. & Herbst, D. 2008. *Evaluation of Literacy Teaching in the Primary Schools of the Limpopo Province*. For the Limpopo Department of Education and Irish Aid. Pretoria: Human Sciences Research Council in association with the Department of Language Education at the University of Limpopo.

Reddy, V. 2006. *Mathematics and Science Achievement at South African Schools in TIMSS 2003*. Pretoria: Human Sciences Research Council.

RSA. 1996. The Constitution of the Republic of South Africa. Pretoria: Government Printer.

Ridge, S. 2000. Mixed motives: Ideological elements in the support for English in South Africa. In Ricento, T. (Ed.) *Ideology, Politics and Language Policies: Focus on English* (pp. 151-172). Amsterdam: John Benjamins Publishing Co.

Roberge, Paul. 2002. Afrikaans: considering origins. In R. Mesthrie (Ed.) *Language in South Africa* (pp. 79-103). Cambridge: Cambridge University Press.

Satyo, S. 2001. Personal Communication, 24 July.

Setati, M. 2008. Access to mathematics versus access to the language of power: The struggle in multilingual mathematics classrooms. *South African Journal of Education, 28,* 103–116. Retrieved from http://www.sajournalofeducation.co.za/index.php/saje/article/view/150/99

Taylor, N. and Vinjevold, P. (Eds.). 1999. *Getting learning right. Report of the President's Education Initiative Research Project*. Johannesburg: The Joint Education Trust.

UNESCO. 1953. *Report on the Use of the Vernacular in Education*. Paris: UNESCO.

Wa Thiong'o, Ngugi. 1981. *Education for a national culture*. Harare: Zimbabwean Publishing House.

Chapter 7
The Malawian Experience in Language Planning
Atikonda Akuzike Mtenje

African countries including Malawi have been working towards policies that include local languages in their education systems. This paper examines the experience of Malawi as it was developing the language in education policy. The paper firstly examines the development of language policies in Malawi from the colonial era to the post independence (one party state) era all the way to the democratic era showing how Chichewa had an advantage over other local languages in the country during the one party state. The paper then explains the declaration from the Ministry of Education in Malawi which includes local languages in the early stages of primary school i.e. Standards 1-4 and observes that even though the Malawi government made this declaration, the approval and implementation of the policy has not yet been done. It is cited that the country has made strides in working towards the policy by conducting surveys, having symposia, sensitising the media and publishing materials. However, the implementation of the policy has met challenges such as improper planning, lack of political will, elite's negative attitudes towards African languages and lack of public sensitisation. The paper finally observes that other African countries working on similar policies can learn from Malawi that there is need for proper planning, proper sensitisation and commitment from all stakeholders in order for a policy to be approved and implemented.

Introduction
The need to incorporate African languages in language policies of African states has been a cause of interest among linguists and other stakeholders all over the continent. This has been the case after observing that African languages can be used to mitigate hindrances of social economic development such as poverty, gender inequality, illiteracy, environmental degradation, violation of minority rights just to mention a few. It has therefore been argued that the numerous African languages should be seen as a resource and not a curse.

More specifically scholars have debated on the medium of instruction to be used in schools and research has established that there are pedagogical and cognitive advantages of using the mother tongue especially in the early years of primary education. Children also show increased accuracy in the acquisition of literacy and numeracy when they learn in their mother tongue. (c.f. UNESCO

1953 report; Bamgbose (1984), Fishman (1989), Mtenje (2002), Prah (1998), Brock-Utne (2009). Several African countries such as South Africa, Tunisia, Tanzania, Ethiopia and Namibia have adopted policies that use mother tongue instruction and in most cases the exoglossic languages are English and French which are taught as subjects in the early stages.

In 1996, the Malawi government issued a directive that local languages of Malawi should be used as media of instruction from grades 1-4 while English should be taught as a subject. Stakeholders such as linguists, teachers, the media, Ministry of Education and the general public were to work together in order to come up with a proper language policy to be approved by government. Nevertheless even though a draft policy is in place, the policy has not been approved 15 years down the line.

As African countries are considering developing language policies for their various countries, lessons can be drawn from the experience of other countries by examining their achievements and setbacks concerning the implementation of such policies. This paper explains the experience of Malawi as the country was coming up with a language in education policy. It looks at the development of language policy issues in Malawi, the achievements and the challenges that the language in education policy has faced and the lessons that other African countries can learn from the Malawi experience.

History of Language Policy in Malawi
The development of language policies in Malawi can be categorised into the following three:
    i)   Colonial period
    ii)   Post independence (The One party state)
    iii)   The Democratic era

Colonial Period
In this era, the language policy stipulated that English was the official language. As a result, it was used in official domains such as the judiciary, the legislature, government offices and in trade. Chinyanja (which is the present Chichewa) and Chitumbuka were the languages of instruction in the lower levels of primary school and English was

taught as a subject in these levels. English was used as the medium of instruction in the upper levels of education.

Post – Independence (One party state)

After Malawi gained independence in 1964, this language policy was adopted. However, in 1968, at a Malawi Congress party convention, the then president Hastings Kamuzu Banda declared that English and Chichewa become the official languages of Malawi. He also decreed that the language Chinyanja change its name to Chichewa and that Chichewa should also serve as the national language in order to unify the country. He outlawed the use of Chitumbuka in schools and in the media where it was previously used. According to Kishindo (1994) and Vail and White (1989), the elevation of Chichewa to official and national language status led to the under development of other local languages in the country. Moyo (2001) observes that Hastings Kamuzu Banda failed to recognise the fundamental role and function of other indigenous languages. These other indigenous languages and cultures were marginalised to village use and tribal identity. The choice of Chichewa was based on the fact that Banda was a Chewa by tribe where the dialect of Chichewa was used. As Kamwendo (2010) argues Banda never missed an opportunity to favour his mother tongue (Chichewa) over Malawi's other indigenous languages in the guise of strengthening nationhood through one unifying language.

Democratic Era

Malawi voted for multiparty democracy in 1994 and this led to the respect of people's rights alongside linguistic liberalism. Major local languages such as Chilomwe, Chitumbuka, Chiyao, Chitonga and Chisena were allowed in news bulletins in the local media. More importantly to this paper, the Malawi government through the Ministry of Education authorised teachers from Standard 1-4 to use local languages pupils were familiar with as media of instruction. The communiqué from the Ministry of Education read as follows:

> The Ministry of Education would like to inform…that with immediate effect, all standards 1, 2, 3 and 4 classes in all our schools be taught in their own mother tongue or vernacular language as a medium of instruction. English and Chichewa will however, continue to be offered as subjects in the primary

curricula. In the past, Chichewa was used as both medium of instruction and subject, making it difficult for beginners to grasp ideas. However, English will be used as a medium of instruction beginning standard 5 (Sec for Education's letter. Ref. No. IN/2/14 quoted in Kayambazinthu, 1998).

The Malawi government had the following motivations for the issuing this directive:
i) Research from other countries had shown that pupils learn better in a familiar language than a foreign one.
ii) The Ministry of Education had observed that teachers use other dominant local languages of an area as media of instruction even though the existing policy recognises only Chichewa as a medium of instruction from standard 1-4. The Ministry of Education therefore wanted to regularise the practice.

Implementation of the Policy

The directive from the Ministry of Education received a lot of criticism through the media from various stakeholders. Mtenje (2011) quoting documentation from Mtenje (2002) and Chauma, Chimombo and Mtenje (1997) summarise the criticisms as follows:
a) Most of the teachers in service lacked the relevant training and competence in multilingual education.
b) The policy would be too expensive for a poor country like Malawi to implement.
c) The introduction and encouragement of indigenous languages would lower the standards of English which were already deteriorating.
d) There were no instructional materials in local languages to sustain the policy.
e) There was no comprehensive research that had been conducted in Malawi to justify the supposed advantages of mother tongue education.
f) Indigenous languages were too underdeveloped for use in science and technology.
g) The policy would enforce feelings of ethnicity since teachers would be allocated in their areas of origin. Furthermore, smaller groups of people will want to identify themselves with their mother tongue.

h) The public was not consulted on the matter.
i) Children learning in an indigenous language will get inferior education.
j) The decision was political because the then ruling party, United Democratic Front (UDF), did not want anything to do with the former ruling party which made teaching in Chichewa compulsory.
k) The policy does not account for children staying with their parents in areas where their mother tongue is not dominant.
l) The policy had been introduced to save face for there are some teachers who are not well conversant with English.

The government of Malawi in trying to address the criticisms that were raised came up with various activities to look into issues concerning the implementation of the policy. The most notable was the establishment of the Centre for Language Studies (henceforth CLS) which was mandated to look at issues concerning language in the country but also to carry out sociolinguistic surveys which were going to determine teachers', pupils', parents', guardians' and other stakeholders' attitudes towards the use of mother tongue instruction. CLS was also authorised to standardise orthographies and compile dictionaries of the major local languages. All this was to be done as preparation for the introduction of the new policy.

Achievements
Since 1996 there have been some achievements that have been made towards the language in education policy. Below is an outline of these achievements.
1. The Centre for Language Studies together with the Malawi Institute of Education conducted several sociolinguistic surveys from 1996-2007. These include the following:
    a) A sociolinguistic survey aimed at determining the extent to which mother tongue education would be accepted by stakeholders such as teachers, pupils, parents/guardians. The study also wanted to find out the level of preparedness of teachers to teach in local languages, the availability of teaching and learning materials in languages other than Chichewa and other training needs. The major results of these surveys are presented below:

    i) Most of the subjects supported the introduction of local languages as media of instruction in the early years of primary education. They however insisted that this should be implemented provided that English continues to be offered as a subject.
    ii) Malawians suggested that Chichewa be offered as a subject because they saw that it was appropriate as the lingua franca for broader communication.
    iii) The majority of teachers indicated that they would be willing to teach in the local languages.
    iv) There is great need for training teachers in local language teaching methodologies.
    v) Other Malawian languages apart from Chichewa and Chitumbuka did not have adequate teaching and learning materials.

b) A language mapping survey was also conducted with the main objective of determining the number of languages spoken in the country, where they are spoken and the number of speakers for each language. The major finding of the survey was that there are 18 languages spoken in the country. CLS has provided maps for the languages spoken in each district and the entire country.

c) Other research that has been conducted has been on orthography revision, effectiveness of teaching primary school Social Studies and Mathematics in local languages as opposed to foreign languages, the influence of language on pupils' failure, repetition and drop out cases.

2. The Centre for Language Studies from 1999-2007 also held several symposia following the results from some of the studies above. The symposia provided a platform for the discussion of matters concerning multilingual education in Malawi. Participants included linguists, international scholars, primary school teachers, legal practitioners, publishers, the media, education officials, traditional chiefs and many others. A crucial result of these symposia is the formulation of the draft language in education policy which provides for the use of mother tongues and where it is not possible dominant languages as media of instruction from standards 1 – 4. Mtenje (2012: 4) outlines the following as the major issues in the current draft language in education policy.

- The policy maintains English as a subject from grade 1 to tertiary level. It is compulsory in primary and secondary schools because it is an international language and a language of socio-economic privileges in Malawi.
- Local languages will be used as media of instruction from grades 1-4 and thereafter English takes over up to tertiary level.
- Other foreign languages which are considered to be of socio economic and political significance to Malawi will be taught as optional subjects depending on the availability of human and other resources.
- Chichewa shall continue to be taught as a subject from grade 1 up to end of secondary school because it is widely spoken.
- Wherever circumstances permit (for example where teachers are available), other local languages shall be permitted as optional subjects from grade 4 onwards.
- In linguistically mixed areas, local communities shall choose the medium of instruction after carefully weighing the relevant factors.

3. CLS in 2007 also held a sensitisation workshop with the media. The aim of the workshop was to make the media aware of the contents of the language in education policy so that they can further sensitise the general public.
4. CLS have published the first Chichewa monolingual dictionary and it has an online Chichewa dictionary.
5. According to the CLS website, the following are the projects the centre is working on:
    - Development of scientific terminology in local languages
    - Compilation of monolingual dictionaries for Ciyao and Citumbuka
    - Compilation of orthographies for Citonga, Cisena, Cinkhonde, Cilomwe
    - Measuring literacy levels in Malawian local languages
    - Linking language, literacy and livelihoods

- Development of a multilingual database for Malawian languages.
- Compilation of bilingual English-Chichewa dictionaries.

Much as there have been considerable achievements that have been done especially by the Centre for Language Studies, the draft policy still has not been approved and implemented since the directive from government was made in 1996. We now turn to a discussion of the setbacks that the implementation of this policy has faced.

Challenges
The following are the challenges that this paper recognises as the major challenges that have caused the non implementation of the language in education policy in Malawi:

Improper Planning
One of the major issues that have led to the non implementation of the language in education policy is the lack of proper planning. Kaplan and Baldauf (1997) argue that in order to come up with an appropriate model for language use in a country, there is need for proper status, corpus and acquisition planning. However this was not the case in Malawi, the use of mother tongue instruction came as a directive with no sociolinguistic surveys to determine the linguistic situation of the country and also to assess stakeholder's attitudes towards such a policy. In addition, there was no survey conducted in order to research on the pedagogical problems that were going to be faced with the introduction of such a policy and the availability of teaching and learning materials, and teacher training needs. Kayambazinthu (1999) notes that such important surveys constitute proper language planning for education. However, in the Malawi situation, research on all these issues was done after the directive for the policy was made. Bamgbose (1985) notes this as a common problem in African countries; he notes that 'no preparatory steps are taken to identify problems. Rather the decision often precedes the fact finding '. This problem in Malawi has also been noted by Kamwendo (2008) and Mtenje (2012). It is no wonder that the directive received a lot of criticisms.

The other problem concerning planning for this policy is that language policies in Malawi have largely been politically motivated. Kayambazinthu (1998) and Moyo (2001) also note this. Soon after independence, President Hastings Kamuzu Banda elevated Chichewa to official language status mainly because it was the language of his tribe and he imposed the language and its culture on people who are not from the Chewa ethnic group. When Malawi voted for multiparty democracy in 1994 and when President Bakili Muluzi came to power, there was a lot of ethnic consciousness and some quarters were against the dominance of Chichewa and the marginalisation of lesser used languages. Muluzi therefore wanted to distance himself from Kamuzu Banda's autocracy and he wanted to gain political mileage with people from other ethnic groups. This led to the improper planning of the implementation of the policy because everything was done in an ad hoc manner.

Lack of Political Will
One other major problem that has led to the non implementation of the draft policy in Malawi is that there has generally been lack of will on the part of the government to implement the policy. The Centre for Language Studies which is the secretariat of the implementation task force and other stakeholders such as academics are the only ones that have been left to make public statements about the policy. Government has not made any public comments on it after it made the directive in 1994. The draft policy is in place but the Ministry of Education has not yet presented it to cabinet for discussion and approval. As a result, the policy remains in draft form more than a decade down the line. The government that came after Bakili Muluzi's government was also not fully committed to implementing the policy. This was mainly because they might have thought that Malawi has other major economic problems than to deal with issues to do with language. Mtenje (2011) further notes that considering that the directive of the policy was introduced during the reign of Bakili Muluzi who later on became an arch enemy of President Bingu wa Mutharika, his government may not have wanted to implement some policies that came from him.

It is yet to be seen what the recently inaugurated government of President Joyce Banda is going to do concerning the policy. So far there has not been any information from government concerning the matter.

Lack of political will for the implementation of a policy is problematic because politicians are the crucial people who approve policies and they are the ones who approve funds to be used for the implementation of the policies. If there is no political will, a policy just like the language in education policy in Malawi may never be approved.

Elite's Negative Attitudes Towards African languages

The Malawi Government in its 2020 vision report noted that one of the major things that may hinder development in the country is that Malawians have a low self-esteem and they have no confidence in their local products and culture. It should be noted that this mentality has extended towards their perception on Malawi's local languages. The language in education policy has been criticised mainly because the elite deem indigenous languages as inferior, underdeveloped and incapable of use for scientific and technological development. This stance has been vehemently advanced by the elite and these people are preoccupied with safeguarding English by thinking that local languages will lower the standard of English. Since these elite feel that English is superior anything that threatens its status must be opposed and in this case it is the indigenous languages of Malawi. These attitudes have also been observed in other African countries and have been attributed to colonisation. Prah (2002) notes that most educated Africans have remained neo-colonially trapped in the usage of colonially or imperially received languages which are treated as inherently superior to indigenous African languages and that one of the worst side effects of colonial education on the African elite has thus been the denial and dislike of their culture and languages.

English has gained so much socio-economic importance in Malawi since it is used in official domains, it is a prerequisite for white collar employment, passing of Malawi School Certificate of Education, entry into universities in the country and it is a language for global communication. These facts make the Malawian elite oppose the language in education policy further because they see the indigenous languages as being of no socio-economic importance.

Luckett (1995), Chumbow, Tadajeu and Tamanji (2003); Alexander (2004) have argued that the negative attitudes of the elite has been one of the factors leading to the delay of policies in mother tongue instruction in the various African countries and indeed this has been the case in Malawi too. This is because the elite mostly hold key positions in government and are therefore crucial in the approval of policies.

Lack of Adequate Public Sensitisation

One of the issues very important when advancing for change in policy is that the stakeholders or implementers should truly understand the contents of the policy. This therefore involves public sensitisation. Mtenje (2004) argues that in the formulation of a policy that will concern multicultural societies like those in Malawi, there is need for the public to be informed of the pedagogical advantages a mother tongue or multilingual policy like the one proposed for Malawi.

When the directive for mother tongue instruction was made, it received a lot of criticism mainly because people did not really understand what the policy was saying. To this day, there are some quarters that still do not understand what the policy involves. Sensitisation of the policy was solely left to the Centre for Language Studies for they were the ones who responded to some of the criticisms that were raised in the press. CLS also organised a workshop for the media which was done in order to let them know about the policy and urge them to further sensitise the public about the advantages of the policy. The Ministry of Education on the other hand have not made any statements concerning the policy.

Much as there has been some work in this sensitisation especially by CLS, there is more that still needs to be done. Unfortunately, talk about the policy has subsided. Since much of the talking and the defending of the policy was left for academics while other stakeholders like the Ministry of Education remained silent in the public, some of the academics are now 'tired'. There was a lot of talk about the policy between 1996 – 2007/8, which is not heard anymore. During this period, the Centre for Language Studies held symposia where stakeholders debated on the policy and issues concerning it. However, these symposia are not conducted anymore. Lack of talk on the policy has contributed to the policy still lying at the Ministry of Education waiting for approval. There is need for talk concerning the policy to be revived so that government can work towards this policy otherwise the policy will always remain in draft form.

These are the major challenges that Malawi has faced over the approval and the implementation of the language in Education policy. However, not all hope should be lost for Malawi, because what the country needs is to once again be committed to the implementation of the policy. The country therefore needs to tap into the opportunities that it has. For instance, there is now considerable research on several language issues in the country, there is need to build up on that research. The Centre for Language Studies and the public universities in Malawi have resources that can pursue such further research. Mtenje (2012) also notes these other opportunities: major stakeholders in education such as teachers, parents, guardians and pupils supported the policy as seen from the 1997-1998 sociolinguistic survey by the Centre for Language Studies. There were some development partners and international organisations that are willing to provide financial support for the implementation for the policy and that Malawi is a signatory to international protocols and agreements that promote the development and use of local languages in education. These opportunities can be used in Malawi and other African countries that have similar opportunities. Malawi and Africa in general therefore still have work to do in order to ensure that linguistic liberalism is ensured on the continent and that the children of Africa are getting an education that is developmental for their continent since as Chumbow (2002: 171) notes 'The effective mobilisation of the masses …for national development requires the democratisation of access not in an exoglossic (foreign) language but in a language (or languages) the people know best - an African language.

Lessons to be Learnt from the Malawian Experience

The achievements and the setbacks that Malawi has experienced can be used as lessons from which other African countries that are pushing for similar policies can learn. Below are the major lessons that can be learnt from Malawi:
1. There is need for proper planning before coming up with a policy. Research should be done on the advantages of having mother tongue instruction, and on the sociolinguistic situation

of a country so that it is known which languages will be used in the policy. There is also need for research which will determine the readiness of the country in the implementation of the policy in terms of the availability of teaching and learning materials for the different languages to be used for instruction. There is also need for research on the people's attitudes towards the introduction of such a policy.

Proper planning is crucial because most criticisms that arise stem from questions on whether there has been proper research which will determine whether it is important for a policy to be adopted. When proper research is done, the public have confidence in the policy rather than when there are so many questions unanswered.

2. It is also important that people are sensitised about the contents of the policy and its advantages. When people understand the contents of the policy they are more likely to accept and support the policy.
3. More importantly, there should be commitment from all stakeholders especially government on the implementation of the policy. This is because once all stakeholders are involved it will ensure that the policy is approved and the running of the implementation is smoothly done. Once there is no political will from government chances are high that a policy will not be implemented.

Conclusion

This paper has examined language policy issues and their progression from the colonial era to the present. It has focused mainly on the language in education policy by looking at the major achievements that have been made in preparation for the policy and the setbacks that have led to its non implementation. It has also highlighted the main lessons that other African countries can learn from the Malawian experience and it argues that not all hope is lost because the continent can tap on the opportunities that it has in order to implement policies that involve local languages.

References

Alexander, N. 2004. The African renaissance and the African academy of languages: Developments around the African

Academy of Languages and the significance for applied language studies. Keynote address delivered at the International Conference of the Southern African Applied Linguistics Association (SAALA). University of Limpopo, 13-15 July.

Bamgbose, A. 1984. Mother tongue medium and scholastic attainment in Nigeria. *Prospects.*
14 (1), 87-93.

Bamgbose, A. 1985. The role of linguistic research in moulding language policy. Seminar paper presented at the International Seminar concerning Current Problems of Linguistic Research in Africa and Caribbean Countries. Paris: UNSECO, 24-27 September 1985.

Brock-Utne, B. 2009. The adoption of the western paradigm of bilingual teaching – Why does it not fit the African situation? *In Multilingualism an African Advantage: A paradigm shift in African languages of instruction policies*, In K. Prah and B. Brock-Utne (Eds.), 67, 18-5. Cape Town: CASAS.

Chauma, A., Chimombo, M. and Mtenje, A. 1997. Introduction to vernacular languages in primary education: The Malawian experience. In Proceedings of the LICCA workshop in Dar es Salaam. 37-46. Sept 1996.

Chumbow, B. S. 2002. The language question and national development in Africa. In *African*
Intellectuals: Rethinking politics, language, gender and development. Mkandawire T. (Ed.), 169-192. London: Zed Books.

Chumbow, S., Tadadjeu, M. and Tamanji, P. 2003. The Intellectualisation of African Languages: The Cameroon experience. Paper presented at the Towards the Intellectualisation of African Languages. Cape Town, South Africa, 8-12 July.

Fishman, J. A. 1989. *Language and ethnicity in minority sociolinguistic perspective.* Clevedon:
Multilingual Matters.

Kamwendo, G. 2008. The bumpy road to mother-tongue instruction in Malawi. *Journal of Multilingual and Multicultural Development* 29 (5): 353-363.

Kaplan, R., B. & Baldauf, R. B. Jr. 1997. Language planning: From practice to theory, Clevedon: Multilingual Matters.

Kayambazinthu, E. 1998. The language planning situation in Malawi. *Journal of Multilingual Development* 19 (5&6), 369-436.

Kishindo, P., J. 1994. The impact of a national language on minority languages. The case of Malawi. *Journal of Contemporary African Studies.* 12 (2), 127-150.

Lora-Kayambazithu, E. 1999. Formulating a language policy: Theory and practice. In *Towards a National Policy for Education.* Proceedings of a national symposium on language policy formulation. University of Malawi. 7-11 July.

Luckett, K. (1995). Additive Bilingualism: New Models of Language Education for South African Schools. Johannesburg: ELTIC Publication.

Moyo, T. 2001. Changing language policies and reversing language roles in Malawi: From colonial times (1891-1964) to the present. Per Linguam 17(2):1-11

Mtenje, A. A. 2011. The Language in Education Policy of Malawi: An analysis of the strides and setback in the implementation process. Paper presented at the African Renaissance, Integration and Development Conference. Pretoria, November 2011.

Mtenje, Al. 2012. Developing a Language Policy in an African country: Lessons from the Malawi experience. Paper presented at the South Sudan Conference on Language in Education, Juba, March, 2012.

Mtenje, Al. 2002. The role of language in national development: A case for local languages. Inaugural lecture delivered on July 26 2002, at Chancellor College. University of Malawi.

Mtenje, Al. 2002. Implementing mother tongue education in Malawi: Problems and prospects. Paper presented at the ADALEST conference, University of Pretoria. July, 2002.

Prah, K. K. 2002. A tale of two cities: Trends in multilingualism in two African cities: The cases of Nima-Accra and Katatura-Windhoek. In *Multilingualism an African Advantage: A paradigm shift in African languages of instruction policies.* K.K. Prah and B. Brock-Utne (Eds.), Cape Town: CASAS.

Prah, K. K. 1998. *Between distinction and extinction: The harmonisation and standardisation of African languages.* Cape Town: CASAS. UNESCO. 1953. The use of vernacular languages in education. Monographs on fundamental education. UNESCO. VII. Paris.

Vail, L. and White, L. 1989. Tribalism in the political history of Malawi. In *The creation of tribalism in Southern Africa*. Vail, L. (Ed.), 151-192. London. James Currey.
www.unima-cls.org/pmwiki/pmwiki.php/Projects/Projects.

Chapter 8
An Overview of the Ethiopian Language Policy and Planning
Bekale Seyum

This study attempts to give an overview of the Ethiopian language policy and planning, past and present. Data are gathered from document analysis and from different secondary sources, including the author's own previous field work; and descriptive method is used. The article is organised on the basis of the different historical periods in the country. Language policy during the earliest historical period, the Pre-LP Era, is characterised by the development and spread of Ge'ez, then the language of the monarchs, while the other Ethiopian languages were used in oral communication by their native speakers until it was replaced by Amharic. The Imperial and the Derg periods covered the time in which Amharic, which by policy became the hegemonic sole national official language of the country within a unitary state, where the one-language-one-state policy was the rule. All other Ethiopian languages were marginalised. During the current period, however, the country's linguistic plurality is recognised. Despite some implementation problems, many Ethiopian languages have been developed, reduced to writing, and used as LOI and as official languages in their respective administrative areas as well as in the mass media.

Introduction

Africa has a large number of social, political, economic and technological problems. Language is related to all these non-linguistic problems. There is no human affair that does not require language as a means of expression. Language is also one of the most salient factors that help to identify individuals, groups, or communities. Besides it has several other important functions in human society. Language carries the accumulated knowledge and skills of generations of speakers. It represents all the human culture and helps society to transmit that culture from generation to generation. Without language human beings could not have interacted with the world around them. This makes language vital in the life of people.

Language diversity is a typical characteristic of most countries in Sub-Saharan Africa. Nearly all countries in this part of the continent are multilingual. This may pose a number of challenges to national socio-economic advancement, social stability, and educational progress. Ethiopia is not an exception. Multilingualism and multiethnic reality are real challenges faced by Ethiopia. Communication, social and vocational mobility, global economic interrelationship, and development of urbanisation and industrialisation in the linguistically diverse communities in the modern world increase more and more. This may result in various types of changes in languages. Some languages tend to become dominant and spread, while others, particularly non-populous[44] languages tend to become subordinate and face language shift or struggle for maintenance. Some may even face the danger of extinction. All these call for careful language planning (LP)[45]. Therefore, to make proper use of the various language varieties so that society can benefit, a sound LP must be put in place.

Ethiopia is a unique country in the world in respect to its distinct art, music, poetic forms, its calendar, writing system, numeration system and its history. It is also a diverse country in terms of its geographical structures, ecological conditions, ethnic composition, religious multiplicity and linguistic composition. Currently Ethiopia has a federal system of government constituting nine regional states and two chartered cities. These include the regional states of Tigray, Afar, Amhara, Oromia, Benshangul-Gumuz, Gambella, Harari and the Southern Nations and Nationalities Region (SNNPR). These regional states are divided on linguistic basis and it is also considered by some as following a system of Ethnic Federalism. The two chartered cities are Addis Ababa, the capital city and Diredawa. Ethiopia is the second most populous country in Africa. Its population was 73,750,932, which has an annual growth rate of 2.6 % according to the 2007 national population and housing census. About 84% of this population is rural. Eighty percent of the total population is found in the three largest regional states of the

---

[44] In this study the term minority language is intentionally avoided as it is assumed derogative and for it implies that the so called minority languages are defective and inferior. Where the term minority is to be used the terms non-populous or less populous are used only to indicate that these languages have small population size.

[45] Different scholars define the terms language planning and language policy differently, and thus the two terms are confused in the literature. In this study the definition by Spolsky (2004) is adopted. According to Spolsky, LP is an intervention of a government or other influential body in order to influence or change the language practice and the language ideology prevailing in the society in question; while Language policy constitutes the actual language practice in the society, the linguistic ideology the community upholds, as well as the language planning in the society.

country, namely, Oromia, Amhara, and the SNNPR (CSA 2010). Religiously, Ethiopia is also heterogeneous and according to the 2007 census, 43.5 percent of the total population is Orthodox Christian, 33.9 percent Muslim, 19.6 percent Protestant, 3.1 percent traditional and 0.8 percent is Catholic. The remaining 0.7 percent of the population belongs to other religions (CSA, 2010).

Language Policy and Planning in Ethiopia in the Past

The brief history of the language policy and planning (LPP) in the country before the current government is presented in this section. It is organised with respect to the different historical periods in the country. The pre-LP Era will be treated first, which will be followed by the LP during the Imperial Era and finally by the LP during the period of the Derg.

The Pre-Language Planning Era

The Pre-LP Era covers the language policy (LPo) of the earliest historical period of Ethiopia that had started from the early Axumite period to the time of about the first half of the reign of Emperor Haileselassie. The middle of Emperor Haileselassie's regime was taken as the point of departure between the LPo of the pre-LP Era and the second period, referred to here as the Imperial Era. The disciplines of sociolinguistics or applied linguistics and in relation to them researches and studies of LPP were started only about the time of the Imperial Era. Concepts, theories, frameworks, models, etc. in the discipline were developed from various empirical and some theoretical studies during the Imperial Era and these had their influence on LP in Ethiopia. None of these existed during the pre-LP Era. Therefore, in regard to the pre-LP Era, we will only make brief descriptions of the sociolinguistic situations, the language practices and the language ideologies without attempting to evaluate them since LP as we know it in the literature today was not practiced.

During the Axumite period, it is believed that "Ge'ez, the language of the ancient Axumite empire" (Hetzron & Bender, 1976: 25), played the role of the language of the monarchs, commonly referred to as the role of *lisane negus* (literally, 'language of the king'). Prior to it three languages, namely, Greek, Sabean, and Ge'ez were inscribed on the old stone monuments that declared the victories of the monarchs in different expeditions of warfare. Greek was supposed to be the international language of wider communication (LWC) at the time, Sabean to be the language of the monarchs, and Ge'ez the language of the people in and around Axum (see Cooper, 1976: 300). The other Ethio-Semitic languages (and apparently the predominant non- Semitic languages in the region too) are said to have been used by different groups of speakers side by side with Ge'ez during the Axumite period (Hetzron & Bender, 1976: 25). First Sabean and Greek were the written languages while Ge'ez and the other Ethio-Semitic and non-Ethio-Semitic languages did not have a written tradition. But later Ge'ez was also reduced into writing and was developed into a language of the monarchs of the Axumite Empire replacing Sabean.

Even though it is difficult to reconstruct the history of the spread of Ge'ez during the Axumite period, scholars assume by mere speculation that it was marked by most of the general features which characterise the spread of Arabic, Greek or Latin. According to Cooper (1976: 292),

> Ge'ez spread with the spread of the Axumite Empire, whose power and cohesiveness lasted for centuries. Although we do not know what degree of linguistic diversity existed on the plateau among the peoples conquered by the Axumite emperors, it is not unlikely that Ge'ez has spread among peoples speaking several different Cushitic languages and that it has served as a lingua franca. And knowledge of this imperial language must have been a material advantage."

Bahru (1991) also attests that during the Axumite period, Ge'ez was the language that served as *lisane nigus* 'the language of kings' and as a lingua franca among ordinary people with some kind of official status. Since the time about 330 A.D., Ge'ez has also served as the language of education in the Ethiopian Orthodox Church (Ayalew, 2000, cited in Zelalem, forthcoming). The time between the 13th and 17th centuries was the golden time of Ge'ez during which it had flourished with full dominance particularly in literary functions. It is assumed that "it probably existed together with Amharic in a diglossic relationship, perhaps Ge'ez serving the literary and ecclesiastical as well as the ceremonial functions enjoying higher status, and Amharic (and presumably other Ethiopian languages) serving as spoken languages in the day-to-day life of the people, with relatively lower status" (Cooper, 1976: 289). According to Cooper (1976: 287), Ge'ez became extinct as a mother tongue between the 9th and 12th centuries, when the centre of power moved to the south to the Amhara area – after which for most of the time the Amharas have been the politically dominant forces in Ethiopia.

Some evidence indicates that Amharic was already reduced to a written language by the 13th century. Although the predominance of Ge'ez was felt until the late 16th and early 17th centuries, Amharic had some literature like the imperial songs written in the 14th century in praise of the monarchs like Dawit, Yishaq and Amda Tsion. As noted by Manuel de Almeida, a Portuguese Jesuit traveller (Levine, 1971: 15, cited in Cooper, 1976: 293), Amharic had been a lingua franca in most parts (presumably of northern Ethiopia) about the early 1620s. In the late 16th and early 17th centuries, Amharic had been employed in religious polemics between the Portuguese Jesuits and the clergymen from the Ethiopian Orthodox Church. However, little was written in Amharic between the time of the expulsion of the Jesuits and the coming of Tewodros II to the Ethiopian throne in the middle of the 19th century (Cooper, 1976: 290). Other Ethiopian languages were apparently used by their ethnolinguistic groups, except that the Oromo expansion in the 16th century has left some traces of its influence in some areas in the north in the form of personal and place names, such as Rayya, Kobbo, Kombolcha, Worrehimenu, Worrebabbo, Mecha, Ilmanna Densa, etc. and in lexical items like /abba wärra/ 'head of the family', /angaffa/ 'eldest', /guddifäcca/ 'adoption of a child', onne 'courage', etc. which still persist in Amharic. Tigrinya in the north and Afan Oromo in the south used to serve as important lingua francas to a lesser extent than Amharic (Cooper, 1976: 293).

The reign of Emperor Tewodros II was marked with Amharic coming to be used as *lisane negus* and also for its being used as the main written language in Ethiopia (Pankhurst, 1969). The Ethiopian royal chronicles, which used to be written in Ge'ez between the 13th up to the early 19th centuries, were written in Amharic for the first time during the reign of Tewodros II (Cooper, 1976:290). Bahru (1991:34) also testifies that the reign of Tewodros was significant for the birth of Amharic literacy. It is possible that Amharic spread over northern Ethiopia during Tewodros II's reign over the various communities speaking different languages which belonged to Cushitic and perhaps to the Nilo-Saharan families. Ge'ez still continued to be the language of literature and ecclesiastical practices in the Ethiopian Orthodox Church and the language of education in the church schools. Besides, Pankhurst (1976: 309) notes that parallel to the use of Ge'ez in the Orthodox Church, Arabic was used for religious and educational purposes in other parts of the country where Islam had spread.

Emperor Menelik II was the next monarch who further carried over Tewodros' efforts of nation building using Amharic as a unifying force. According to McNab (1989),

> A century after persistent conflicts, the Amharas were united under this Emperor, who around the second half of the 19th century subjugated the peoples speaking various languages in South Ethiopia. These conquests were carried out with a marked degree of brutality and led to the depopulation, the development of a slave trade, and the institution of a feudal system by the Amhara landlords who willingly incorporated some leaders of the subjected ethnic groups into the state so as to avoid potential conflicts.

Cooper (1976: 292) also states that by the early 20th century, Menilik, an Amhara from the southernmost part of the highlands, doubled the empire by annexing the areas to the south, west and east of Showa. He expanded his territory to a large extent making Showa, which was the southernmost part of the traditional Ethiopian Empire to become the centre and started to spread Amharic over the speakers of various other Ethiopian languages within the boundaries of this large empire. Like Tewodros, Menelik also used Amharic for writing his chronicles. Pankhurst (1976) notes that the Emperor Menilik took the first steps to create modern education, to establish the first school in his palace, where instructions in good manners, reading, writing, calligraphy, religion, Ethiopian history, law, (presumably in Amharic), and Ge'ez were given. In the first modern school, operated by the government, French, English, Italian and Arabic were studied, and reading and writing in Amharic were set as criteria to enrol in this school while there was no any Ethiopian language included in the list of subjects. French medium schools were later opened by the Alliance France. The introduction of printing, the publication of some books, and the printing of the Amharic newspaper *Aemero* 'the mind' in Amharic and the importation of some publications of the British and Foreign Bible Societies in several Ethiopian languages, as well as the use of

Amharic in the administrative affairs and in correspondences were features of the language policy (LPo) during Menilik's reign. The role of Christian missionaries during the time of Menilik was also significant. They spread education using French, Amharic and some of the local languages like Afan Oromo, but their trainees remained at the levels of clerks and interpreters (Pankhurst, 1976: 314-317).

The conquest of the Italian invaders by Menilik II's army, and the attempt to establish Ethiopia's national boundaries, was followed by a long period of attempt for national consolidation. After the end of Menilik II's rule in 1909, following a subsequent struggle for power, the process was carried forward by Emperor Haileselassie, during his regency until he was crowned Emperor. The national consolidation movement even continued till it was disrupted between 1935 and 1941 by the short lived Italian occupation of Ethiopia. In 1923, Haileselassie established a printing press, issued the first Amharic newspaper in his reign B*irhanenna selam*, literally, 'Light and Peace", and he made significant advances in education and literacy in Amharic (Pankhurst, 1976: 318,320).

In summary, the LPo of this era can be described as one of the development of Ge'ez, which like the other Ethiopian languages was a spoken language of its mother tongue (MT) group, favoured by the monarchs of Axum and was transformed into the privilege of a *lisane nigus* and played some role of a lingua franca after which it was reduced into writing. Then Amharic, which gradually developed into a written language, came to replace Ge'ez at the status of *lisane nigus* leaving Ge'ez to play the roles of a language of traditional literature and of religion and also played some role of a lingua franca. It was at the time of Tewodros' rising to power that Amharic was attempted to be used as a means of national consolidation in what is today Northern Ethiopia. But during the reign of Emperor Menelik II, Amharic spread over the garrisons of his army in what is today the southern part of Ethiopia where the army which was primarily ethnically Amhara settled. In all these periods, there was no evidence of any measure taken by the monarchs of the different times by design to impose Ge'ez or Amharic on the speakers of the other indigenous Ethiopian languages, to refer to the events as LP. From this it follows that there was LPo, i.e. language practice and language ideology, but there was no LP, an intervention by an authoritative body to influence or force other Ethiopian languages to change in favour of Ge'ez or Amharic. Hence the period is referred to as the Pre-LP Era.

The Imperial Era

The second half of the reign of Emperor Haileselassie is classified as the Imperial Era in the history of LPP in Ethiopia. In this study, even though the LP during the time of the Italian occupation (the five year unsuccessful attempt to colonise the country) had a feature of its own, it is treated within this Era. The Italian invasion of 1935 halted the educational progress, and changed the policy pursued so far by successive periods. In 1936, the Italians inhibited the privilege Amharic enjoyed, and determined that teaching should be in the main local languages of their six colonial administrative units: namely, Amharic in the Amhara administrative unit; Amharic and Afan Oromo in Addis Ababa; Tigrinya in Eritrea; Harari and Afan Oromo in Harari; Afan Oromo and Kefa in the administrative region they named "Galla-Sidama"; and Somali in Somalia, the Governor-General being empowered to establish the use of any other local language by decree (Pankhurst, 1976: 322). The Italian colonial LP is attested by many authors (Tekeste, 2006; Bahiru, 1991, to mention a couple of examples) to be part of its segregationist racial policy developed to suit their divide and rule strategy.

The Italian expulsion from East Africa was followed by the gradual inclusion of Eritrea in the territory of the Ethiopian empire in the form of a federation. Emperor Haileselassie reinstituted the education system and continued the national consolidation process using Amharic as a unifying language. Mohammed (2004: 1) describes the time as "...a historic moment for the re-birth of earlier local initiatives and a more vigorous approach to education, nation building and modernisation."

The Imperial Era corresponded to the beginning and flourishing of LPP studies in the world, which yielded a number of new notions and concepts in LPP, empirical knowledge about LP practices, and some theoretical studies in the new discipline, which seems to have influenced to some extent the Ethiopian LP of the time. Smith (2008: 217) notes that, "It was especially in 1941, after the end of the Italian occupation, that the LPo assumed a formalised role in the state- and nation-building projects of Haileselassie". This was also the time in which an explicit, written LP was promulgated for the first time in the country in the 1955 Revised Constitution. Later a LP central agency authorised to perform LP under the name 'the National

Amharic Language Academy', the first of its kind in the country, was instituted in 1972, (Negrit Gazeta, No. 79/1972), and explicit status planning activities were carried out for the first time. Influences from the theories and empirical studies of the time are reflected in the establishment of the Amharic Language Academy, the implementation of the LP by means of diffusing it through the school system and the mass media, etc.

The government was the main agent of LP in Ethiopia during the Imperial Era. The Amharic Language Academy was the central organ that was established to carry out LP by the government. But this institution was nominal and has produced nothing in its life. McNab (1988: 143-4) shows the lack of attention from the government in general or the emperor saying, "…The Academy had been established but did not have any professional staff apart from its Secretary General". Other agencies of LP during the time included the Haileselassie I Foundation and the different educational institutions. The Haileselassie I Foundation awarded prizes to outstanding works of Amharic literature. The modern schools that spread in the main centres of the provinces, the Faculty of Arts in the Haileselassie I University (HSIU), the only institution of higher learning in the country during the era, with a department for Amharic, and the Ministry of Education and Fine Arts (MOEFA) with its Division of Curriculum, the Education Materials Production Unit as well as the Department for Adult Education were promoting the LP of the time considerably. In this authoritarian system, people had no role at all in the language decisions. LP was formally endorsed by the nominal parliament but the actual decisions were of the Emperor (see Marcus 1994: 134). But implementation was by the various government organs. The National Amharic Language Academy itself was also proclaimed following the same procedure. But there were some private individuals who have tried to voice their ideas or to produce works that can contribute to the LP of the Era. Authors like Mersie Hazen WoldeKirkos, Teklemariam Fantaye, Haddis Alemayehu, etc. are the prominent ones.

The central document for the LP of the Imperial Era was the Revised Constitution of 1955, which had only a single statement of LP that stated that Amharic was the only national official language (NOL). Many questions were unanswered about the LP by this single short statement. Neither were details of the policy articulated in any other LP document. Of course one may infer from the range of LP practices, and from the implications in other documents that the goals of the LP were to build a strong modern nation united and consolidated under a single common language following the one-state one-language ideology; to spread Amharic language and its literature over the whole territory and to assimilate all other ethnic languages in the country towards it; and to maintain the purity of the language. Cooper (1976: 301) asserts in his statement that, "the spread of Amharic in Ethiopia is a clear example, unique in Africa, of the expansion of an indigenous national language, in a highly multilingual country, as a principal factor in national integration". Mohammed (2004: 1) on his part tries to show the concern of the Imperial government which assumed the country could disintegrate without a single language. He said,

> ... Since 1941, the Ethiopian government has made a series of attempts to create a national framework within which the society could develop towards a greater degree of cohesion and integration. It appears that for the bulk of the subsequent times, the official attitude was to discourage the development of multilingualism due to the apprehension that it might eventually lead to disintegration and political disunity...

According to Smith (2008: 217-8), making Amharic the national language was critical for consolidating central power and promoting the bureaucratic efficiency that Haileselassie desired as in the newly incorporated regions of southern, eastern and western Ethiopia, where most subjects were non-Semitic speakers and either Muslims or were practicing traditional religions. The Imperial LP was also characterised by the absolute discrimination of all the Ethiopian languages. It was led by the Amharic only policy which promoted, developed and spread only Amharic at the expense of all the other indigenous languages. "Other Ethiopian languages were never recognised, rather they were deemed to assimilate to Amharic", (Lema Aritty, cited by McNab, 1989). Smith (2008: 219), also asserts that, "In general, the LPo under Haileselassie fostered a strong sense of pride in Amharic among MT speakers of the language, who had privileged access to employment, unrestricted mobility and the resources of the state both at corpus planning and status planning of Amharic..." She cited Keller (1989), Boothe and Walker (1997), and Mekuria (1997) as noting that the other languages were suppressed, were proscribed to be taught or to be used for public purposes (Smith, 2008: 217).

So, the regime intended to promote the use, development and spread of Amharic as the sole national language, and as an emblem of Ethiopian nationalism. This has been pronounced as the objective in the proclamation issued by the regime to provide for the establishment of the Amharic Language Academy in 1972 which read as follows: "i) to foster the growth of the Amharic language; and ii) to encourage the development of Amharic literature" (Negarit Gazeta, No. 79/1972). Indeed the institutional support provided to promote the national language was also immense. They have been instrumental in defusing Amharic through the education system (McNab, 1984:5; Tesfaye & Taylor, 1976). The use of Amharic as the language of instruction in the literacy program, and as the major medium in the mass media, the widespread use of Amharic as the medium of communication in local businesses and industries, the spread of Amharic in the urban centres, the role Amharic played as criteria for entry into higher education, etc. have all played significant roles in defusing Amharic in all spheres of life throughout the country. All government administration, the mass media, the judiciary, etc. used Amharic as the sole language of communication.

Education is the most decisive institution in the spread of a LP. Following the declaration of Amharic as the national official language in the Constitution, the language in education policy was also changed in 1958/9 (E.C[46].), and Amharic replaced English as the language of instruction (LOI) at primary level of education following the Emperor's indigenisation policy of the education personnel, while English remained the LOI as of grade seven (at secondary and tertiary levels) (Tesfaye & Taylor, 1976: 373). Cooper (1976: 190) argues that, "The assignment of Amharic as universal elementary school medium will provide a powerful impetus to the spread of Amharic as increasingly larger proportion of children enter and complete elementary school". A literacy campaign entitled *yäfidäl särawit*, (in Amharic) literally meaning 'the army of literacy' was also proclaimed and implemented by an ad-hoc national committee in the medium of Amharic.

Another major means of diffusing Amharic was its use in the mass media. According to Cooper, "with respect to the languages

---

[46] E.C. indicates that the preceding year is in the Ethiopian calendar.

chosen for the governmentally operated mass media, Amharic is the language used most often in both the government press and radio, although there was some use of foreign languages, Arabic, English, and French, as well as some use of indigenous languages such as Afar, Somali, Tigre and Tigrinya" (Cooper, 1976: 190). The fact that some languages were given short air time to broadcast in the mass media owned by government does not reflect the government's recognition for the languages. It was simply a step intended to calm the resentment when it takes its highest form. Smith (2008: 219) offers evidence to this by saying:

> ...though there was a small opening in the late 1960s when four ethnic groups – Tigrinya, Tigre, Somali and Afar – began to be broadcast by government-owned radio stations, these were not real attempts to reinvent or redefine the content and nature of belonging to the Ethiopian nation-state. Significantly, the continued ban on the use of Oromo, with by far the largest group of any language speakers in the country, provides compelling evidence that this practice was not intended to allow a flourishing of cultural and linguistic identities.

McNab (1989) also reinforces the same view. She remarks that Amharic had 2 weekly and 4 daily newspapers and 7 hours of air time while only a few other languages whose speakers have strong rebel groups were given a short air time in the national radio (Tigrinya one hour, Somali, Afar, and Tigre thirty minutes each), and only Tigrinya had a newspaper.

The Imperial Era even used the Christian missionary organisations as agents for spreading its Amharic dominant LP. The proclamation issued a few years earlier prohibiting Christian missionaries to utilise languages other than Amharic in predominantly non-Amharic and non-Christian areas has turned the missionaries into a major agent of this assimilative policy (Cooper, 1976: 189; McNab, 1984: 4; 1989: 45; Negarit Gazeta, 1944).

As Cooper (1976: 190) noted, there is no doubt that the aim of the LP of the time was to spread the Amharic language. "In general, this review of the central government's activities with respect to language and language use suggests that government policy is consistent with the aim of promoting Amharic as the national language of Ethiopia". However, it had also the associated goal of assimilation, that of forcing all the other ethnic languages to shift towards the dominant language. Smith (2008: 219) says, "There was little doubt that Amharic hegemony was a critical pillar on which the Amharicisation policy stood".

Assimilating the various languages of the country towards Amharic was thus the aim of the LP of the period. This is verifiable from the fact that Amharic was proclaimed as the sole national official language with no mention of any other Ethiopian language in the 1955 Revised Constitution. The change of the official languages in Eritrea into Amharic, which during the colonial period were Tigrinya and Arabic, and the LOI and administration in the single institution of higher education in Eritrea into English and Amharic, respectively, (Negarit Gazeta, 1944, Decree 3, cited in Cooper, 1976a), also demonstrate the same. Several authors (Kapeliuk, 1980; Cooper, 1989; McNab, 1989, Cohen, 2000, Smith, 2008, etc.), characterise the strong measures taken by the Imperial Era to assimilate all other Ethiopian languages towards Amharic as 'Amharicisation'.

> ...It was no accident that Haileselassie became the great champion of a national language. Building a centralised and modern state required taking radical political steps to reduce the power of regional nobility and this was a primary accomplishment of his reign. However, it was not only his state-building vision, but his vision of a nation of Ethiopians that propelled Haileselassie towards Amharic. It was the package of policies systematically applied by the regime of Haileselassie, under the rubric of Amharicisation, and prominently including Amharic language acquisition, which explain the tremendous historical significance of language identity and language policy in Ethiopia (Smith, 2008: 216-7).

The assimilation of the Ethiopian languages into Amharic during the Imperial Era, labelled as Amharicisation created a supra-ethnic national identity to all citizens of Ethiopia. This means that Amharic, the most hegemonic and prestigious language of the country, which was the MT of one ethnolinguistic group, the Amhara, is taken as a supra-ethnic national language to represent the nation as a symbol. In this way, this policy of Amharicisation imposes the symbolic identity of Amharic on all citizens of the country. In short, to claim oneself as an Ethiopian one must manifest that he/she can speak Amharic proficiently. The imperial law which demanded that "foreigners must know Amharic 'perfectly, speaking and writing it fluently' in order to become Ethiopian nationals" (Cooper, 1976: 189) is good evidence to show that by the government policy citizenship is marked by the national language identity. That was why in those times when an individual in the non-Amhara areas of Ethiopia who spoke Amharic perfectly was often referred to as an Amhara, rather than his true ethnic background. This means that the assimilation turns the non-Amharas to Amhara, verified by their proficiency in Amharic.

The imperial urbanisation policy was one of the major strategies of promoting the assimilation of the Ethiopian languages and cultures towards Amharic.

> Amharic, then, was Ethiopia's most important urban language. It was claimed by the largest number of speakers...even in traditionally non-Amhara areas, there are urban centres in which substantial proportions of Amharic mother-tongue speakers were found. This means that throughout the country there are towns which can serve as agents for the diffusion of Amharic into the countryside surrounding them. (Cooper, 1976: 197-198).

The third goal of the LP during the Imperial Era was to purify the Amharic language from the pollution by elements of the other ethnic languages of the country. Citizens who learned it as a second language (L2) had to be proficient enough to the level they did not influence it. Quoting Lemma Arity, McNab (1989: 59) shows how this Amharic purification process affected speakers of other ethnic languages. "The superior-inferior culture concept was so intensely applied to the languages that it became a major factor of dehumanisation and subsequent alienation of groups speaking the non-official language. Children from the non-Amharic speaking groups were not only ashamed to speak their languages in public, but also changed their given names into Christian/Amhara names." In this manner, Amharic was fast spreading, becoming mainly the language of the educated and the urbanised. Bayleyegn (2002 (E.C.): 105), in his article on the history of the Ethiopian Language Academy, quotes a statement from the Academy of Ethiopian Languages (1986), as paraphrasing the idea contained in the order in the Negarit Gazeta,

No. 79, in 1972 to reinstitute the National Academy of the Amharic Language, as follows:

> ...we realise that in as much as Amharic language is the national language of Ethiopia, it is essential that this language while being faithful to its traditions and preserving its purity, should become a vehicle for the expression of the knowledge, learning and thought engendered by modern civilisation...There is hereby established an autonomous Public Authority having separate judicial personality to be known as the National Academy of the Amharic Language...

This clearly shows that the regime also aimed at working for the purification of Amharic from contamination by other indigenous languages. Note that the French LP was typical of this goal and as the Imperial government of Ethiopia had taken France as its role model, it had also adopted the same in its LP.

In general, linguistic pluralism was perceived as a threat to national integrity and development during this Era. The need to develop through modernisation, (modernisation is taken synonymously with westernisation) has influenced the directions of the monolingual LP of the country, which also used international language(s)- first French, then English (without undermining the role of Amharic which is realised by the growing use of Amharic in different domains, particularly in the official function in the government organisations and in primary education, and in the intention to scale it upwards).

Other studies, however, revealed that Amharic did not spread to the extent that was aspired by the regime. It was indeed far from what was expected. For instance, another survey carried out by Cooper, Singh and Abraha Ghermazion (1976: 222) on data gathered from both rural and urban areas on household use of language in two predominantly Oromo speaking areas of Jimma and Arsi revealed that people in urban areas speak largely Amharic as their first language, while in the rural areas Afan Oromo is the first language of the people. The urban centres were characterised by linguistic diversity with at least the local languages and Amharic, while the rural areas were characteristically linguistically homogeneous in the local languages. This suggests that the government LP is practiced in the urban centres while the practice by people in the rural areas is different from that of the government LP. To many of the rural people who speak either their ethnic language or who use another common indigenous language which is predominant in the area, Amharic was totally unknown by many of the rural population. For example, in a study conducted in 1965 by the Central Statistics Office in the Wolayta Soddo area in order to determine the extent of the Amharic spoken in the area, it was learned that out of the entire population of 597,371, which excluded the population of the main town Soddo, only 1.5 per cent could speak Amharic (McNab, 1984: 6). One could imagine how small the influence of Amharic was in the rural areas. This is particularly significant when we contrast the size of the rural population to that of the urban areas. The urban population of the country in 1967, according to a conservative estimate by the Ethiopian Statistical Agency in 1968 was about two million, which is about 8% of the country's total population (Cooper & Hovarth, 1976: 192).

Besides Amharic, international languages of wider communication (LWC) had significant places in the Ethiopian situation. According to the literature, since Ethiopia must use other than Ethiopian languages for the purpose of international communication, there have always been languages that served the country in this regard. During the height of the Axumite Empire, Greek appears to have served this function. During the decline of the Axumite Empire, the function was fulfilled by Coptic, and later by Arabic. Italian and French were the principal LWC used in Ethiopia later when greater communication was needed with the outside world. Finally the function was served by English (Cooper, 1976: 300).

Later during the Imperial Era, the role of French declined considerably and English took the role of a language of international communication and education in Ethiopia. "...English has a negligible number of native speakers in Ethiopia, but at the present time, it has a crucial position in education, commerce, government, and international communication, and from this point of view it can be regarded as a major Ethiopian language" (Bender, et al. 1976: 12). Even the educational textbooks published for England, and later for the USA were simply imported and used in the Ethiopian modern school system. English, which had replaced French during the Imperial Era, has had a significant position in the LP of the Empire. It played the role of the medium of international communication and international business, LOI at secondary schools and the university, and even as additional official language in some modern government institutions, such as the banks, communication and postal services, the Ethiopian Airlines, etc. It has also developed an elite class that is separated from the mass of the people (Cooper, 1976; Cooper & Singh, 1976; Cooper and King, 1976; McNab, 1984).

The Derg Period
As the revolution which brought the Derg[47] into the political forum started, the LP question was at the forefront. The regime had to address it as quickly as possible. Aware that the people's main demand is centred at the need for self-determination, the regime tried to halt the uprising by proclaiming the rights of people to use all the languages of Ethiopia in its Program of the National Democratic Revolution (Transitional Military Administration of Ethiopia, 1976) and in its Constitution (People's Democratic Republic of Ethiopia, 1987). The Constitution however, also declared that Amharic is the sole official language of the country, along with the recognition of the equality as well as the equal development of all the languages of the different nations and nationalities. But as in the previous Era, the aims of the LP in the Derg Period were not explicitly stated in any documents. They were not articulated in any LP legislation or in any published directive.

Cooper (1989) and Smith (2008) argued that the Derg had LP as a means of exerting control over the people. According to these scholars, the goal of the LP of the Derg was to get a temporary respite through appealing to the interests of the radical students, who were instrumental to oust the regime of Emperor Haileselassie and who had long supported the demand for ethnic self-determination. The regime saw that the vocal opposition of the radical students was a big threat for its strong desire to control power. So it articulated loudly that it stands for the self-determination of the nations and nationalities. Cooper asserts that the truth was that Derg was not willing to grant self-determination as proved by its successive acts. Rather, the regime was aware about the power of language in social control and exploited this by using its rhetoric and paying lip service to people's interests in

---

[47] The name Derg was used to refer to the regime by the military government of Colonel Mengistu as it came to power. The term literally means 'committee' in Amharic. Mengistu was the ring leader of the group of soldiers who organised themselves and took of the leadership of the popular revolution and filled the vacancy of power as there was no organised political organisation to lead the revolution during the time.

regard to language rights and making some cosmetic changes to win the hearts and minds of the people and particularly the radical students.

Thus, the centre of the LP of the Derg Period was the Mass Literacy Campaign (MLC), which was also considered as instrumental to disperse the radical opposing students from the centre. It was the major program in the educational reform of the period. Fifteen indigenous languages (including Amharic), were used as media of the MLC which is claimed to have covered about 90% of the population. Amharic, Afan Oromo, Tigrinya, Afar, Gedeo, Hadiyya, Kefa-Mocha, Kembata, Kunama, Saho, Silte, Sidama, Somali, Tigre, and Wolayta were the languages used in the campaign (see McNab, 1989: 57; Bender et al. 1976: 12). Orthography was developed for most of these languages on the basis of the Ge'ez script and basic literacy materials were produced. However, the use of the fourteen local languages was limited to the non-formal education, and only Amharic continued to be the LOI at primary schools, while English still served as the LOI at secondary and tertiary levels (McNab, 1984: 9). Ge'ez still remained the language of the Ethiopian Orthodox Church and Arabic served as a medium of Islam in some parts of the country, although they were under strong religious and cultural suppression.

Many of the MLC languages had not previously been written down, or had been transcribed using the Latin-based script by various missionaries or in some cases the Ge'ez-based script by Ethiopians who were serving the missionaries. The other major task undertaken was the elaboration of Amharic, so that it could fulfil its functions as the language of state and of primary education in a nation undergoing revolutionary change (McNab, 1988: 139). Bender (1985), states that the Derg followed much the same LPo as its predecessor in promoting Amharic as the official language of the country. Smith (2008) also describes it in much of a similar manner. She says:

> The Emperor's policy of Amharicisation has essentially been continued. While the rhetoric of the state's rulers has changed, the state's problems have remained. Or rather they have been exacerbated. The tendency towards fragmentation, normally found at the demise of an old regime, is found today. Not only were the new rulers faced with old problems of separatist rebellions by Tigres in Eritrea and Somali in the Ogaden, but they

were soon faced with new rebellions among Tigress in Tigray province and Afars in the Danakil and by the rekindling of Oromo rebelliousness in Bale Province...

Cooper (1989: 28) also agrees by describing the consistency between, on the one hand the regime's denial of true ethnic self-determination (which it accepts only rhetorically) and its attempt to exert central control over the multilingual empire that was created by the preceding regime, and on the other hand its adherence to the policy of Amharicisation promoted by the previous regime. Therefore from these we can realise that the second goal of the LP of the Derg regime was to perpetuate the assimilation of all other Ethiopian languages into Amharic, as did the previous Era in its Amharicisation project.

While the Derg LP is also assimilative, in that it forced all the Ethiopian languages to shift in favour of Amharic, it differs slightly in the way this process took place. The assimilation of the Ethiopian languages into Amharic during the Imperial Era, labelled as Amharicisation tried to impose a supra-ethnic Amhara national identity on all citizens of Ethiopia. In the assimilation policy of the Derg, however, while national identity is marked by Amharic, still a supra-ethnic symbol of identity, Amharic was not considered to be the language of any ethnolinguistic group in Ethiopia; it was taken just as the language of Ethiopia in general. That Amharic is no one's language was promoted with the help of the myths, first defined by the head of the regime, President Mengistu, that the term Amhara refers to any person living on a mountain, which may not necessarily be in Ethiopia. Thus people living on the Alps in Europe, Himalayas in India, Andes in Latin America or Kilimanjaro in Kenya are Amharas, just like people living on the highlands of Ethiopia. So an Ethiopian must be identified in the Derg Period by speaking the supra-ethnic language called Amharic, which belonged to no specific ethnic group. An individual who shifts into Amharic from any other ethno-linguistic group in Ethiopia will get the new identity of 'Ethiopian' through speaking Amharic. Hence the assimilation of the various languages of Ethiopia towards Amharic in the Derg Period is better labelled Ethiopianisation rather than Amharicisation.

Another major step in the LP of the Derg Period was transforming the former 'National Amharic Academy' into 'The Ethiopian Languages Academy' and transferring it from the MOEFA to the Ministry of Culture and Sports in 1971 E.C. (Ethiopian Language Academy 1986, cited in Bayleyegn, 2002 (E.C.):110). It had a council of intellectuals with members drawn from various organisations, more than seventy full-time professional members of staff in the secretariat's office, and some committees made up of members from academic and professional institutions like the HSIU. Later, another organ called the Institute of Nationalities was also organised. However, it is not clear from the reports to what extent the different sections of society, particularly the grassroots of the members of society have been involved in the LP activities. As the regime was suppressive of all kinds of religious practices, religious institutions could not have participated. Since it was an autocratic regime, it could be speculated that popular participation might not have been well realised. It was however true that the LP of this period involved a significant number of scholars from different fields of study.

The specified duties of the Academy included eradicating the weaknesses in the cultures of the people and building 'new popular cultures', conducting different researches on Ethiopian languages, developing the country's LPo, extending the studies of linguistics, documenting and studying the different oral literature, compiling the dictionaries of the different "significant" languages of Ethiopia, etc. The institution was rapidly expanded and resourced and its contributions in developing some of the local languages were considerable. The Academy had various outputs based on its short- and long-term projects.

The Academy had proposed improvements to the Amharic orthography and had carried out works on linguistics, oral literature, Ge'ez poetry (qine) and literature, translation and terminology. Orthography was developed for the languages Silte, Sidama, Kafa-Mocha, Afar, Ari, Gumuz, Agnuwa, Saho, Aan Oromo, and Harari. Some works were done on sociolinguistics. Grammatical descriptions of Hadiyya, Gumuz, Ari, Amharic, Gedeo, Harari, and Agnua were also carried out. Large corpora of oral literature of Oromo, Amhara, Tigray, Wolayta, Sidama, Hadiyya, so called Gurage, Kambata, and Gedeo were collected. Collections of Ge'ez poetry (qine) and biographies of famous Ge'ez scholars were published. The Dictionary of Marxist Leninist Terminology in Amharic and works on the compilation of 5 dictionaries of Afan Oromo, Tigrinya, Wolayta, Sidama and Amharic were started. A number of symposiums and conferences were organised and considerable research papers in the various areas of LP were presented and proceedings were compiled

(Bayleyegn, 2002 (E.C.: 110-112). Although the LP recognised the plurality of the country theoretically, this was not realised at all on the ground. All the cosmetic changes did not alter the state of assimilation of the indigenous languages of Ethiopia towards Amharic, which also prevailed during the previous era.

Among the indigenous languages Amharic, Afan Oromo, Tigrinya, Somali, Afar, Tigre and Harari were broadcasted on the Ethiopian radio from Addis Ababa, Harari and Asmara, while French, English and Arabic were also used in the mass media among the non-indigenous ones. A weekly Oromo newspaper, bariisaa 'down' started to be published in 1975. It had institutional provisions to support the LP activities, the main ones being the Institute of Nationalities, the Institute of Language Studies which is reinstituted in the Addis Ababa University from the former Ethiopian and Foreign Languages Departments of the Faculty of Arts of the HSIU, the reorganisation and strengthening of the Institute of Curriculum, the Educational Materials Production and Distribution Unit and the Department of Adult Education in the Ministry of education, and the different additional schools opened in some of the provinces.

During the Derg Period the world was divided into the two main camps of the Eastern Bloc and the Western Bloc. Ethiopia's relations with the Western bloc during the cold war period were reversed and a new relation with the Eastern bloc was started. Even though the use of English as a medium of international communication continued during the period, the government's new relations with the Eastern bloc resulted in some linguistic influences from the east. To enhance the regime's solidarity with several Eastern bloc countries, languages like Russian and German as well as some East European languages were used and taught to Ethiopians. This was further extended by the scholarship opportunities provided for more and more Ethiopians in the East European countries. Relations with the west deteriorated, and the American Peace Corps Volunteers Program was discontinued. Employment of expatriate teachers, which was reduced due to the indigenisation of the teaching personnel as a result of the shortage of resources during the previous era, was totally halted during this period. Despite these facts, however, English continued as the LOI from the secondary school on wards with a diglossic relationship with Amharic that used to be in the previous regime. But the frustrating situation in classroom communication and in the proficiency of teachers and students due to incompetence in

English increased even more during this era. Coupled with other changes in the education system which had the goal of orienting the system towards the communist ideology, the quality of education was negatively affected.

Language Planning During Post-Derg Ethiopia

Immediately after the overthrow of the Derg from power in May 1991, a four-day conference was held in Addis Ababa between the Ethiopian People's Revolutionary Democratic Front (EPRDF), the main rebel force that overthrew the regime from power, and a number of other organised rebel movements in the country. The central issue of the conference was to develop a Charter that was to govern a transitional period of three years just like a Constitution. According to this Charter the country came to have a federal state then named the Transitional Government of Ethiopia (TGE) which consisted of nine regional states and two chartered city administrations, basically divided on linguistic criteria. This Charter recognised the LRs of all the indigenous languages of the country but neither proclaimed specific NL nor allocated any language as OL for the country. Article 2a of the Charter stated it as follows: "The right of nations, nationalities and peoples to self-determination is guaranteed. Accordingly, each nation, nationality and people shall have the right to: ... maintain and to get its identity respected, to develop its history, as well as to use and develop its language" (TGE, 1984 E.C.). The LP exercise .during this short transitional period laid the basis for the current LP in Ethiopia, whose basic principles were later stipulated in the Constitution of the Federal Democratic Republic of Ethiopia (FDRE, 1995). Therefore, in this study, the LP during the transitional period is considered not as a separate LP period but as the first stage of the Post-Derg LP Period.

Based on the provisions of the Charter, a new education and training policy (ETP) was also declared by the TGE, and the acquisition planning (AP) of the period is governed by the provisions in the ETP. The ETP (MoE 1994: art 2.1.12) states that the objective of the policy is "to recognise the rights of nations/nationalities to learn in their language, while at the same time providing one language for national and another for international communication". Articles (3.5.1 – 3.5.8) state the stipulations of the policy as follows:

3.5.1. Cognizant of the pedagogical advantage of the child in learning in mother tongue and the rights of nationalities to promote the use of their languages, primary education will be given in nationality languages.

3.5.2 Making the necessary preparation, nations and nationalities can either learn in their own language or can choose from among those selected on the basis of national and countrywide distribution.

3.5.3 The language of teacher training for kindergarten and primary education will be the nationality language used in the area.

3.5.4 Amharic shall be taught as a language of countrywide communication.

3.5.5 English will be the medium of instruction for secondary and higher education.

3.5.6 Students can choose and learn at least one nationality language and one foreign language for cultural and international relations.

3.5.7 English will be taught as a subject starting in grade one.

3.5.8 The necessary steps will be taken to strengthen language teaching at all levels. (MoE, 1994)

According to the ETP, 8 years of primary education as well as teacher training programs for the level were to be given in the MT after the necessary preparations are made in each of them; Amharic was decided to be given as L2 for non-Amharic MT students in all regional states; and English is supposed to continue serving as the LOI as of secondary school and also to be given as subject starting from 1st grade. The ETP has also left some important questions unanswered. Issues like the LOI at kindergarten and at technical and vocational education and training (TVET) levels, and the level of education at which Amharic shall be started as L2 are not clearly spelt out. In reference to primary education, Heugh et al. (2007: 5) describes that, "... the current MoE policy of eight years of MT medium schooling is one of the best on the continent and promotes sound educational practice".

According to Boothe and Walker, 1997: 5, (cited in Smith, 2008: 222), a national referendum was to be held on the question of national official language (NOL). But later a constitutional assembly consisting of members of the different ethnic groups from all over the country was called by the TGE and the outcome was the new Constitution of the Federal Democratic Republic of Ethiopia (FDRE

1995). This Constitution declared that all the languages of the country have equal rights as far as the government is concerned and also provided for Amharic to be the OL of only the Federal government, at the same time decentralising the power to determine the OLs of the regions to the respective regional states. This is stated in article 5 of the Constitution as follows:

1. All Ethiopian Languages shall enjoy equal state recognition.
2. Amharic shall be the working language of the Federal Government.
3. Members of the Federation may by law determine their respective working languages. (FDRE, 1995: article 5)

According to this Constitutional article, therefore, there is no single language or a group of languages allocated NL status in the LP of current Ethiopia. Amharic as the OL of the Federal government serves in oral and written communications within all the federal institutions and the two city administrations of Addis Ababa and Dire Dawa, as well as among the regional states and the federal government. This language decision does not assign any symbolic function to the OL as it is limited only to this communicative function in the government. The provision in article 5 of the Constitution is further strengthened by article 39, which is stated as follows:

1. Every nation, nationality and people in Ethiopia has an unconditional right to self-determination, including the right to secession.
2. Every nation, nationality and people in Ethiopia has the right to speak, to write and to develop its own language; to express, to develop and to promote its culture; and to preserve its history.
3. Every nation, nationality and people in Ethiopia has the right to full measure of self-government which includes the right to establish institutions of government in the territory that it inhabits and to equitable representation in state and Federal governments. (FDRE 1995: article 39)

The Constitution has recognised all the languages in the country at equal status, accepting the linguistic plurality of the country at the same time dismissing the former view that a single NL serves a unifying role. It rather confirmed that recognition, respect and use of the indigenous languages were the guarantee for national integration.

Thus it follows that there is no more single Ethiopian NOL according to this Constitution.

Goals of the Language Planning

As it was the case in the previous periods, the LP of this period too had no specific LP document and lacked any explicitly specified LP goals. To understand the underlying goals of the LP of the period, therefore, one would need to examine actual LP exercises during the period and to refer to related documents to infer the goals from them. Thus, beside the Constitution (FDRE, 1995) and the Education and Training Policy (MoE, 1994), reference can be made to other basic government documents to deduce the goals of the LP of the period. From all these it is possible to deduce at least three basic goals of LP pursued in the current period: a) to realise the linguistic human rights of the citizens; b) to ensure the active participation of all members of the society in the political, economic, social and cultural life of the country; and c) to promote a mass education system (as opposed to the elitist system of education that used to be practiced) where all citizens get access to information and education through a language they command very well.

The federal policy document entitled Issues on the Development of a Democratic System in Ethiopia (Ministry of Information, 1994 E.C.: 151) states the following:

> All peoples have their own languages, cultures and history that identify one from the other. The languages, cultures and history of the Ethiopian people are the sum total of these nationality values which are the results of their interrelationship. No single group of people is superior or inferior from any other people; the behaviours and values that make the identity of the peoples must enjoy equal recognition and protection so long as it is accepted that all peoples are equal. Therefore, all the peoples will have equal rights to use and develop their languages. All the peoples have equal rights to expand and develop their cultures. All the peoples have equal rights to entertain and learn their histories. (translation is the researcher's).

From this, one can deduce that one of the main goals of LP of the Post-Derg Period should be to ensure the rights, including the language rights of the people. The necessary legal frameworks are in place in the form of a Constitution (FDRE, 1995) and other policy documents, such as the Education and Training Policy, (MoE, 1994) and the Cultural Policy (the Ministry of Youth, Sports and Culture, 1995 E.C.). Secondly, the institutional support to put these frameworks into practice is made available both at federal and regional levels and it is generally made part of the system already, though their efforts are not coordinated due to lack of centrally organised LP agencies.

The other policy document of the Federal government (Ministry of Information, 1992, E.C.: 29-30) emphasises the need for active participation of all the citizens in political, economic, social and cultural affairs of their country, and for them to be beneficiaries of the results of developments in each sphere. This is stated in the document in the following words:

> ...our task of building a democratic system requires one who has complete knowledge of his/her own rights and obligations, an educated citizen who has democratic thinking and culture and a professional who can manipulate adequately the democratic administrative institutions. In the same manner, our rural and agricultural development activities, our urban and industrial development activities, etc. also require a human resource that has been trained at different levels and has industriousness and discipline. The goal of our education and training program is to fulfil this. The centre of our development activities is also producing this type of human resource adequately and deploying it in the various development works. (Translation is the researcher's).

By implication from the fact that such communication cannot take place in a language vacuum, LP must serve the goal of enabling all individuals from all walks of life and from all the ethnolinguistic groups in the country to become active participants in the socioeconomic activities of the country.

In a multilingual community where most of the languages are marginalised access to education is open only to members of the community who have access to the dominant language. Thus education will remain the domain of a small elite group which has access to the dominant language and excludes members of the non-dominant language groups. But if mass education was required the LP must break the linguistic barrier in and outside classroom communication and create self-concept and self-esteem in the use of one's own language, as well as allow all the languages including the marginalised ones to enable access to education through them. The Ministry of Information (1992 E.C.: 34-5), highlights the claims of the government. "In this regard, we are making efforts with the view that primary education must be available to all citizens. Our construction of the democratic system will get to a reliable level when we have citizens who have full knowledge of our Constitution, understand their rights and obligations, and possess at least the level of primary education". The same document adds,

> ...The fact that the completion of primary education has been raised to two grade levels and that the education to be offered at this level is intended to attain highest level, starts from two basic reasons. First, primary education should be available to all citizens; and in order to do so primary schools should be constructed not only in towns but also in the countryside, in the Kebeles, and in the vicinities and as a result to do away with the condition that the largest majority of the citizens who have began primary education should not discontinue as it used to be before; and it also takes into account the fact that at the present level of our development the largest majority of the students cannot pursue their study above this level... (Ministry of Information 1992, E.C.: 43, translation is the researcher's).

Thus, this statement, coupled with the statement in the ETP (MoE, 1994), which states that primary education shall be offered in the MT, the government LP intends to realise mass education rather than an elitist one. One can therefore deduce from this that one of the goals of the LP of the period is to replace the elitist education system with a mass education system.

Status, Corpus and Acquisition Planning
Various status, corpus and acquisition planning activities have been carried out during the Post-Derg Period. LP in general was carried out

both at the federal and at regional, (including at zonal and *woreda*[48]) levels. This has been enhanced by the federal arrangement of the government and by the decentralisation policy pursued during this period. The lower government levels were authorised to give immediate decisions to the various issues that dealt with their regional, zonal or *woreda* affairs, including the LP under their jurisdiction. So each regional state decided the OL of its respective region and promulgated it in its own constitution. Accordingly, the regional states of Amhara, Benshangul-Gumuz, Gambella and the state of SNNPR determined Amharic as their regional OL. The Regional States of Oromia, Tigray, Somali, Afar and Harari chose the languages Afan Oromo, Tigrinya, Somali, Afar-Af, and Harari and Afan Oromo, respectively as their OLs. Some of the regional states have further decentralised the power to determine the OLs to some of the zonal administrations believed to have higher competence while abiding the use of regional OL during transactions outside their respective zones. In accordance to this provision, the Oromia Zone in the Amhara Regional State, as well as the zones of Sidama, Gedeo, Wolayta, and Kaficho, in the state of SNNPR chose the languages Afan Oromo, Sidama, Gedeoffa, Wolayta and Kafinoonno, respectively (for details see the regional constitutions including the Afar National Region 1994 E.C.; ANRS 1994 E.C.; Gambella People's National Regional State 1995 E.C.; Harari People's Region 1997 E.C.; NRS of Benshangul-Gumuz 1995 E.C.; Oromia National Regional Council 1994 E.C.; SNNPR 1994 E.C.; Somali National Regional State 1994 E.C.; and the TNRS, 1994 E.C.).

According to Bekale (2012) the state of Ormia is engaged in the works of standardising the technical terminology and the orthography of the OL. So far 35 languages (including Amharic, Ge'ez and Tigrinya which were already written languages) have already been reduced to writing with their own orthographies developed on the basis of the Ge'ez script or the Latin script. Many other regional states and zonal administrations within them are busy on works of lexicography and collection of oral literature in their OLs. Codification of the grammars is being carried out in Oromia and

---

[48] Zonal and *woreda* administrations are the lower levels in the hierarchy of government structure under the regional states. Each regional state is structured into several zones and each zone is composed of several *woredas*. Where the zones and *woredas* are of specific ethnic area such zones and woredas are named as special zones (or nationality zones) and special woredas, and are granted considerable autonomy.

Harari Regions, while universities with departments for linguistics and with language research centres are engaged in language descriptions. The notable one is the Addis Ababa University (structured under the Federal government) in its Department of Linguistics and in the Ethiopian Languages Research Centre (now renamed as the Academy of the Ethiopian Languages and Cultures) with focus on the grammatical descriptions of less studied Ethiopian languages and on the documentation of the languages that are threatened by extinction. The Summer Institute of Linguistics (SIL), an NGO engaged in works of linguistics makes contributions in some works of language descriptions and orthography development. The SIM mission is assisting financially as well as technically the compilation of Wolayta dictionary in the zonal administration.

At the level of the federal government the Ministry of Communications and Information Technology is promoting, developing and regulating IT uses in the different Ethiopian languages. It has so far developed softwares for standard computer keyboards in the Ge'ez script to be used by Ethiopian languages for IT. The Ministry had commissioned scholars to develop IT terminology for use in the Internet for Amharic, Tiginya, Afar and Somali. We now have cell-phone services that use some Ethiopian languages, like Amharic and Afan Oromo. These are new developments that seem to be enhanced and expanded to the other indigenous Ethiopian languages.

Following the stipulations in the ETP, among the languages having orthography as many as 29 indigenous Ethiopian languages including Amharic and Tigrinya are currently in use at primary level as LOI. These include Hadiyissa, Sidama, Silte, Shekinonno, Bench, Kambata, Kafinonno, Konta, Wolayta, Dawro, Qabena, Gamo, Gedeaffa, Afan Oromo, Gamo, Nuer, Agnuwa, Majang, Berta, Gumuz, Shinasha, Himtanga, Awgni, Argobba, Somali, Afar-Af and Harari. Some of these languages are also used as LOI or as subjects at the regional teacher training colleges. Afan Oromo, Amharic and Tigrinya have programs offering degree at several universities. Three other languages (Korette, Saho and Kunama) are introduced as subjects of study in the primary curriculum in their respective zones and *woredas*. Amharic is introduced as L2 to all non-Amharic medium schools and English is given as FL as of grade one for all schools in the country. In all the secondary schools and in the institutions of higher learning in the country, English has continued to be the LOI. In higher educational institutions, some programs of FLs have started in addition to English (such as the programs in French, Italian, German, Arabic, and Chinese in AAU).

The use of the indigenous languages in the mass media has been higher during this period, than ever before. According to records in 2009, from the Federal Government Communications Affairs Office (cited in Bekale, 2012), private press are working for the first time in the history of the country. In respect to the print media, there are 42 newspapers and 19 magazines (a total of 61 print outputs) with different themes (religious, sports and entertainment, health, business, social, cultural, and political) published by the private press with license at federal government level. Out of these one is monthly, six are weekly and one is daily (totally 8) while all the rest of the newspapers and the magazines are only monthly. All the private publications are in Amharic. Among the government press outputs at Federal level, the Ethiopian press agency publishes one newspaper each in Amharic, Tigrinya, Afan Oromo, English and Arabic, all established during the previous regimes. In addition one Amharic magazine is also published.

In respect to the broadcast media, each Regional State has air time in some TV channels and in radio broadcasts through the Ethiopian Radio and Television Ageny's stations in their respective OLs. The Ethiopian Radio and Television Agency itself broadcasts news, information and entertainment programs in Amharic, Afan Oromo, Tigrinya, Somali, Afar, Harari, French, Arabic and English in the TV, while it broadcasts in Amharic, Afan Oromo, Tigrinya, Somali, Afar, English, Arabic, and French in the radio. It also has FM radio broadcasts for audiences in Addis Ababa and the surroundings in Amharic. Government sponsored regional mass media agencies in the states of Amhara, Tigray, Oromia, SNNPR, and Harari also have FM radio broadcasts to audiences of their respective regions. Radio Fana, formerly possessed by the EPRDF has been licensed now as a share company and broadcasts programs in Amharic, Afan Oromo, Somali and Afar languages in its own radio station. It has FM radios also to Addis Ababa, Gondar and Bahirdar and their surrounding audiences in Amharic, also to audiences in and around Jimma in Afan Oromo. Recently, community radios are established in the different regional states, zones and woredas in the different parts of the country by government to broadcast programs of information, entertainment and education in almost all the indigenous languages including those which were hitherto never used in any press media.

Conclusion

This study has attempted to give a brief picture of the LPP in Ethiopia during the different periods of administration. It has revealed the different features of LPP in the country at different times. The development from the hegemonic Amharic monolingual assimilative LP of one-language-one-state ideology during the imperial Era to the perpetuation of the same with some reforms during the Derg Period to the basically pluralistic LP that respects the linguistic rights of all indigenous Ethiopian languages have been described. The study has shown the positive developments and achievements in the current period. However, this does not mean that the current LP is free of any problems.

In Bekale (2012) the key problems of the LP of the current period have been identified. The federal constitution has laid down the foundation for the LP of the present time based on basic democratic principles. However, the central problem of the current LP has to do with the lack of knowledge and skills in LP concepts, principles and theories by the experts in the organs of both federal and regional governments, who are also expected to offer professional advice to policy makers. As a result, most LP activities are carried out haphazardly, and without having any central LP agency both at federal or regional state level to coordinate, oversee, and regulate. So, the well formulated principles in the federal constitution show some failures sometimes at the implementation stage. Practices were sometimes inconsistent to the federal constitutional provisions and even to the ETP proposals. For instance, while the federal constitution has given equal recognition to all languages of the country, populous or non-populous, having written or oral tradition, in some of the regions some non-populous languages are not officially recognised as belonging to the particular region. According to the ETP the LOI at primary education level and at teacher training colleges was supposed to be the MT. However, in practice the MT is LOI at eight years or at complete primary education level only in three of the regional states, which includes the states of Oromia, Tigray and Somali. The rest have either four years of MT education (the states of SNNPR, Gambella, Afar, Benshangul and Gumuz), or six years of MT education (Harari State, DireDawa and Addis Ababa City administrations) or mixed

(MT and English) LOI in the Amhara Regional State. Other shortcomings are also available, but this overview is limited by scope to go further into more details. However, the prevailing general political and policy environment can be considered a great asset to potential positive developments of the LPP if properly exploited by language planners in the country in the future.

References

Afar National Region. 1994 (E.C.). *The revised Afar National Region constitution,* Addis Ababa.

ANRS, 1994 (E.C.). *The revised constitution of the Amhara National Regional State:* Addis Ababa.

Bahru, Zewde. 1991. *A history of modern Ethiopia, 1985-1997.* London, Athens and Addis Ababa: James Curry, Ohio University Press, Addis Ababa University Press.

Bayleyegn, Tasew. 2002 (E.C.). 'yä'ityoPiya q^{w}anq^{w}awocc akkadämi käyät wädä yät,' in Zena Lissan: *Journal of Ethiopian Languages Research Institute,* Vol.XXI, No. 1:94-122.

Bekale, Seyum. 2012. 'Linguistic pluralism and the challenges of government language planning in Ethiopia'. Unpublished PhD Dissertation, Addis Ababa University: Addis Ababa.

Bender, M. L., et al. (Eds.). 1976. *Language in Ethiopia.* London, Oxford University Press.

Cohen, Gideon P.E. 2000. *Identity and opportunity: the implications of using local languages in the primary education system of the SNNPR, Ethiopia.* Unpublished PhD Thesis, University of London.

Cooper, Robert. 1976 'The Spread of Amharic', in Bender, M.L. et al. (Eds.), 289-301.

_____.1989. *Language Planning and Social Change.* Cambridge: Cambridge University Press.

Cooper, Robert L., and B.N. Singh. 1976. 'Language and factory workers'. In Bender, M.L. et al. (Eds.), 264-272.

Cooper, Robert L., B.N. Singh, and Abraha, Ghemazion. 1976.'Mother tongue and other Tongue in Kefa and Arusi'. In Bender, M.L. et al. (Eds.), 213-243.

Cooper, Robert L., and Michael King. 1976. 'Language and university Students'. In Bender, M.L. et al. (Eds.), 273-280.

Cooper, Robert L., and Ronald J. Hovarth. 1976. 'Language migration and urbanisation'. In Bender, M.L. et al. (Eds.), 191-212.

CSA (Central Statistical Agency). 2010. *Summary and statistical report of the 2007 population and housing census*, Addis Ababa.

Department of Geography, n.d. 'Introduction to the geography of Ethiopia'. Unpublished teaching material, AAU,

FDRE. 1995. *Constitution of the Federal Democratic Republic of Ethiopia*. Addis Ababa.

Gambella People's National Regional State. 1995 (E.C.). *Revised constitution of the National Regional State of Gambella*.

Harari People's Region. 1997 (E.C.). *The revised constitution of the Harari People's Region*.

Heugh, Kathleen, et al. 2007. 'Final report, study on medium of instruction in primary schools in Ethiopia' (Commissioned by the Ministry of Education), Unpublished.

Hetzron, Robert, and Bender, Marvin L. 1976. 'Language policy in Ethiopia', in Bender, et al. (Eds.): 23-33.

Kapeliuk, Olga. 1980. 'Language policy in Ethiopia since the Revolution of 1974'. *Asian and African studies*, 14: 269-78.

Marcus, Harold G. 1994. *A history of Ethiopia*. Berkley, Los Angeles, London: University of California Press.

McNab, Christine. 1984. 'From traditional practice to current policy: The changing patterns of language Use in Ethiopian education'. *Proceedings of the 8th International Conference of Ethiopian Studies*, Addis Ababa, 26-30 November.

_____.1988. 'The Application of language planning theory to language planning practice in Ethiopia'. *Proceedings of the 19th International Conference of Ethiopian studies*, Vol. 3:139-151.

_____.1989. 'Language policy and language practice: Implementation Dilemmas in Ethiopian education', Unpublished PhD Dissertation, Institute of International education, University of Stockholm.

Ministry of Information. 1992 (E.C.). *The FDRE implementation capacity building strategy and program*. Addis Ababa, Mega Printing Enterprise.

_____.1994 (E.C.). *Issues about the development of democratic system in Ethiopia*. Addis Ababa, Mega Printing Enterprise.

Ministry of Youth, Sports and Culture. 1995 (E.C.). *Cultural policy of Ethiopia*, Addis Ababa.

MoE (Ministry of Education). 1994. *Education and training policy.* Addis Ababa.

Mohammed Habib. 2004. 'Issues and trends in the development of language policies of the Ethiopian government since 1941'. In *Proceedings of the 15th Annual Conference of the Institute of Language Studies*: 1-5.

Negarit Gazeta, No 79. 1972. Proclamation to provide for the establishment of the National Amharic Language Academy: Addis Ababa.

NRS of Benshangul-Gumuz. 1995 (E.C.). *Revised constitution of the National Regional State of the Benshangul-Gumuz.*

Oromia National Regional Council. 1994 (E.C.). *The revised constitution of the Oromiya Region.*

Pankhurst, R. 1976. 'Historical background of education in Ethiopia', in Bender, M.L. et al. (Eds.). 305-323.

_____.1969. 'Language and education in Ethiopia: Historical background to the Post-War Period'. Unpublished essay, HSIU, Addis Ababa.

People's Democratic Republic of Ethiopia. 1987. *Constitution of the People's Democratic Republic of Ethiopia*, Addis Ababa.

Smith, Lahra. 2008. 'Politics of contemporary language policy in Ethiopia'. In *Journal of Developing Societies*, 24,2: 207-247.

SNNPR. 1994 (E.C.). *The revised constitution of the SNNPR.*

Somali National Regional State. 1994 (E.C.). *The revised constitution of the Somali National Regional State.*

Spolsky, Bernard. 2004. *Language policy.* Cambridge: Cambridge University Press.

Tekeste, Negash. 2006. *Education in Ethiopia: From crisis to the brink of collapse*, Uppsala: Nordiska Afrikainstitutet.

Tesfaye, Shewaye, and Taylor, Charles V. 1976. 'Language curricula'. In Bender, M.L. et al. (Eds.), 371-399.

TGE, 1984 (E.C.). *Charter of the transitional government of Ethiopia*, Addis Ababa.

TNRS. 1994 (E.C.). *The revised constitution of the Tigray National Regional State.*

Transitional Military administration of Ethiopia. 1976. *The program of National Democratic Revolution.*

Zelealem, Leyew. Forthcoming. *The nexus in the Ethiopian language policy: A typological overview.* AAU, Addis Ababa.

Chapter 9
An Overview of Sudan Language Policy and Planning
Abdelrahim Hamid Mugaddam

This paper gives an overview of Sudan language policy and planning. Efforts made to address the problem of language in Sudan will be the main focus of the paper. We discuss the problem of language in two different periods: colonial period and the post-colonial one. Language of education, arabicisation of education and the status of indigenous Sudanese languages are among the issues specifically addressed by this paper. A number of efforts made by Sudan's successive governments to organise the use of language/languages in different domains will also be reviewed. The paper emphasises on the prolonged debate on Arabicisation between scholars and decision makers in the North and the South. The paper concludes that indigenous languages in Sudan (North and South) will remain marginalised and that Arabic will maintain its dominance in the North while English will gradually assume the role of a hegemonic language in the South.

Introduction

In the last two decades of the 20th century a number of very important world events have thrust language planning into prominence: the collapse of the former Soviet Union and the unification of the multilingual Europe. In both cases feelings of language loyalty have aroused in a number of countries, presupposing the creation of a well-formed language planning to cater for the new linguistic situation. According to Kaplan (1995), language planning has often been viewed as a sort of monolithic activity, designed primarily to account for one specific kind of linguistic modification at a particular point in time. This conceptualisation assumes the development of one dominant language at the expense of many other languages. The ideal situation should be considering a wide range of languages for modifications and development. Language policy and planning can be at a pan-national, national, regional or local level. Cooper (1982) provides a comprehensive account of language planning and policy in terms of" who does what, for whom, when, where, how and why". Kaplan (1995), on the other hand, outlines various stages in language planning activities together with some complexities on implementation. Fishman (1991) and Phillipson (1992), on the other hand, have emphasised the influence of social, economic and political dimensions on language planning and policy.

However, for almost two decades language planning has been presented as a cure-all for culturally and linguistically diverse communities in the developing African, Asian and other non-western countries (Kachru, 1996). The term was over used and its applications were exaggerated. But this tendency was not shared by all; some practitioners were quite conscious of the limitation of the claim and complexity of the task. This attitude, according to Kaplan (1995), has played a substantial role in reassessing and re-evaluating the earlier claims. This results in a better understanding of the linguistic, political, social, and attitudinal constraints on language policy formation. Kachru (1996) argues that language planning efforts share the following generalisations:

First, the main concern is for learning and teaching a language of a wider communication: a language that can go far beyond political and linguistic boundaries providing its users with a neutral code (e.g. English).
Second, the language of a wider communication sought is in most cases a nativised colonial one.
Third, slogans such as unification and national identity usually result in de-emphasising minority languages (as in Asia, Africa, Australia and the U.S).
Fourth, in addition to issues relating to language of education and lingua franca, the area of concern also includes language standardisation, developing specialised registers and providing acceptable technical terminologies.
Fifth, there is no general consensus as to the application of western notions of language planning to third world countries.
Sixth, in most multilingual countries there is an interesting love-hate relationship between the languages served by the language policy and speakers of minority languages.

One might add to the above generalisations the fact that the choice of an indigenous language to assume the position of the national language in a multilingual country is very difficult if not impossible. This is true even in the countries where one language is spoken as a lingua franca by a vast majority of the population. The choice of a given language in such a case may not be accepted by speakers of the remaining languages. This is the situation in Ethiopia, where Amharic used to be the official language during the Amharic' political domination before the 1973-1974 revolution (Scotton, 1983).

Amharic became dominant for political and historical reasons. The hegemonic situation of Amharic was as the only official language in Ethiopia opposed by a number of ethno-linguistic groups in Ethiopia.

A similar problem is found in Sudan where about 120 languages are spoken with Arabic dominating all aspects of communication. Ethnic differences in the country might bring into question the suitability of the language for assuming the role of the official language as stated in Addis Ababa accord of 1972 and the 1973 Sudan constitution. This rather complex situation presupposes a prior existence of a clear language policy to cater for the linguistic and cultural diversity of the country. Unfortunately, such a policy is lacking in the minds of the country's decision-makers. Although the 1973 Sudan constitution clearly states that Arabic is the official language of The Republic of the Sudan, it gives no attention to the necessity of establishing a coordinated language policy capable of addressing the present and future status of the remaining Sudanese languages. Organisations and academic institutions like the *Academie Française* or The National Swahili Council have no equivalents in Sudan. One more problem with language policies in Sudan is that they are concentrated in the southern part of the country. Very little attention was given to the language situation in the north. Even within that context, all efforts were made on the language of education and the 'national language, should it be Arabic, English or a Sudanese language. Such arguments were initiated in the first place by Southern intellectuals who believe that the South has its unique cultural and linguistic heritage that should be given a very special consideration (will be discussed in details in the following sections).

To give a clearer picture about Sudan language policy, it would be convenient to discuss the issue in two periods during which the problem of language received special attention: the colonial period and the post-colonial one.

The Colonial Period
Historically speaking, the British colonial authorities were the first to adopt a well-defined language policy in Sudan (Abu Bakar, 1995). The main objective sought by the British was to suppress the spread of Arabic language and culture in Sudan in general and the South in particular. To achieve this, the British tried very hard to adopt English as an official language in both southern and northern parts of Sudan

besides selecting some local languages to develop and use instead of Arabic in the South. During this period a number of measures were taken to hinder the spread of Arabic language and culture in the South. Among these procedures are:

The Rajaf Language Conference

This conference was organised by The International Institute of African Languages and Cultures (now International African Institute) in 1928 in London. A number of linguists, politicians and policy makers were invited to discuss the possibility of adopting a unified orthographic system in writing the languages spoken in South Sudan (Abu Bakar, 1995). The main objective of the conference was to consolidate and promote local languages so that they should assume a significant role in the different patterns of language use and subsequently suppress the ongoing spread of Arabic language and culture. The conference came out with some recommendations the most important of which is that all languages in South Sudan should be written in Roman scripts. The conference also recommended that Juba Arabic be written in Roman scripts in order to be used in different domains. Six languages: Shilluk, Dinka, Nuer, Bari, Latuka and Zande were chosen for development in order to function as media of instruction in the Southern schools. These languages were to be introduced in the first two years of education with English taught as a subject. When students reached grade three, they would use only English as a medium of instruction (Abu Bakar, 1975). In summary, the following measures were taken to further enhance the new language policy:
1. Local vernaculars should be used as media of instruction in the first and second years of primary education in the South.
2. English should be taught as a subject in the first and second years of primary education in the South.
3. English should be the medium of instruction right from the third year of primary education.
4. Arabic should not be used as a medium of communication in education and official transactions.
5. Non-Arabic speaking individuals should be employed in the public services.

6 Arabic-speaking employees should be dismissed from their post and replaced with native southerners.

The Creation of No-Man's Land
The second measure taken by the British to impede the spread of Arabic language and culture was the creation of what is known as 'the no man's land'. This measure was meant to isolate the Southern people completely from any kind of contact with the Arabic-speaking communities. To this end, southern tribes were forced to desert their neighbouring Arabic-speaking tribes and resettle southwards.

The Closed Districts Ordinance of 1929
To further reinforce the intended isolation of the South from the influence of Arabic language and culture, a rule called 'The Closed Districts Ordinance' was made. The rule strictly prohibited northern Sudanese citizens from entering the South and the Nuba Mountains without a prior permission from the British authorities. According to Mahmud (1983), this rule failed to achieve its intended goals because of the contradictory nature of the British policy in the area. Whereas the British were trying everything possible to stop the spread of Arabic in the South, their economic policy created bilateral economic ties between the Southern tribes and their northern counterparts. The transformation of the economy to a capitalist one caused Southern producers to export their products to the nearest markets in the north. In this case there would be no more choices for southern producers better than dealing with the Arabic-speaking merchants through the Arabic language.

Despite all these efforts the British failed to suppress the spread of Arabic in the South in the way they planned. As a result, they abandoned the 'Southern Policy after 1945 adopting a new language policy with a high level of consideration for the unique situation of Arabic in the South and Sudan as a whole. The new policy was executed in 1949 when the legislative assembly passed a resolution calling for the adoption of Arabic as the official language of The Republic of Sudan. As a result, there had been two distinct media of instruction in the South. First, use of local languages in grade one and grade two with English and Arabic as subjects. Second, use of Arabic as the medium of instruction in grade one with English as a subject starting from grade five.

The Post-Colonial Period
When Sudan gained its independence in 1956 the problem of language had occupied a wide area of discussion among politicians and educational authorities. The debates focused on the issue of the national language and arabicising the language of education all over the country. In this period local languages and cultures were totally ignored. As a direct result of this policy anti-Arabic language and culture campaigns evolved among vernacular speaking communities in the South. In 1969 the government called a conference to discuss the future of education in the Sudan (The National Conference for Education) resulting to the following recommendations (Abu Bakar, 1995):

1. Instruction in Arabic should commence immediately in the schools located in cities and villages characterised with linguistic diversity in the South.
2. Local languages written in Arabic scripts should be used as media of instruction alongside with Arabic in grade one and grade two.
3. Local languages should be studied and developed in order to maintain the country's linguistic and cultural heritage.
4. Establishing national boarding schools in which students from all over the country could be enrolled.
5. Arabic should be introduced gradually in the English medium schools so that students' academic performance would not be affected negatively.
6. More efforts should be made to train and qualify Southern cadres to teach Arabic in their native lands.

Another serious step towards adopting local languages was made in accordance with the declaration of June 9th, 1969 on the regional autonomy of the South. The minister for The Southern Affairs asked Dr. Yousif Al-khalifa Abu Baker to study the possibility of promoting one of the local languages to function as the national language for the South (Abu Bakar, 1975). It was difficult to choose a certain language to assume the role of the national language in the South as it required clear answers to difficult questions such as which language to select and why? Would speakers of other languages accept it? How would the social, economic and educational consequences be like? The problem became even worse as every language group believed that its language was the best candidate.

Although the problem of the national language has been settled by the 1973 Sudan constitution and the Addis Ababa agreement which stipulate that Arabic is the official language of the country as a whole and English is the principal language in the South, voices calling for a national language for the South were heard among the Southern intellectuals. Sir Anai Keludjang (cited in Mahamud, 1984) argued that whereas Addis Ababa agreement solved the political problem of the south, it did not offer any solution for the cultural one embodied in the question of the national language. He believes that the southern people were purely African with their own African cultural heritage that should be represented with an African Language. The most appropriate language to do the job, according to Keludjang, was Swahili because it was a well-developed international language. Some Southern intellectuals then viewed Arabic as a real threat to their own languages and cultures. They believe that the Arabic speaking southerners would behave like Arabs, think in Arabic and subsequently lose their cultural identity. Such views ignore the fact that Arabic is the lingua franca of the southern people used by a vast community in the South.

By the year 1974 Southern intellectuals became even more interested in the problem of the language of education. This time local languages were excluded from the discussion and the debated issue was whether to adopt English or Arabic as the medium of instruction in the educational system. The candidature of English appeared during the Regional Popular Council proceedings when Jusho Oudyo, a member of the council, proposed the reintroduction of English as the language of education in all southern schools starting from the school year 1974/1975. This was because, according to Oudyo, the adoption of English as the language of education in the South would help implement one of the very important resolutions of Addis Ababa agreement that 'English is the principal language of the South.' Since education is an official domain, adopting English in it as a medium of instruction, according to Oudyo, was a practical step in implementing the agreement. In addition, a better level of education could be guaranteed through English as it was associated with science and modern technology.

As for the Southern voices calling for the introduction of Arabic as the language of education in the South, their arguments were based on the linguistic situation in the South and the legal interpretation of the Addis Ababa agreement. The language situation suggests that Arabic is the lingua franca of all Southern language groups, which makes Arabic a very difficult figure to ignore especially in the context of education. Lawrence Lowal Lowal, a prominent Southern politician, argued that more than 75% of Southern children would prefer Arabic as the language of education because they started their education in Arabic and were more familiar to it than English. If English was reintroduced in the schools, Lowal continued, the children would be deprived of good education because their English would be too poor to enable them receive knowledge in it. Furthermore, the adoption of English as the language of education in the South would be an explicit violation of Addis Ababa agreement that clearly states that: "Arabic is the official language of the Sudan and English is the principal language in the South". Any violation of this kind would seriously damage the relation between the South and the North (ibid).

Since the Addis Ababa agreement in 1972 no serious step was made in connection with the problem of language till 1989 when the National Dialogue Conference for Peace was held in Khartoum. Although the conference's prime objective was to find a peaceful solution to the ongoing conflict in the South, it did not ignore the language problem in Sudan in general and the South in particular. A significant consideration was given to local vernaculars as evident in article 27 of the recommendations which highlights the following points:

1. Whereas the Federal Government is responsible for the educational policy, the cultural diversity of the country should strictly be considered when dealing with related questions.
2. The historical role of Arabic as a lingua franca for a considerable number of Sudanese ethnic groups and as an official language for the country as a whole should not be ignored in the educational system.
3. The role of English as a language of a very special status should also be given its due consideration.
4. Local languages can be used as media of instruction in the first year of primary education.

The government's concern for local languages was once again expressed with the approval of the ordinance of the National Council for language planning by the Cabinet of Ministers as well as the National assembly in 1997. The main objective of the council is to find an effective answer to the problem of language in the Sudan with special focus on the position of local languages. This requires that decision makers should deeply understand the problem of language and the significant role local languages play in enriching the country's linguistic and cultural heritage. To this end, the council should have the necessary fund and qualified cadres that help it carry out its assigned mission more conveniently.

Arabicisation of Education in Sudan
The prime objective of any government in a multilingual country is to achieve national integrity at both economic and social levels. Education, its content and language is considered one of the most important factors influencing the national cohesion in any given community. This necessitated the establishment of a well-formed educational policy that directly addresses these issues in order to consolidate the country's social and political unification. Again, such a policy does not exist in Sudan to organise the use of Arabic and other local languages in education as well as other aspects of life. There has been some sort of linguistic chaos: Arabic was used as the language of instruction in the schools and English was used in university education. Sometimes, in the south, both languages were used as media of instruction in schools interchangeably.. This situation continued for a long time despite the fact that Arabic was recognised explicitly as the official language of Sudan by Sudan's permanent constitution of 1973 and Addis Ababa agreement of 1972.

According to Hurreiz (1984), the first call for arabicising the language of education was made in 1955 when The International Committee for Secondary Education recommended the use of Arabic as a medium of instruction in secondary schools. The committee's main task was to find a way in which the decline of students' academic performance could be stopped. After long discussions it recommended immediate Arabicisation of education in secondary schools. This was because, according to the committee, students would understand subjects when taught in the language they master pretty well. However, no practical step was taken to implement this recommendation. Nevertheless, efforts aiming at Arabicising secondary education continued till 1965 when the first Conference for Secondary Schools Teachers was held in which a very strong decision was made concerning Arabicising the language of education in secondary schools. The conference made it clear that Arabic should be used as the medium of instruction in secondary education effectively from June 1965. To guarantee a positive response from the Ministry of Education, the conferences threatened that they would boycott the Secondary School Certificate Final Examinations. As a result, ministerial directives came out approving the implementation of Arabicisation as proposed by the conference. Not so much care about the possible drawbacks and problems of such an abrupt decision relating to timing, teacher training and textbooks was given.

Shortly after the implementation of Arabicisation at secondary schools, people started talking about doing the same thing in higher education as an essential step towards strengthening the country's national sovereignty. The first call in this regard was expressed in an essay written by Dr. Mansour Khalid who urged the Ministry of Education to think about Arabicising university education and the importance of planning for it as quickly as possible (ibid). The call was reinforced by the vice chancellor of the University of Khartoum in the opening sessions of 'The English Teachers Conference' in 1966. The vice chancellor focused his speech on Arabicisation and the expected problems upon implementing it such as the lack of qualified teachers using Arabic as the medium of instruction and the scarcity of Arabic references and textbooks. In 1970 the Ministerial and Technical Committee of the University of Khartoum held a conference in which the problem of Arabicisation was discussed thoroughly. The conference concluded that there was no reason for using English as the language of instruction in the university. Something serious should be done to put things in the right way. After long discussions and debates, the conference forwarded the following recommendations (ibid):

1. Arabic should be adopted as the language of instruction in the university and no other language is allowed to be used without a prior permission from the University Senate.
2. The university should work in collaboration with the Arab universities in order to find effective answers to the problems of references, textbooks, and teacher training.

3. A living language should be introduced as a subject so as to help students with their research work.
4. Arabic should be the university official language by translating all university regulations and principles into it and by using Arabic as the language of communication in the university senate meetings as well as the other academic and administrative committees.

Unfortunately, according to Hurreiz (1984) none of the issues recommended by the committee found its way to implementation due to several reasons including delay and hesitation. Nevertheless, debates on Arabicisation continued and committees were formed to find out the best ways for adopting Arabic as the language of instruction in the university. Among these committees was the one formed by the Faculty of Arts in 1976. Besides studying the possibility of arabicising the language of instruction, the committee was asked to prepare a detailed report about the departments that could be Arabicised, the effects of Arabicisation on students' academic standard, and to review the similar experiences attempted in the Arab world. The committee went on with its proceedings for days during which different views and arguments were discussed openly and a number of recommendations were forwarded. In addition to these efforts, a ministerial decision was signed in 1980 concerning the formation of a national committee for Arabicisation. Again, no practical advance was made regarding the implementation of Arabicisation in higher education.

In 1990 a presidential decree was signed stating that Arabic should be adopted as the language of instructions in all universities and institutions of higher learning starting from the academic year 1990/1991. The decision was implemented as scheduled without any concern for problems such as securing Arabic references and textbooks, teacher training and possible strategies and procedures of implementing Arabicisation effectively. However, a special committee of Arabicisation was formed purposely to provide universities and institutions of higher learning with Arabic references and textbooks covering all fields of social and applied sciences.

In 2005 a new language policy came into being as part of the comprehensive Peace Agreement (CPA) signed by the North and South. The language issue was included in one of the protocols entitled power sharing. Five important statements addressing the language problem have been stipulated:

- Arabic is the widely spoken national language in the Sudan,
- Arabic is a major language at the national level, and English shall be the official working language,
- All the indigenous languages are national languages which shall be respected, developed and promoted,
- In addition to Arabic and English, the legislature of any sub-national level of government may adopt any other national language(s) as additional official working language(s) at its level,
- The use of either language at any level of government or education shall not be discriminated against.

The CPA statements on language suggest that all Sudanese languages are granted the status of languages, their speakers are free to use in whatever domain, and protected against any sort of discrimination. This means that all Sudanese languages have the right to survive and flourish. But, in practice one can seriously question the vitality of these statements. While the agreement explicitly emphasises the importance of the Sudanese languages and their right to survive, it keeps silent on the strategies and procedures necessary for making this a reality.

Now, six years later the agreement the agreement regarding the language issue has not been implemented. The South has seceded with more than fifty languages of the former united Sudan and the situation remains as it is - dominance of Arabic in the north and empowerment of English in the South. In March 2012 a conference on language in education was organised by the British Council in Juba. Scholars from all Anglo-phone Africa were invited to discuss the issue of mother tongue education with special reference to South Sudan. One of the striking recommendations made is that children in South Sudan will receive education in their mother tongues with English as a subject up to grade four. From grade five up to university level, English will be the only medium of instruction. All indications suggest that English is going to be the language of education in the South instead of Arabic. This means that the situation remains as it used to be, dominance of English and marginalisation of Southern languages leading to their ultimate demise in the near future. This will seriously question the thesis that Arabic is used as a tool for killing the indigenous languages and cultures of the South, which was regarded as one of the strongest reasons for the long war between the South and the North.

Conclusion

This paper reviews the language policy and planning in Sudan. Issues of Arabiciation, language of education and the different efforts made by the governments to solve the problem of language were discussed. While the general tendency in northern Sudan was to empower Arabic, voices in the South strongly called for the maintenance of indigenous languages. The opposing views to Arabic emphasised the issue of marginalisation of other languages and cultures in favour of the mainstream language policy of the successive governments in Khartoum. The paper concludes that Arabic will continue its dominance in the North as no practical steps were taken to cater for the remaining languages while English will assume a similar hegemonic role in the South, given the new language policy adopted after the 2012 Juba conference.

References

Abu Bakar, Y. 1995. Elsiyasaat aluqawija filsudan. *Majalat Dirassat Ifriqqiya* 12: 125-152.

Abu Bakar, Y. 1975. Language and education in Southern Sudan. *Direction in Sudanese Linguistics and Folklore*. Khartoum: Khartoum University Press.

Cooper, R. 1991. A Framework for the study of language spread. Bloomington: Indiana University Press.

Fishman, J. 1997. *"What do you lose when you lose your Language"*. Centre for Excellence in Education, Stabilisation of Indigenous Language.

Hurreiz, S., H. 1964. Linguistic diversity and language planning in the Sudan. *African Research Seminar, Sudan Research Unit*.

Kachru, B. 1986. The power and politics of English. *World Englishes* 5: 121-140.

Kaplan, R., B. 1995. Iceberg tips and first steps: A call to action. *TESOL MATTERS* 9:16-26.

Mahmoud, U. 1983. *Arabic in Southern Sudan: History and spread of a Pidgin-Creole*. Khartoum: FAL Advertising Co.Ltd.

Mahmoud, U. 1984. Didd altcrib. A paper presented to the first International Linguistics Conference. IAAS. Khartoum, 13-17 October.

Miller, C., & A. Abu Manga. 1992. Language change and national integration: *Rural Migrant in Khartoum*. Khartoum: Khartoum University Press.

Phillipson, R., and Skutnabb-Kangas T. 1986. Linguistic human Rights and English in Europe. *World Englishes* 5: 27-43.

Scotton, C., M. 1983. The Negotiation of identities in conversation: a theory of markedness and code choice. *International Journal of the Sociology of Language 44*: 81-118.

Perspectives for Cameroon

Chapter 10
Towards a National Language Policy for Cameroon
Blasius A. Chiatoh and Pius W. Akumbu

> If language constitutes a fundamental defining feature of human existence, then it means that a country's language policy options signal the development orientations established for that country. Accordingly choosing between foreign and indigenous languages directly implies choices between development and underdevelopment. In this light, the underdevelopment of Africa crucially hinges on the inappropriate choice of language policy adopted at independence or the failure to ensure the implementation of those considered to be significantly appropriate. In Cameroon, the case is clear. Despite the country's rich linguistic diversity, we have continued to implement a language policy that is based on foreign languages that falls short of responding adequately to the needs and aspirations of citizens. At this historic moment of reunification commemoration, the demands of a thorough review of this policy are enormous and their implications far-reaching. The need for an integrative policy, in fact, one that carefully considers the country's socio-cultural and political landscape is not only real but also urgent.

Introduction

Linguistic complexity plays an important role in the formulation of a language policy for a country. Admittedly, language policy formulation is less challenging in countries with less complex linguistic landscapes. Cameroon's situation can effectively be described as a complex situation par excellence. The country plays host to about 248 languages, a majority of which are minority languages with less than 10,000 speakers each. This makes the task of choosing a national language policy an extremely challenging one. Faced with this complexity, the country has since reunification in 1961, adopted English and French as its only official languages. Such a choice, dictated primarily by purely political concerns has over the years, proven its inherent inadequacies in properly addressing the educational and written communication problems in the country. In fact, despite constitutional and educational reforms, contained in legal frameworks considered by some as language policy, the system has failed to provide adequate solutions to the country's language problems. Today, more than 50 years afterwards, the need for an appropriate language policy is increasingly evident. This need is made even stronger as we commemorate 50 years of reunification, an event that should mark a turning point in the history of the country's development planning.

However, the emphasis placed on the promotion of foreign language policy greatly overshadows any efforts towards putting in place a balanced policy based on indigenous languages. Current policy, which has demonstrated its limits by virtue of its exclusive and discriminatory nature, accounts to a large extent for the country's failure to judiciously harness its resources for the purposes of development. As we celebrate 50 years of reunification, it is incumbent on us to reconsider our language policy options. It is a period for us to take stock of the gains and losses incurred through a language policy based on foreign languages and to reorient our development initiatives. Undoubtedly, 50 years is a really long period in the life of a nation. Failure to plan at 50 invariably represents a resolve to fail forever. In this paper, I attempt a suggestion of theoretical and practical issues worthy of consideration in elaborating an appropriate and operational policy for Cameroon. The basic understanding in the paper is that all development planning issues are fundamentally language policy ones in the sense that they essentially constitute the core of citizenship cultivation and participation in the life of the nation.

On the Value of Language

One of the key causes of wrong choices of policy is the misconceptions people have about indigenous languages. In most minority language contexts, these languages are perceived as problems rather than assets. In Cameroon, for instance, they have for many years been considered as threats to national unity and so relegated to the background (Mba & Chiatoh, 2000: 3). It is thus essential to understand that languages, like all other resources in the nation, are crucial in national development efforts and so should be incorporated into planning processes. But to do this, planners must be convinced that language, whether big or small has value in society. Alexander (2003) identifies four levels of this value, namely; economic, political (democracy), education (learning) and cultural (identity). To these can be included a fifth – ideology. Below, we present each of these value levels briefly.

Economic value: Language policy, through its choice of language for specific functions, can either accelerate or slow down economic productivity. Greater productivity calls for greater efficiency, which in turn necessitates better and improved education for all. So, strong foundations for economic productivity as well as scientific and technological advancement in Cameroon must be laid on a solid educational base.

Educational value: All modern knowledge, skills and know-how are ideally transmitted through the educational system. Given the importance of indigenous languages in the enhancement of learning, it is clear that the strongest foundation for quality education lies in a system founded on the indigenous values, that is, languages and knowledge systems of Cameroonians. In this regard, research informs us that learning is greatly facilitated when instruction takes place in languages that learners master best, that is, their tongues (UNESCO, 1953; Heugh, 2000; Obanya, 2004). For a vast majority of Cameroonian learners, these mother tongues are indigenous languages.

Political value: Language policy is inevitably linked to issues of voice in the definition of power relationships as well as in the distribution of opportunity. By mainstreaming some languages at the expense of others, policy is directly depriving their speakers of the right of voice in the nation. Besides, language planning prioritises equal and equitable management of linguistic resources thus providing an ideal framework for the respect and promotion of rights in the nation. Societies that uphold the values of democracy also endeavour to put in place inclusive or democratic language policies as a means of fostering people participation and the cultivation of responsible citizenship.

Cultural value: The interrelationship between language and identity has been well-documented. Every single individual, community or nation is concerned with issues of identity and belonging. Our identity is essentially embedded in the languages we speak. Since it takes individuals to build communities, and communities to build nations, it is, therefore, incumbent on us to carefully consider the role of indigenous languages in the construction of our national identity. In the present circumstances, Cameroon can only boast of a foreign language national identity based on English and French. It is no doubt that such a choice is ridiculous for a nation with about 248 indigenous languages and ethnic groups. It suggests deliberate measures to impose foreign identity values on the citizens. Of course, today, there is no justification whatsoever for Cameroon to continue to promote such an alien identity among its citizens. Cameroon and Cameroonians need a national identity of their own that reflects their cultural specificities. This can only be achieved through indigenous language promotion.

Ideological value: This is closely related to the political and cultural values of languages. It has to do with the specific needs of defining our national cultural orientations against the overall ambition of fostering national development. More specifically, it involves acknowledging that no country has been truly independent when its educational system is fundamentally founded on foreign languages and values. Independence for Cameroon should be reflected in the choice of its educational system as demonstrated by its language-in-education options. It means recognising that continuous exclusive reliance on foreign languages as media of instruction in our schools renders our independence more of an illusion than a reality. Incorporating our linguistic resources into educational and other important domains thus constitutes a bold step towards re-appropriation of our independence, indeed, our common collective destiny. Decolonisation of our educational system calls for indigenisation, domestication and diversification (Mazuri, 2002: 276) and this ideally takes place through the valorisation of indigenous languages.

On the Nature of Policy

Language policy and planning have the potential of considerably shaping individual and social attitudes and development orientations through the cultivation of a clearly expressed set of values in the nation. Whatever role a language plays in a nation is determined almost entirely by the opportunities created for the languages. For this reason, language policy can either contribute to the smooth development of a country or its systematic destruction depending on the role it is called upon to play. The value of language as a development asset and the consequences language policy could have on society are carefully captured by Cuellar (1995: 179) in the following words:

> A people's spoken and written language is perhaps its most important cultural attribute... Language policy, like other policies, has been used as an instrument of domination, fragmentation and reintegration into the ruling political structure. Linguistic diversity is thus a precious asset of humanity, and the disappearance of any language means impoverishment of the reservoir of knowledge and tools for intra-cultural and inter-cultural communication.

Consequently, policy choice is never the result of haphazard decisions. Rather, it is always the outcome of meticulous reflection and consensus. An appropriate policy for a country, therefore, takes into account a host of factors that together constitute the main thrust for building national consensus on matters of language use. In the particular case of Cameroon, given its linguistic and political complexity, great care must be taken to integrate all possible variables capable of rendering policy a desired development tool for a modern society. For a society like ours, to respond properly to collective needs, some underlying frames must be considered. Outstanding among these are:

a) Historical frame: Cameroon is a bi-cultural country based on its official languages (English and French) inherited from colonial administration. Moreover, harmonious development planning in Cameroon calls for scrupulous respect and safeguarding of Anglophone and Francophone values along 1961 reunification demands. This means not only ensuring true equality of English and French but also revalorising national languages relegated at reunification by making them an integral part of the country's linguistic resources. The celebration of 50 years of reunification provides an ideal framework for thorough overhauling of current policies.

b) Theoretical frame: Language planning should be understood to involve three vital components. It should be understood as involving decisions consciously and explicitly taken about language issues that encompass very highly technical areas such as standardisation of language, reforms of orthographies, terminology development and renovation (corpus planning) and the allocation of functional roles or status to particular languages or varieties of languages (status planning), the teaching of second languages and educational decisions involving minority languages (acquisition planning).

c) Ideological frame: Ideologically, language planning should be understood as representing a strong and genuine national vision. It encapsulates major concerns about the history and future of a nation and what it takes to construct a national spirit of oneness, dignity and pride of citizenship in the nation. Policy should not render citizens strangers or foreigners in their own country. As such, it should provide appropriate answers to crucial questions such as: Who are we? Where are we coming from? Where are we going to? Why should we go there? How do we get there? Underlying these questions must be a firm resolve to protect and project a legitimate cultural image worthy of internal and external admiration.

d) Political frame: All language policy matters are basically political issues. Politically, language policy must pay attention to addressing concerns about harmonious coexistence of citizens from different historical and cultural backgrounds. Our fundamental goal here should be to ensure the building of national unity in diversity rather than the destruction of diversity. Constructing unity in diversity is what we refer to as integration, which is opposed to unification that involves the destruction of difference. Given Cameroon's linguistic and cultural diversity, it would be political falsehood, indeed, national betrayal to opt for unification rather than integration.

e) Linguistic frame: Language policy and planning is a deliberate process intended to provide adequate answers to language problems in a nation. Theoretically, language problems only arise in contexts characterised by bilingualism or multilingualism. It is these situations that necessitate the choice of one or more languages for clearly prescribed functions in society. Cameroon's linguistic landscape is marked by important dichotomies that must be carefully analysed. Accordingly, the languages in this country can be grouped into foreign versus indigenous (national) and majority (vehicular) versus minority languages. Other crucial issues to be considered have to do with the phenomena of language shift and endangerment and then special learning needs for disadvantaged minority groups such as the deaf (sign language) and minority language children. This calls for the use of languages other English and French in official communication. Also, in line with the current process of decentralisation, which grants autonomy to regions, the choice of regional languages becomes an imperative.

f) Educational frame: Language policy invariably involves crucial decisions about educational processes and institutional structures. Important areas of educational promotion such as curriculum development, teacher training, materials development, national assessment and certification are crucially language matters. In a multilingual setting like ours, successful educational planning must provide for the inclusive use of all languages in all teaching and learning processes. National languages shall thus serve instructional purposes (as mediums of instruction and as subjects or disciplines).

g) Legal frame: For language policy to command national respect and adhesion; it must be legally binding, that is, it must enjoy legal backing. One of the major legal dimensions of policy is its recognition of minority linguistic rights. Linguistic rights are fundamental human rights and should be respected irrespective of the status of the languages concerned. It is, therefore, a basic right for each child or community to learn in its own language. While these are not negotiable, different learning models may be adopted depending on the context of policy application. Critical in the legal frame is the need for policy to enjoy constitutional backing that renders its application mandatory.

h) Communicational frame: In modern society, communication in all its forms is vital in the dissemination and marketing of ideas, products and services. The same applies to language policy which enjoys significant market value (Cooper, 1989: 72). For policy to become part and parcel of the daily lives of the citizens, it should be properly marketed through appropriate communication channels and in all forms of media.

On the Choice of Language Policy

Making policy decisions has always been a delicate and challenging process. In fact, a lot of stakes are involved especially given that the choices made directly affect the interests and aspirations of citizens in the nation. Of particular attention here is the fact that language issues are fundamentally sentimental issues since they are central in identity and citizenship construction. Tollefson (2002: 5) aptly summarises the relationship between the symbolic value of language, language policy and human struggles in the following argument:

> [...] Therefore, in order to understand language policy debates and the role of language policy in contemporary states, we must examine the underlying social, economic, and political struggles that language can symbolise. The symbolic value of language can have profound consequences, not only for language minorities seeking to negotiate complex and changing identities, but also for dominant groups seeking to retain various forms of political and economic power.

In a linguistically complex context like ours, therefore, it is not only desirable but equally imperative that our choice of policy integrates different levels of interests with respect to the varying socio-cultural and political realities of the country. Ours should thus be a policy that embraces the allocation of official status to some of our national languages. Only on these grounds can we guarantee more committed national interest in the integration and promotion of indigenous languages and values. Our option, therefore, shall be one that responds to local, national and international demands by valorising all the country's linguistic resources. This can only be possible through systematic cultivation of a culture of linguistic cohabitation, whereby foreign and national languages are required to share socio-cultural, economic and political space.

In making language policy choices, planners should be guided by an in-depth understanding of the different models of language planning. Some of these models are (Haugen's (1983) model cited in (Kaplan & Baldauf; 1997:29) and Hornberger's (2006) model. Haugen's model identifies two key levels of language planning, namely; status planning and corpus planning as presented on the table below:

Haugen's (1983:275) Language planning model

	Form (Policy formulation)	Function (language cultivation)
Society (status planning)	1. Selection (decision procedures)	3. Implementation (Educational spread)
	a. Problem identification	a. Correction procedures
	b. Allocation of norms	b. Evaluation
Language (corpus planning)	2. Codification (standardisation procedures)	4. Elaboration (functional development)
	a. Graphisation	a. Terminology modernisation
	b. Grammatication	b. Stylistic development
	c. Lexicon	c. Internationalisation

Source: Kaplan & Baldauf (1997: 29)

On its part, Hornberger's model is more integrative and proposes besides the two levels of status and corpus planning, another critical level, which is the acquisition planning level. The table below specifies the different components of each of these levels.

Language Policy and Planning goals: an integrative framework

Type	Planning policy approach (on form)	Cultivation planning approach (on function)
Status planning (about uses of language)	Officialisation Nationalisation Standardisation of status Proscription	Revival Maintenance Spread Interlingual communication – international, intralingual
Acquisition planning (about users	Group Education/School Literary	Reacquisition Maintenance Shift Foreign

of language)	Religious Mass media Work	language/second language/literacy
	Selection	**Implementation**
Corpus (about language)	Language's formal role in society Extra-linguistic aims	Language's formal role in society Extra-linguistic aims
	Standardisation of corpus Standardisation of auxiliary code	Modernisation (new functions) Lexical Stylistic
	Graphisation	Renovation (new forms, old forms) Purification Reform Stylistic simplification Terminology unification
	Codification Language's form Linguistic aims	Elaboration Language's functions Semi-linguistic aims

From the two models, we realise that while status planning concerns political decisions on the status (prestige and value) to be accorded languages in for clearly specified functions in society, corpus planning deals with the deliberate intervention on the form of language, that is, the different activities of written development and promotion of the language. As for acquisition planning, it focuses on the users of language, that is, the process through which they learn or acquire a language.

In order to arrive at an appropriate policy for Cameroon, it will be necessary to give serious consideration to some key underlying factors of a general and specific nature as presented below:

General Principles

Adopting a national language policy for Cameroon entails, taking cognisance of important general principles of language planning and policy formulation such as:

1) Standardisation of unwritten languages: Such standardisation is imperative in improving written communication involving indigenous languages. Many Cameroonian languages, especially the very minority ones, are not yet written and so cannot serve written communication functions.
2) Language as a development resource: Languages should be recognised as cardinal resources in holistic human development. In this light, the active presence of indigenous languages in all development planning activities (socio-cultural, educational, religious, administrative, etc.) becomes a necessary imperative.
3) Cultivation and strengthening of national integration: Our choice should be guided by the multilingual and multicultural nature of Cameroon. By respecting all these differences and neatly incorporating them into policy, we shall cultivate and strengthen national integration. Here, emphasis shall be laid on the distinction between national integration and national unity. While the former fits into the Cameroonian situation, the latter is a colonialist option intended to neutralise the identity and values of the different components of the Cameroonian society.
4) Multilingualism and multiculturalism as a national resource: Our language policy should embrace and uphold multilingual and multicultural values as indispensable ingredients for constructing a strong and integrated society. It should promote the learning and use in education (media of instruction) of languages other than English and French. In this regard, it shall recognise minority languages not as a problem but as development assets (Wolff, 2011: 62), indeed, a positive value. This mother tongue-based multilingual policy shall replace the current exclusive and discriminatory foreign official language policy practiced in the country.
5) Coexistence of languages: Both foreign and indigenous languages are indispensable in the definition of our present linguistic reality. While national languages shall constitute the core of our natural existence by ensuring cultural rooting, foreign languages shall enable us to meet instrumental needs of a global society. Our identity and values shall be defined in terms of the coexistence of these two categories of languages.

The role of our language policy option shall thus be to confer legality and legitimacy to this coexistence.

6) Balanced use of English and French: In contrast to current practices, the equality of English and French should be guaranteed through their balanced use in all controlling domains.
7) Mother tongue-based multilingualism: In contrast to the foreign official language bilingual policy, a multilingual policy founded on indigenous mother tongues should be instituted. This approach shall ensure cultural rooting and foster academic excellence in the classroom.
8) National languages in education: The use of national languages in education should be mandatory. These languages shall serve both as co-media (together with English and French) of instruction and as subjects (disciplines) in the classroom at all levels. These languages shall also become permanent instruments of lifelong learning.
9) National official languages: Some of our national languages should be upgraded to the status of official languages. These shall be vehicular languages or languages of wider communication (LWC). A single national official language shall be inappropriate for Cameroon. Rather, we shall need at least three languages. Given their vehicular nature, Cameroon Pidgin, Beti-fang and Fulfulde shall enjoy a place of choice on the selection scale.
10) Regional languages: In line with the on-going decentralisation process and considering the responsibility of regions in promoting national languages, the adoption of regional languages to serve official functions at the level of the regions should become an imperative.
11) Intellectualisation of Cameroonian languages: Cameroonian languages notably the ones to be granted official status should be promoted in the areas of science and technology and other fields of higher learning. Sustained research shall thus be encouraged on these languages to enable them effectively become instruments for the development and promotion of advanced learning.
12) National languages and preservation of indigenous knowledge: Indigenous knowledge systems inform all domains of modern science and development. These systems

(together with the values embedded in them) which are best anchored in indigenous languages should be adequately exploited for national development through in-depth scientific study and use of our national languages.

13) National languages and employability: National languages should be included in the official requirements for employment in both public and private sectors.

14) Place of other languages in education: In order to enable our children to meet the ever-increasing demands of globalisation and African renaissance, other languages (African and non-African) should be encouraged in education.

Specific Principles

More specifically, in formulating a national language policy for Cameroon, measures should be taken to guarantee the respect of the following principles:

a) Explicitness and clarity: The goals of the policy should be explicitly and unambiguously stated. This will facilitate the adoption of strategies, evaluation and feed-back on various stages of implementation. Clear and explicit definition of goals shall help ensure objectivity and so provide guarantees that the security concerns of all the different components of the society are duly taken into considerations.

b) Comprehensive definition of goals: All policy goals should be defined in detail to permit all concerned groups, bodies and institutions to participate freely and actively in the implementation process. Roles of different languages (majority and minority; foreign and national) should also be fully defined.

c) Balance and economy: In the definition of policy interests and actions, steps should be taken to ensure that these reflect overall national needs. Emphasis should be laid on the need for effectiveness and feasibility of action as well as the costs involved in realising the actions proposed.

d) A coordinated approach: Measures should be taken to establish effective and efficient national coordination of activities especially with respect to different organisations, bodies and institutions charged with the enactment of the policy. This coordination shall be ensured by a neutral body made up of members of all the stakeholders.

e) Broad spectrum of policy: Policy should be defined in a way as to make it generally applicable across all sectors and languages of the nation. For instance, each language, its size notwithstanding, shall feel concerned by the policy.

f) Bottom-up-top-down policy approach: For greater efficiency, the process should follow a bottom-up-top-down approach. To this end, the most important voices in decision-making shall be those of the majority of the population (ordinary people) rather than those of the minority political elites.

g) Access to information and services to non-official language speakers: Policy shall guarantee that non-speakers of official languages (foreign and national) shall have free, if not equal, access to all information and services within the nation.

h) Texts of application: The practice of texts of application as prerequisites for policy implementation is regressive and should be reconsidered. Authorities should realise that these texts are more of obstructions than facilitators to effective policy implementation and should either be totally scraped or their speedy elaboration and application should be guaranteed.

Vital Policy Domains Other than Education

Given the linguistically diverse nature of the country and considering the need for the promotion of national languages as development resources, policy should mandatorily cover such vital domains as:

Legal system: The languages of the different communities should be respected as a fundamental human right in the courts and all other forums charged with rendering justice.

Legislation: Deliberations, documentation and reports in parliament should be in all the official languages (national and foreign) of the country.

Civil registry: All civil registration services should employ the languages of the locality alongside the official languages (national and foreign) in the establishment of birth certificates for newly born babies.

Administration: Administration should duly respect the linguistic landscape of the country. Different functions shall be clearly defined for all languages at local, regional and national levels.

National identification: National identification cards, travellers' passport and other related services should be in the official (national and foreign) languages.

Tourism: Tourism is a central income-generation source for Cameroon. Multilingualism shall be promoted in this sector in line with the linguistic realities of the country. At regional levels, regional languages shall be used alongside official languages (national and foreign).

Languages, the Media and Modern Technologies
National languages should be employed in the exploitation and promotion of media networks as well as modern science and technologies. As such, the policy should ensure:
 a) Inclusion of national languages in regular media and science and technology promotion programmes.
 b) Creative use of technology for language maintenance, promotion and learning.
 c) Strengthening of the use of national languages in official (written and audio-visual) media such as the presentation of news in national official languages and a sign language.

A National Literacy and Non-Formal Education Policy
An appropriate language policy for Cameroon should duly take into account the needs of adult literacy and non-formal education for youths. Policy should thus guarantee:
- Promotion of adult literacy with focus on special learning needs.
- Promotion of non-formal education for youths and out-of-school children.
- Gender-sensitiveness in adult literacy and non-formal education.

- Interconnections between adult literacy, non-formal education and formal education

A National Book Policy

A language policy based on national languages must make provision for the promotion of books in these languages. A national book policy should:
- Trigger enthusiasm in book production and publishing in national languages.
- Encourage the creation of a national language book industry for a developing Cameroon.
- Encourage professionalisation through the emergence of publishers, editors, literary and scientific writers, music writers, etc. in national languages.
- Motivate the establishment of national language libraries at local, regional and national levels.

Policy Document and Declaration

There is need for a policy document detailing the main components of the policy statement. The document shall clearly define the goals, strategies and mechanisms of implementation. It shall specify all relevant policy sources such as constitutional and legal provisions. The contents of the document shall be publicly declared by a competent authority most preferably, the President of the Republic.

Translation and Interpretation

An appropriate and operational language policy for a multilingual Cameroon will definitely need to cater for translation and interpretation services. The policy should thus guarantee:
- Institutionalisation of translation and interpretation involving national languages.
- Dissemination of vital development information through translation into and from national languages in domains such as HIV/AIDS, agriculture, health, hygiene and sanitation.
- Professionalisation and job creation in the area of translation and interpretation involving national languages.

Policy Management
Management is an important aspect of language policy effectiveness and success. In our case, the policy should be ensured by:

A Cameroon Language Policy Advisory Board: This board should advices government in matters of policy formulation and implementation. Its membership should comprise researchers, practitioners and specialised institutions. Its main goal should be to provide counselling on strategies and techniques of policy implementation.

A National Language Policy Board: This board should cater for the implementation of language policy in the country. It should be a neutral body created specifically and duly empowered for this purpose. As such, it should enjoy institutional, human resource and financial autonomy. The Board should have regional and local offices.

A National Certification and Qualifications Board: This board should be responsible for assessment and certification at national level. It should work closely with the National Language Policy Board at national, regional and local levels.

Appropriateness of Policy
Given the context of language policy formulation, it seems imperative for us to address the crucial question of appropriate policy. As indicated earlier on, some Cameroonians are of the opinion that the country has a language policy. To this category of Cameroonians, what the country lacks is the political will to ensure implementation. My opinion on this matter is that what others consider as policy; rightly constitutes some important elements of policy but is not policy in purely scientific terms, as stated in Chumbow (1990: 288). From the steps enumerated above and the specifications of each of the steps, we realise that we cannot truly say that Cameroon has a policy worthy of the name. What we have is a set of fragmented pieces of constitutional and legal frameworks that can conveniently be referred to as expressions of intent or as half-baked policy. On-going work by the Ministries of Basic Education and Secondary Education lend credibility to our view. They are currently working on the language policy for the protection and promotion of national languages.

If what Cameroon is currently promoting is not policy enough, what then is an appropriate or ideal policy? What are its fundamental defining features? Bamgbose (1999: 24-28) makes an important contribution to this effect. While recognising the necessity for the participation of all role players and stakeholders in the process of language planning, he stresses on the overarching role of government in ensuring the success of planning actions. According to him, for language policy to be appropriate, it must enjoy the following central ingredients:

1) Government must be convinced of the role of African languages in development: Apparently, the Cameroon government is convinced of the need to promote national languages. However, judging from its rather laissez-faire attitude, it is doubtful if such conviction really exists.
2) Policies must be such as are likely to raise the status of African languages: Present legal frameworks are mute on the status of Cameroonian languages.
3) Policies on development of African languages must be phased: There is practically no goal specification and consequently no clear definition of phases of implementation of policy.
4) Implementation must be specified at the point of policy formulation: Constitutional and legal frameworks provide for the promotion of national languages but nothing is mentioned about implementation.
5) Implementation is best entrusted to specialised agencies rather than to government ministries and departments: So far, ministries exercise overwhelming power in matters of policy design and implementation. Again, there seems to be no indication of government preparedness to surrender implementation to a neutral body.
6) Grassroots' involvement and private initiatives in language development must be encouraged: Here, government neither encourages nor prohibits grassroots and private initiative. However, through its lukewarm attitude towards elaborate formulation and implementation of policy, it clearly discourages private initiative particularly within local community, missionary and civil society levels. They want to engage in actions and processes that enjoy government recognition.

7) Negative attitudes to African languages must be combated through awareness campaigns: Although government is visibly consistent in its promotion of official bilingualism, very little effort is made to improve on the public image of national languages.
8) For policies to succeed, they must be backed by a strong political will: As we have indicated earlier, political will to promote national languages is extremely low.

Policy Formulation Process

Policy formulation is a highly technical process. Given the technicalities involved, it is critical that the process be diligently followed. Rubin (1983: 6-9) identifies four key steps in the formulation of policy which I take the liberty to summarise here as follows:

Fact finding: This is the step set aside for the collection of vital amount of data on the situation in which planning is taking place. Information is needed on the languages in use, their different dialects, other languages used, how these language relate to ongoing socio-economic and political processes (such as education, democratisation, HIV/AIDS prevention, poverty alleviation). In short, information is required on the needs, interests and aspirations of the target population. Here the more the information, the better.

Decision-making: The information collected enables planners to make policy decisions. Decision-making involves several levels and different sets of people. Decisions are made based on prior studies, referred to above as fact finding. One of the decisions should be whether or not to assign official and regional status to national languages. After determining the needs of the target population, decision-makers may prioritise problems involved.

Establishment of goals, strategies and outcomes: Here the goals, strategies and outcomes of policy are specified. Goal specification too takes place at several levels. First, a legislature establishes some general goals and assigns responsibility for implementation. Then the agency or institution of implementation defines these goals more specifically in line with other considerations like funding and staff capabilities. Finally, the implementers may define goals in terms of the local situation. Usually, outcomes are not established in advance even though it would be helpful if they were. The identification of actors, strategies, resources (human and material) as well as the institutional framework for implementation is crucial in this step. Goal specification should be done according to short, mid and long-term needs.

Implementation: This step involves concrete policy actions such as (a) the mobilisation of resources, general finance and personnel management, (b) motivation and supervision of those involved with the management of the programme and the targets, (c) the sequencing and coordination of related aspects of the policy such as the preparation of texts in languages not formerly used as media of instruction. Implementation is a critical variable in the success of the plan. An important clarification concerning implementation is that it shall be phased depending on priorities established by the implementers.

Evaluation: Evaluation involves analysis of trends and general monitoring system as well as specific aspects of a particular programme. The planner must determine whether actual outcomes match projected outcomes, and if not, then why not? This information enables him to know whether or not to modify his strategies in order to achieve predicted outcomes. Evaluation also permits the planner to provide feed-back on the implementation process. Ideally, evaluation should take place in the short, mid and long-terms in line with established policy goals.

Conclusion

For many years now, Cameroon has recognised the need to adopt an alternative language policy to fill the gaps created by the dominant English-French language policy. As we celebrate 50 years of reunification, therefore, the formulation of an appropriate and operational language policy for Cameroon becomes even more compelling. To succeed in this noble journey, government openness to different sheds of opinion is an absolute necessity. But even more importantly, the diagnosis and treatment of language problems in this country must be informed by scientific and inclusive approaches. In this paper, we have attempted to make proposals that could inspire stakeholders in this direction. Whatever the limitations of these proposals, they constitute nevertheless, a scientific basis for more reflections on ways and means of forging ahead with the language policy formulation process. The historical and political implications for urgent action are obvious and should be given serious consideration.

References

Alexander, N. 2003. The African renaissance and the use of African languages in tertiary education, *PRAESA Occasional Papers*, University of Cape Town.

Bamgbose, A. 1999. African language development and language planning. In N. Alexander (Ed.), *Language and development in Africa, social dynamics* Vol. 25, N° 1.

Chumbow, B. S. 1990. Language and language policy in Cameroon. In Kofele-Kale (Ed.), *An African experience in nation building: The bilingual Cameroon Republic since reunification*, West-view Press.

Cooper, R., L. 1989. *Language planning and social change*, Cambridge: Cambridge University Press.

Cuellar, P., J. 1994. Our creative diversity: Report of the World Commission on culture and development, France: Egoprim.

Hornberger, N., H. 2006. Frameworks and models in language policy and planning. In Thomas Ricento (Ed.), *An introduction to language policy: Theory and method*, Malden: Blackwell.

Kaplan, R., B. & Baldauf, R. B. Jr. 1997. *Language planning: From practice to theory*, Clevedon: Multilingual Matters.

Kathleen, H. 2000. The case against bilingual and multilingual education in South Africa. PRAESA *Occasional Papers* N° 6, University of Cape Town.

Mazuri, A., M. 2002. The English language in African education: Dependency and decolonisation. In J.W. Tollefson (Ed.), *Language policies in education: Critical issues*, Mahwah-New Jersey-London: Lawrence Erlbaum Associates pp. 267-281.

Mba, G., and Chiatoh, B., A. 2000. Current trends and perspectives for mother tongue education in Cameroon, *AJAL* N° 1 pp. 1-21.

Obanya, P. 2004. Learning in, with and from the first language. *PRAESA Occasional Papers* N° 19, University of Cape Town.

Ouane, A., and Glanz, C. (Eds.). 2011. Optimising *learning, education and publishing in Africa: The Language Factor*, Hamburg: UIL/ADEA.

Rubin, J. 1983. Bilingual education and language planning. In Chris Kennedy (Ed.), *Language Planning and Language Education*, Park Lane: George Allen & Unwin.

Tollefson, J. W. 2002. Introduction: Critical issues in educational language policy. In J. W. Tollefson (Ed.), *Language policies in education: Critical issues*, Mahwah-New Jersey-London: Lawrence Erlbaum Associates pp. 3-15.

UNESCO, 1953. *The use of vernacular languages in education*, Paris: UNESCO.

Wolff, E. 2011. Background and history – language politics and planning in Africa. In Adama Ouane & Christine Glanz (Eds.), *Optimising learning, education and publishing in Africa: The Language Factor*, Hamburg: UIL/ADEA pp. 49-102.

About the Authors

Kathleen Heugh, Research Centre for Languages and Culture, University of South Australia; and also of the Linguistics Department, University of the Western Cape and the Human Sciences Research Council of South Africa.

Gabriel Mba is Associate Professor of Linguistics in the Department of African Languages and Linguistics University of Yaounde I and has also worked for several years at the National Association for Cameroonian Language Committees.

Atikonda Akuzike Mtenje teaches Linguistics and African Languages at Mzuzu University, Malawi.

Abdelrahim Hamid Mugaddam is Associate Professor of linguistics and the current director of the Institute of African & Asian Studies, University Of Khartoum, Sudan.

Linda Chinelo Nkamigbo teaches in the Department of Linguistics, Nnamdi Azikiwe University, Awka, Nigeria.

Josephat Rugemalira is Associate Professor of Linguistics at the University of Dar es Salaam, Tanzania. He has served as Director of the Languages of Tanzania Project at the university since 2001.

Bekale Seyum teaches in the Department of Linguistics, Addis Ababa University, Ethiopia.

Beatrice Lima Lebsia Titanji teaches in the Department of English, University of Buea, Cameroon.

Coordination:
Pius W. Akumbu is a Lecturer in the Department of Linguistics and also Director of the Centre for African Languages and Cultures, University of Buea.

Blasius A. Chiatoh is a Lecturer in the Department of Linguistics, University of Buea.

www.ingramcontent.com/pod-product-compliance
Lightning Source LLC
Chambersburg PA
CBHW021123300426
44113CB00006B/269